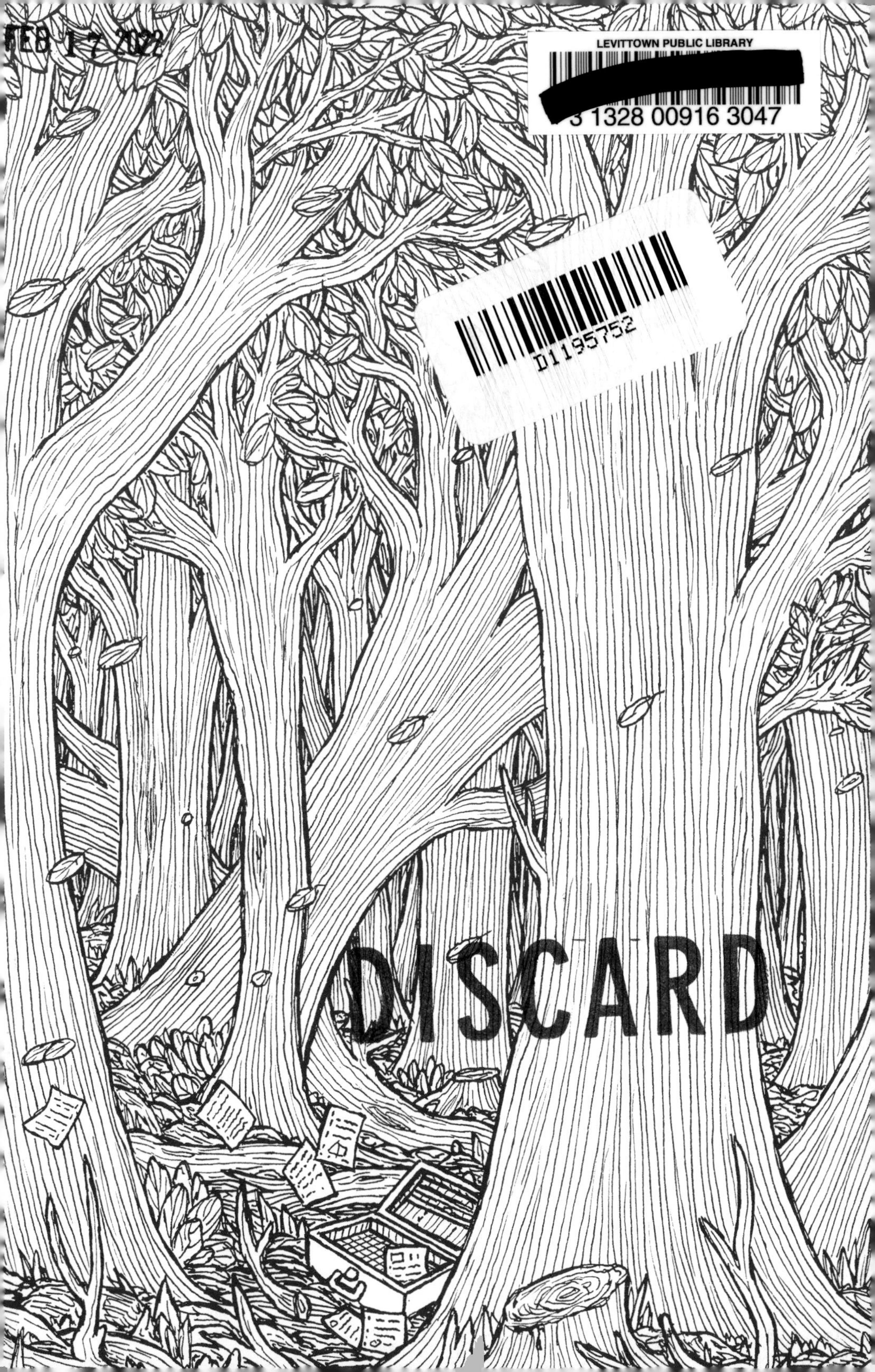

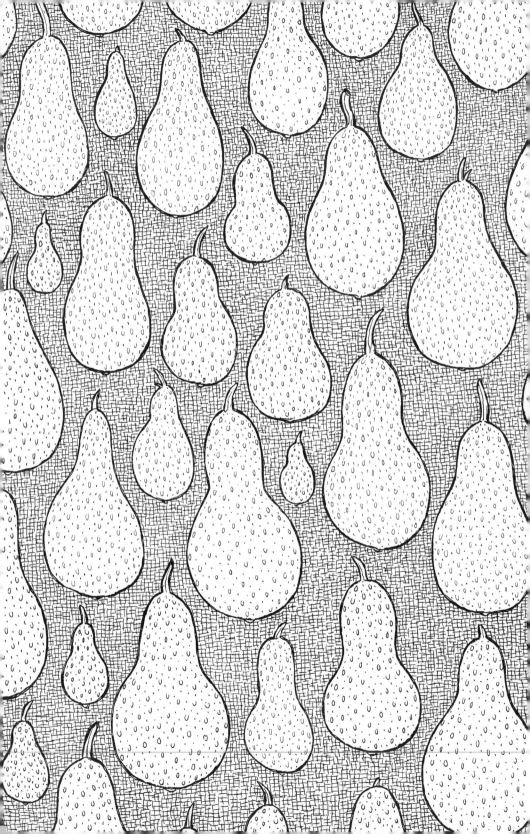

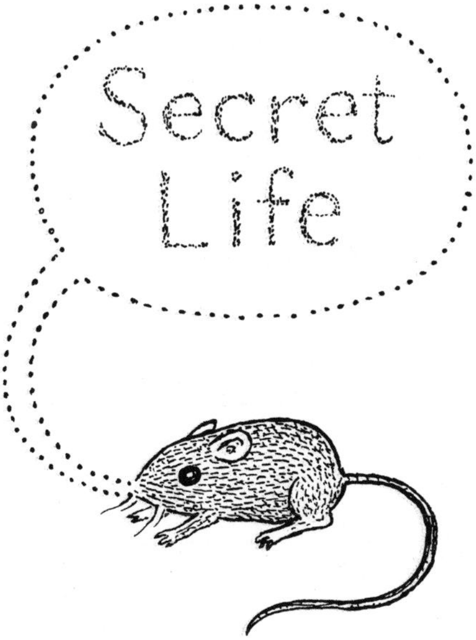
Secret
Life

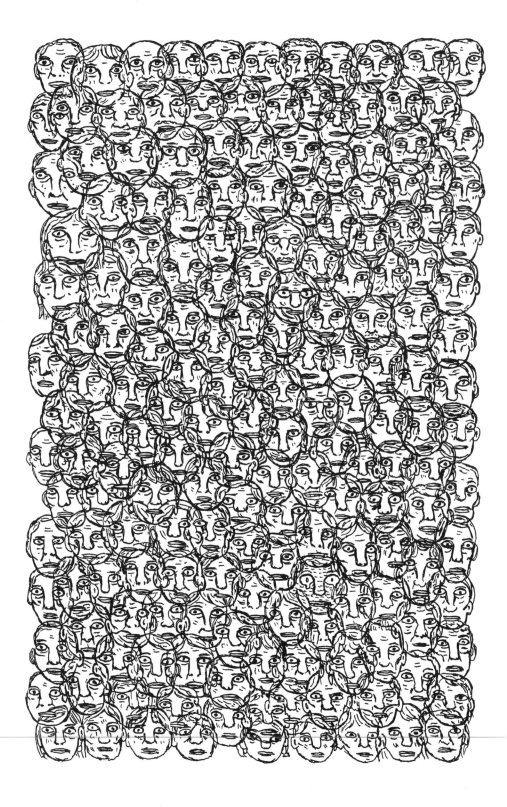

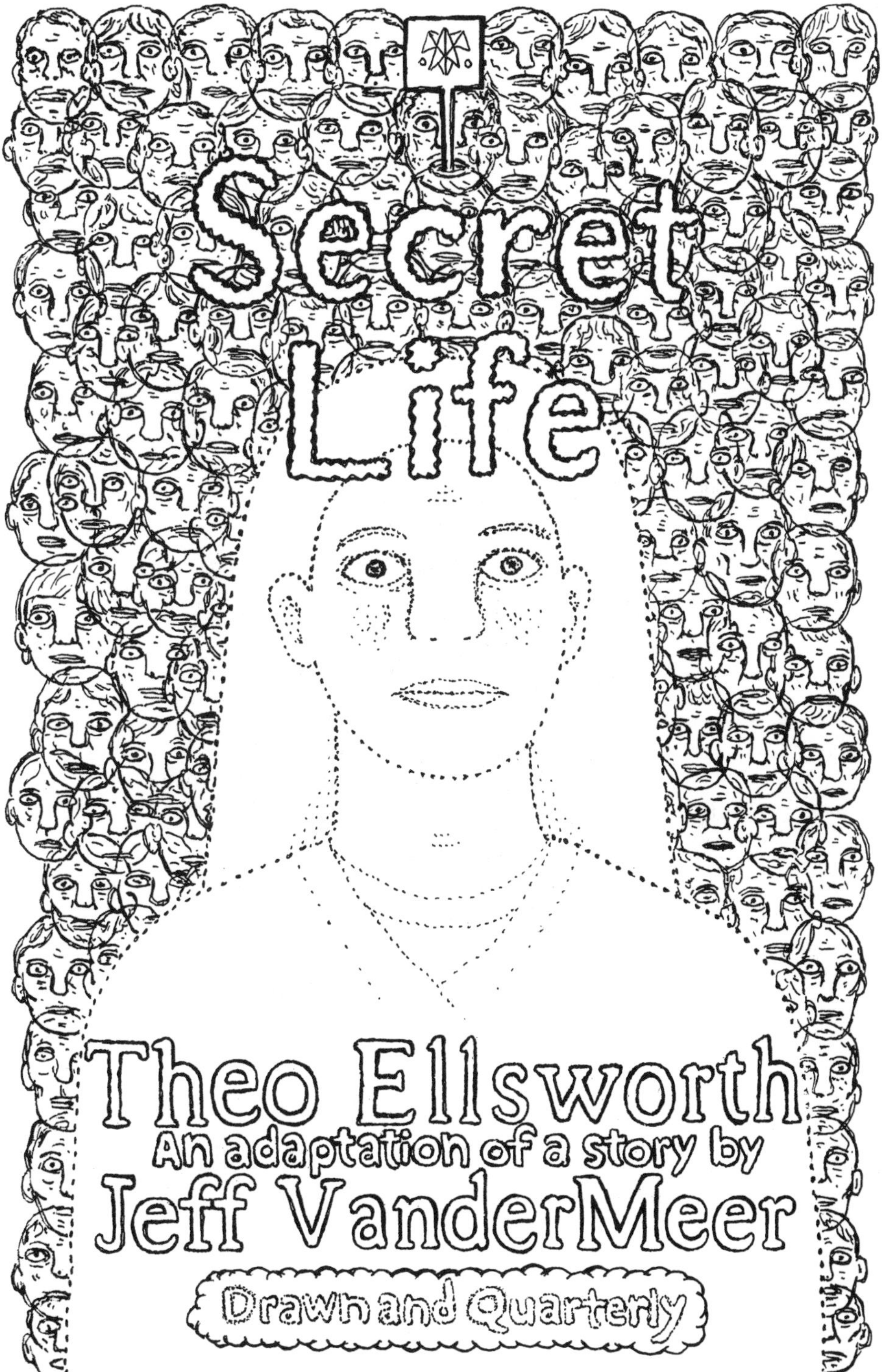
Secret Life
Theo Ellsworth
An adaptation of a story by
Jeff VanderMeer
Drawn and Quarterly

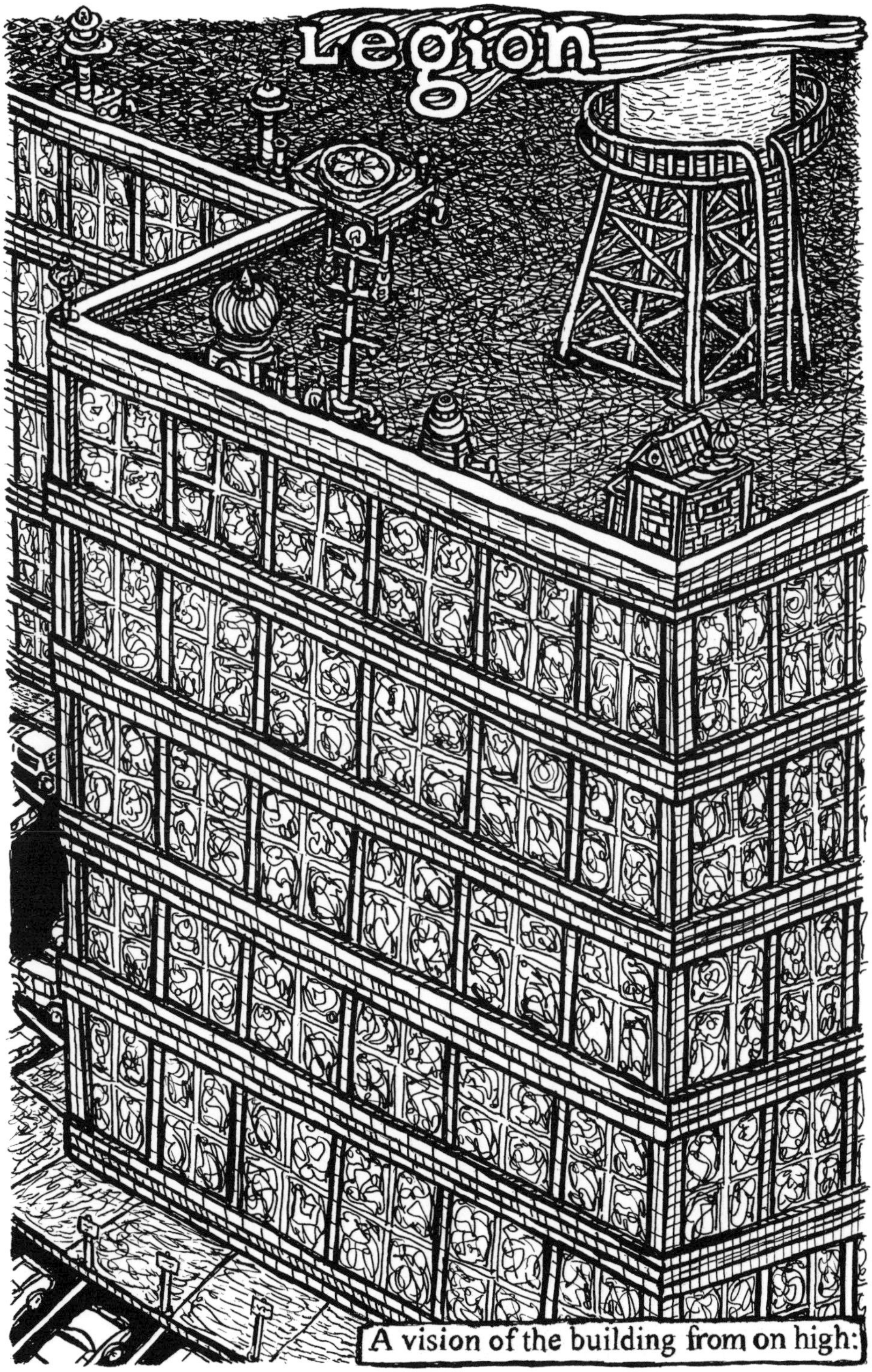
Legion
A vision of the building from on high:

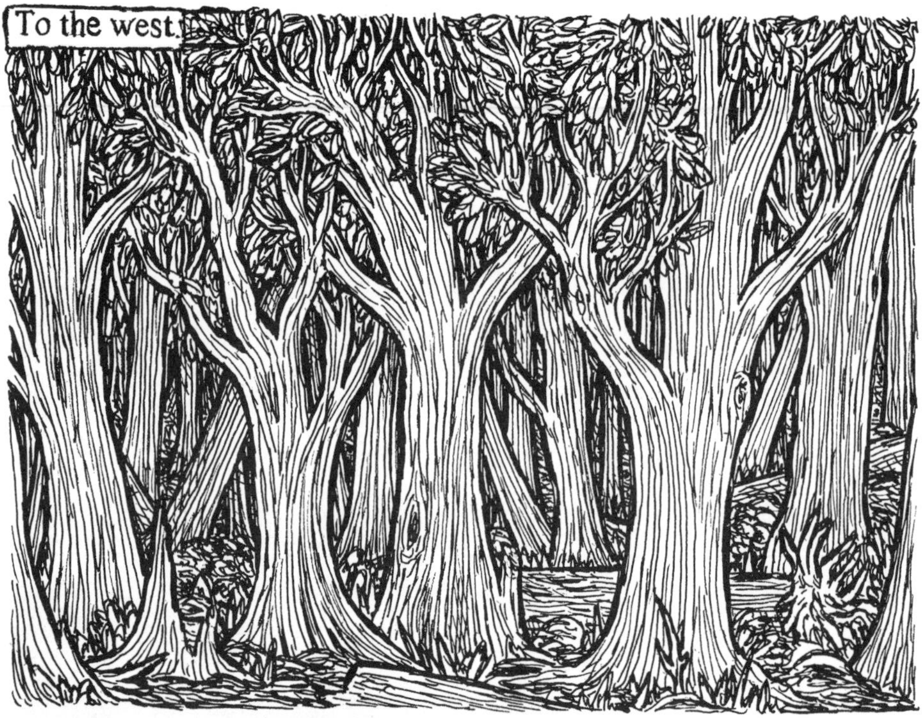
To the west.

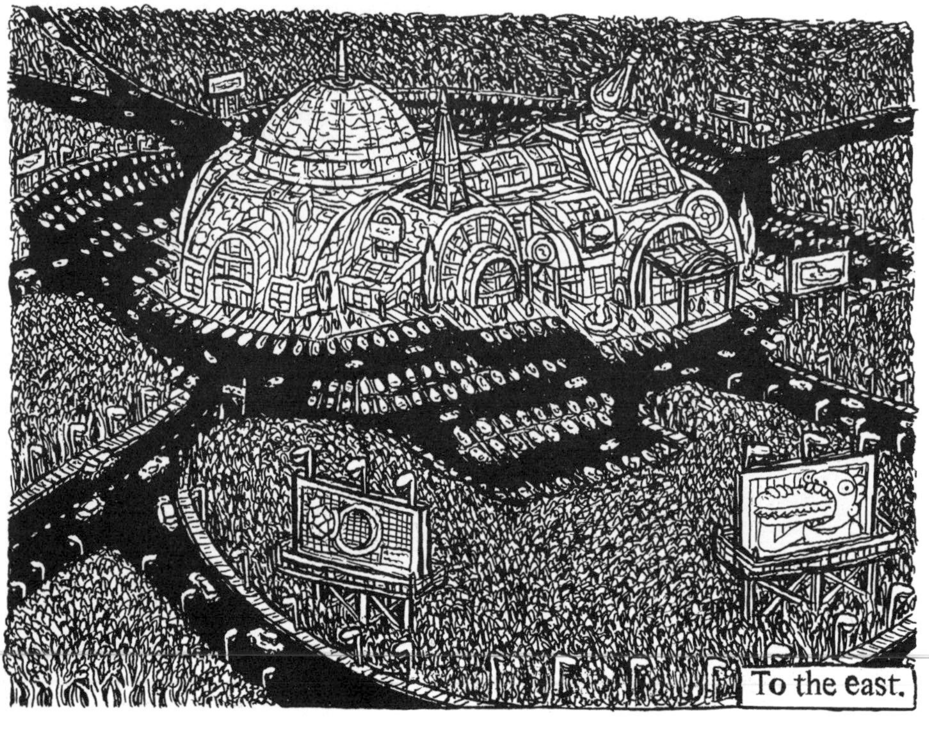
To the east.

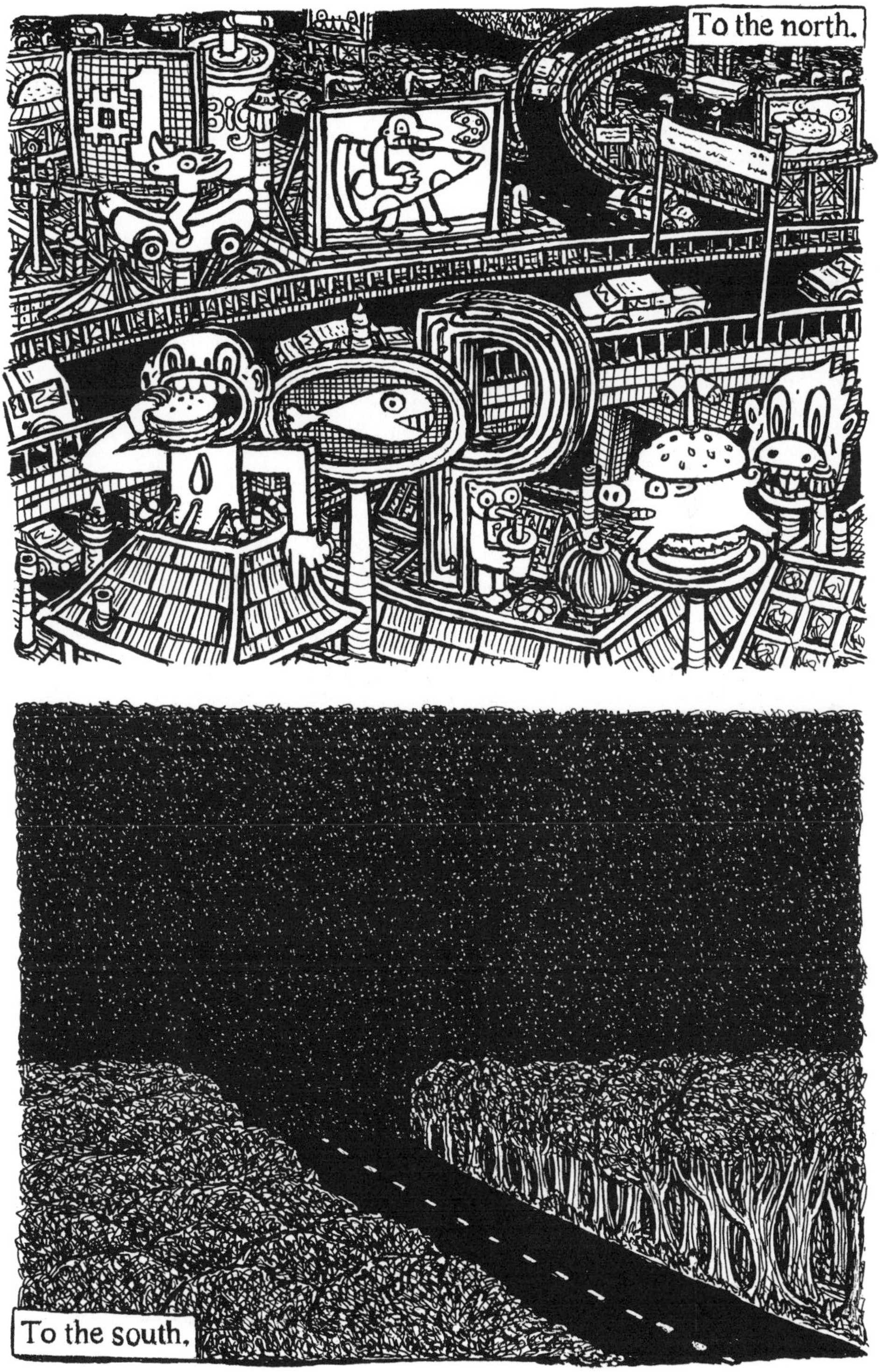
To the north.
To the south.

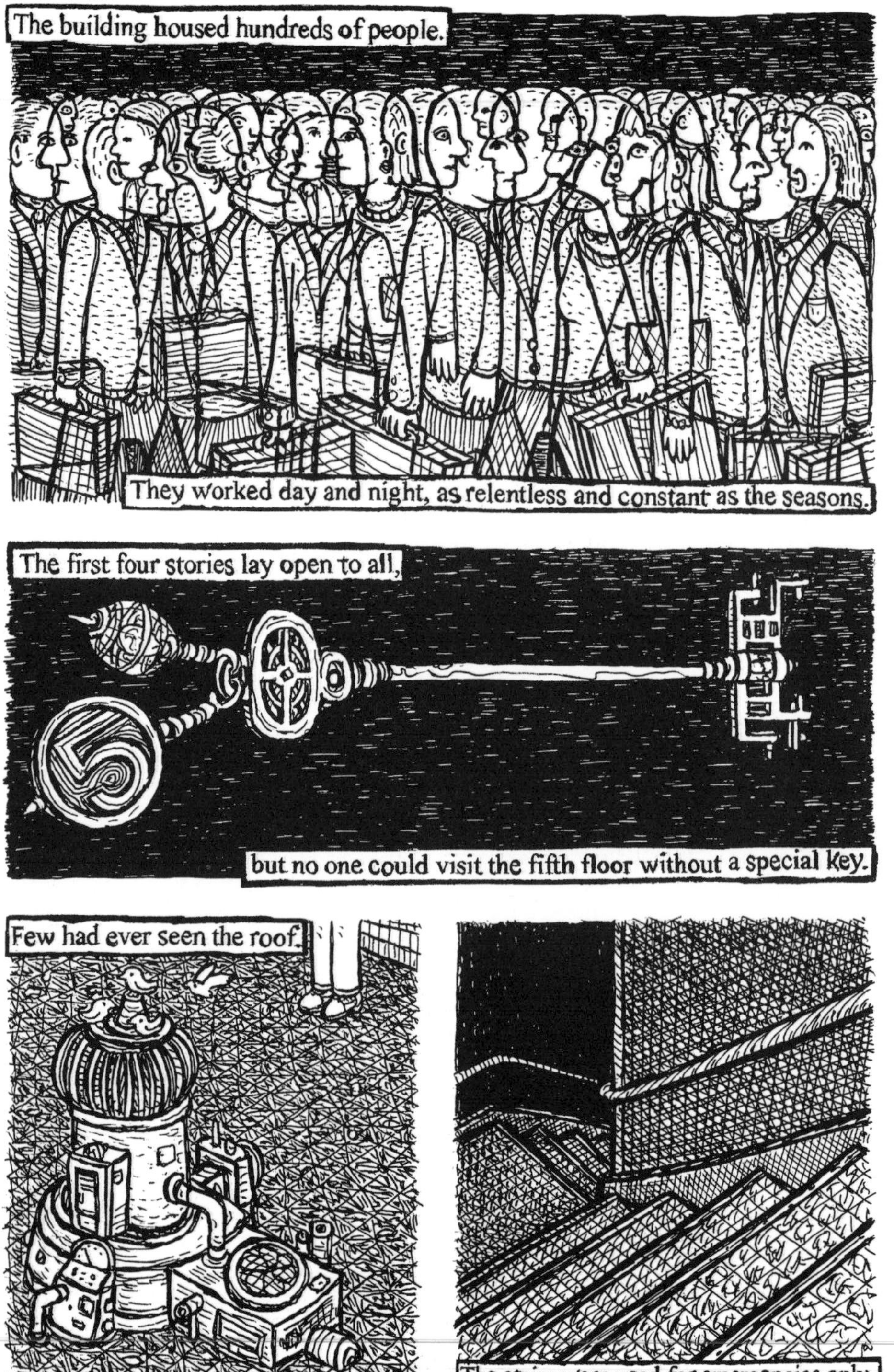
The building housed hundreds of people.
They worked day and night, as relentless and constant as the seasons.
The first four stories lay open to all,
but no one could visit the fifth floor without a special key.
Few had ever seen the roof.
The stairs were used for emergencies only.

Some of the elevators clanked and groaned.

Some of the elevators, quiet and smooth as ghosts, rose and fell with limitless grace.

Most inhabitants of the building, even the custodians in the basement, it was rumored, preferred the noisy elevators.

When the quiet elevators reached the first floor, a scream could sometimes be heard, as of an animal trapped and then crushed beneath their feet.

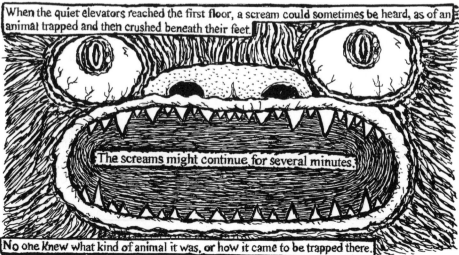

The screams might continue for several minutes.

No one knew what kind of animal it was, or how it came to be trapped there.

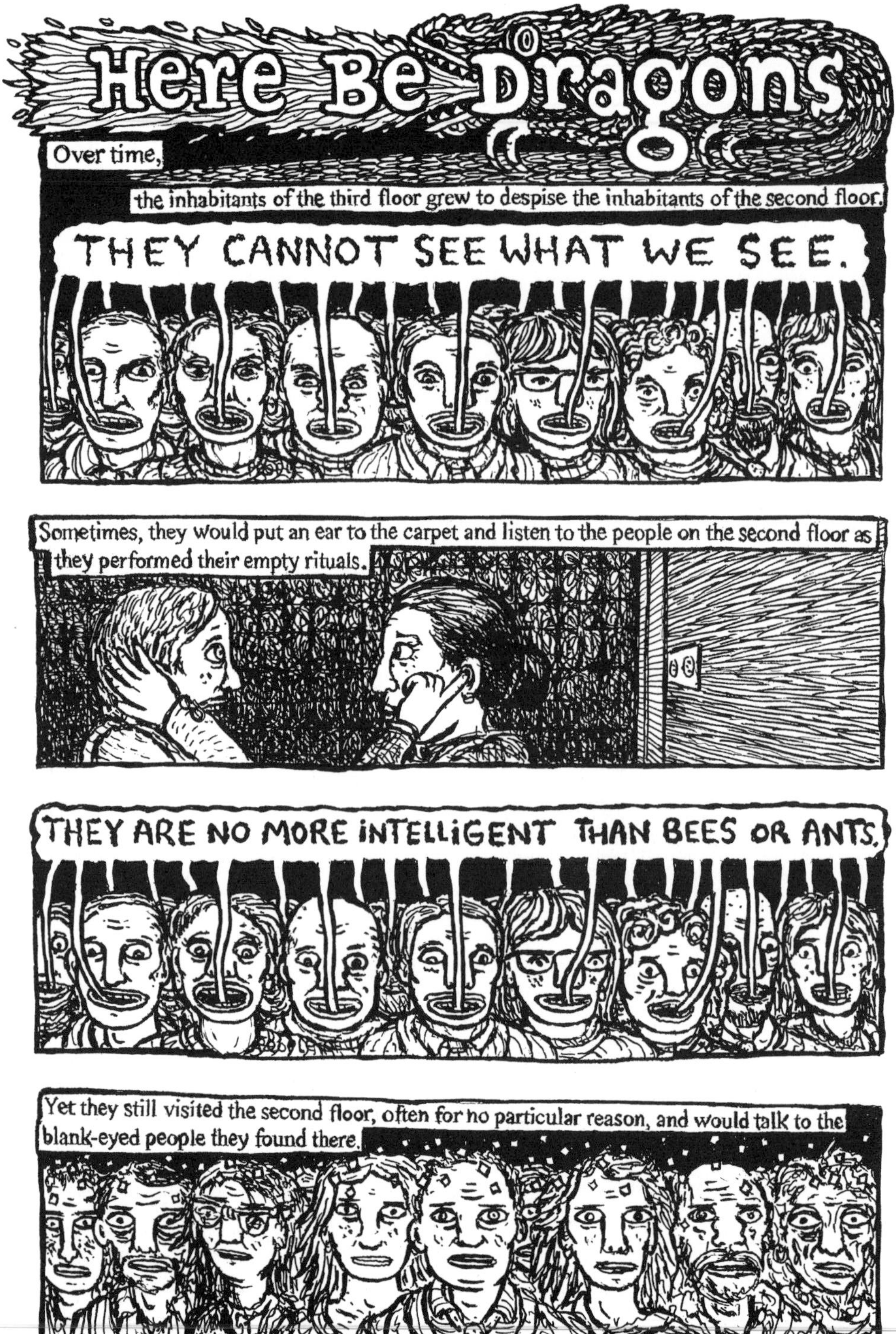
Here Be Dragons
Over time,
the inhabitants of the third floor grew to despise the inhabitants of the second floor.
THEY CANNOT SEE WHAT WE SEE.
Sometimes, they would put an ear to the carpet and listen to the people on the second floor as they performed their empty rituals.
THEY ARE NO MORE INTELLIGENT THAN BEES OR ANTS.
Yet they still visited the second floor, often for no particular reason, and would talk to the blank-eyed people they found there.
After all, they too had once lived on the second floor, before the growth of the company.

Over time,
language fell away from the people of the second floor,

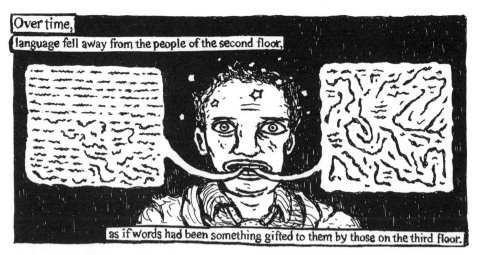

as if words had been something gifted to them by those on the third floor.

Over time,
the words of those on the second floor came to seem like the hum of busy wasps,

or the sound wind makes through corn not yet ready to be harvested.

Over time,
the people of the third floor grew afraid,

for reasons they did not understand.

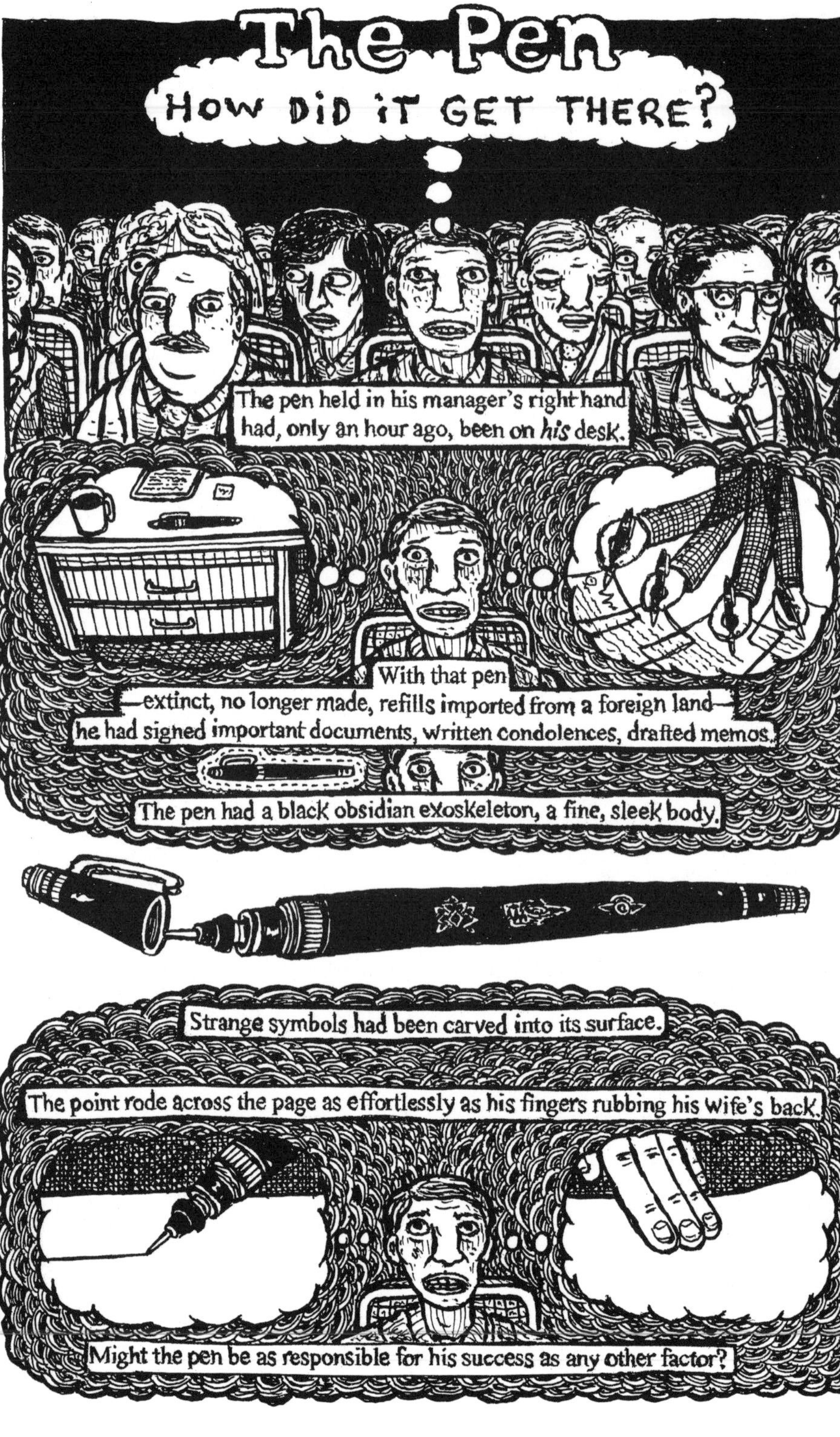
The Pen
HOW DID IT GET THERE?
The pen held in his manager's right hand had, only an hour ago, been on *his* desk.
With that pen
—extinct, no longer made, refills imported from a foreign land—
he had signed important documents, written condolences, drafted memos.
The pen had a black obsidian exoskeleton, a fine, sleek body.
Strange symbols had been carved into its surface.
The point rode across the page as effortlessly as his fingers rubbing his wife's back.
Might the pen be as responsible for his success as any other factor?

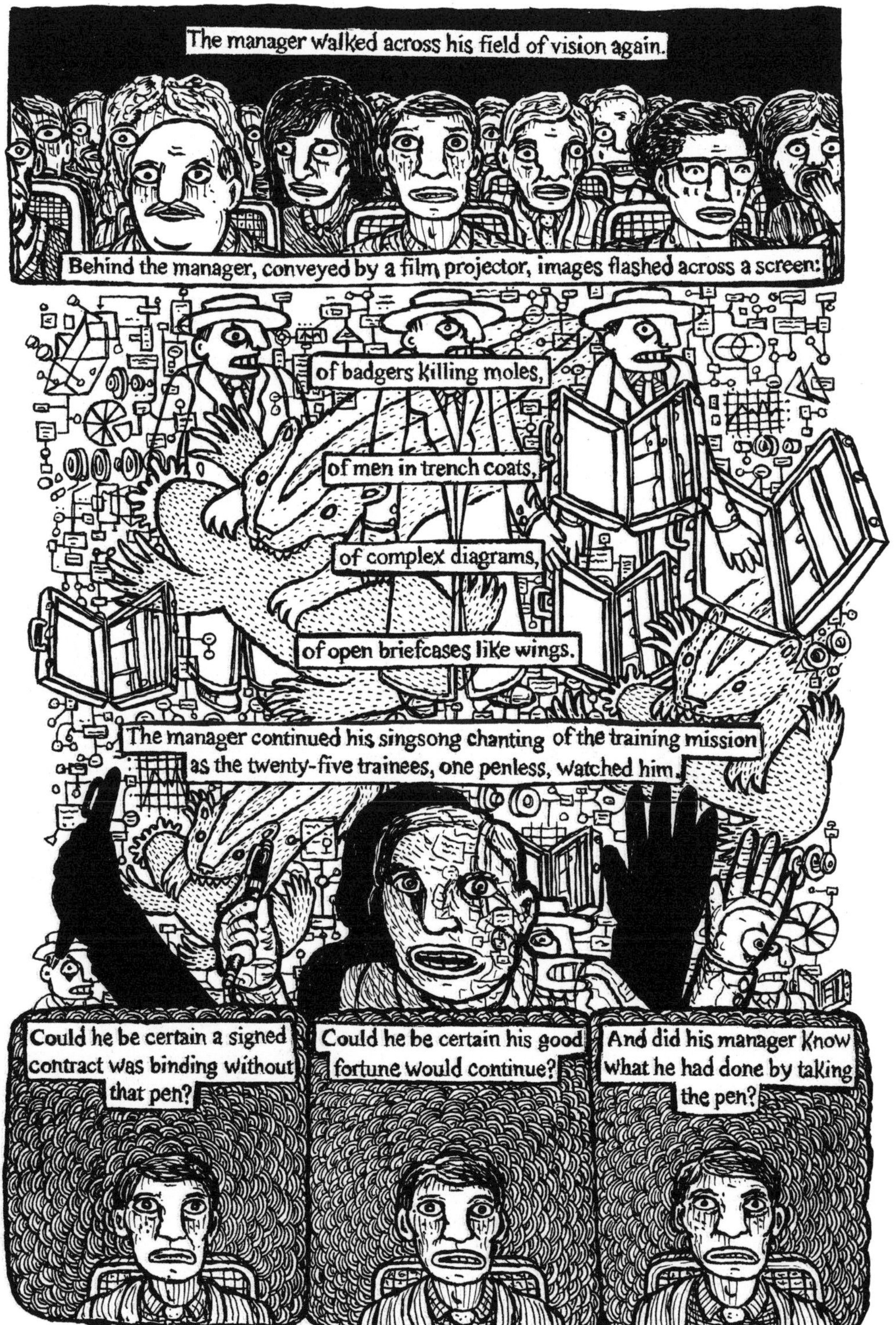
The manager walked across his field of vision again.
Behind the manager, conveyed by a film projector, images flashed across a screen:
of badgers killing moles,
of men in trench coats,
of complex diagrams,
of open briefcases like wings.
The manager continued his singsong chanting of the training mission as the twenty-five trainees, one penless, watched him.
Could he be certain a signed contract was binding without that pen?
Could he be certain his good fortune would continue?
And did his manager know what he had done by taking the pen?

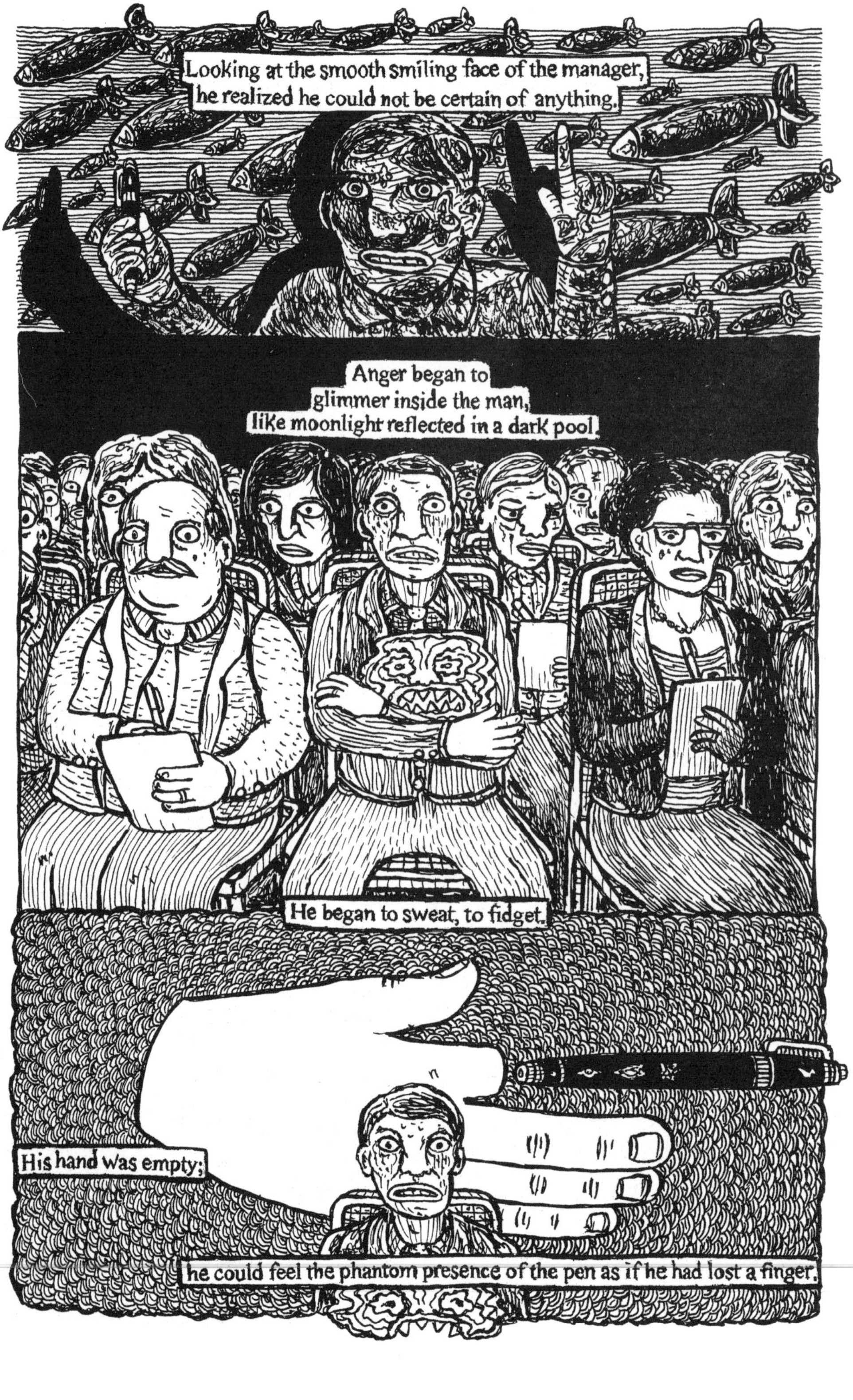
Looking at the smooth smiling face of the manager, he realized he could not be certain of anything.
Anger began to glimmer inside the man, like moonlight reflected in a dark pool.
He began to sweat, to fidget.
His hand was empty;
he could feel the phantom presence of the pen as if he had lost a finger.

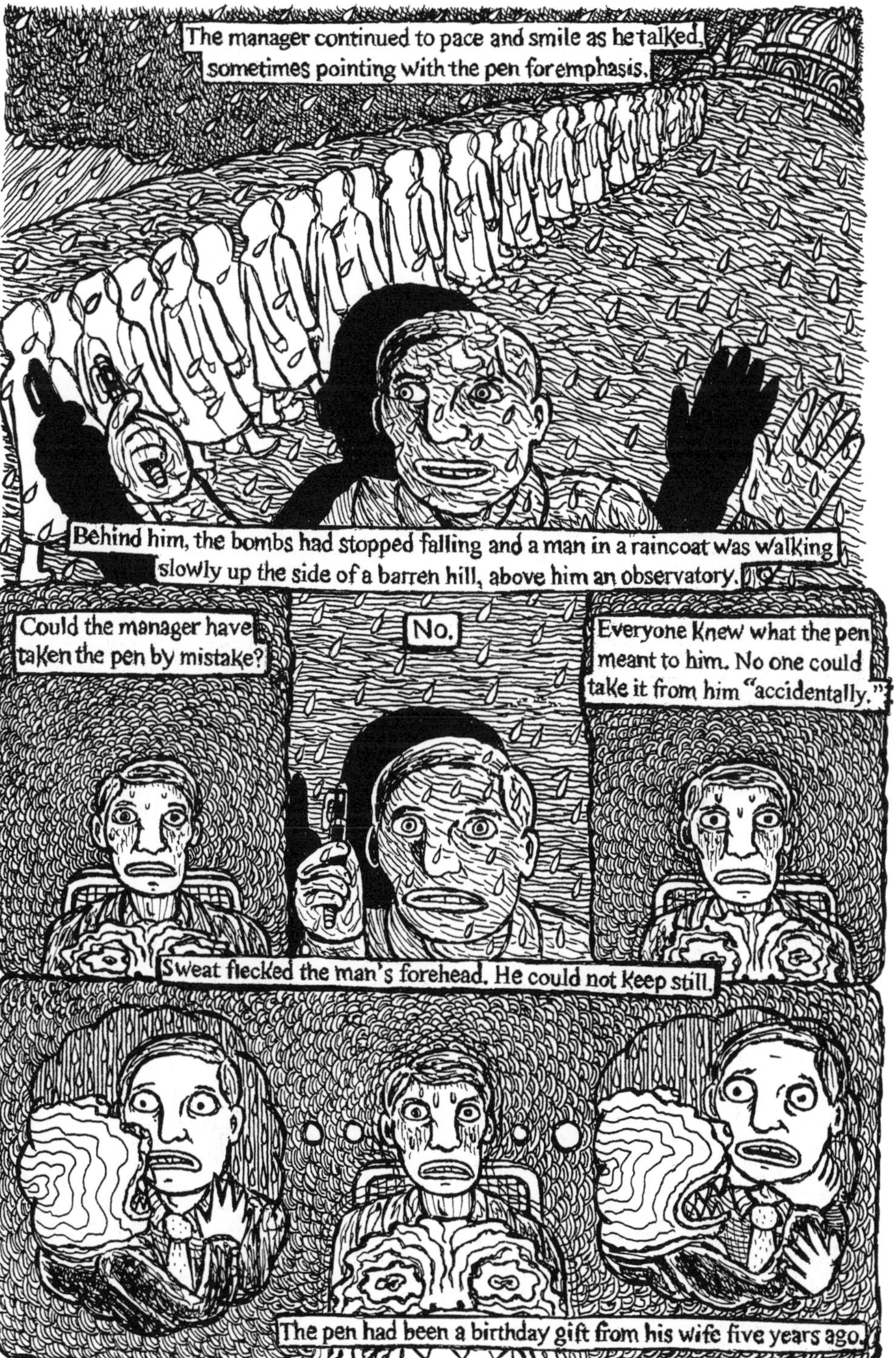
The manager continued to pace and smile as he talked, sometimes pointing with the pen for emphasis.
Behind him, the bombs had stopped falling and a man in a raincoat was walking slowly up the side of a barren hill, above him an observatory.
Could the manager have taken the pen by mistake?
No.
Everyone knew what the pen meant to him. No one could take it from him "accidentally."
Sweat flecked the man's forehead. He could not keep still.
The pen had been a birthday gift from his wife five years ago.

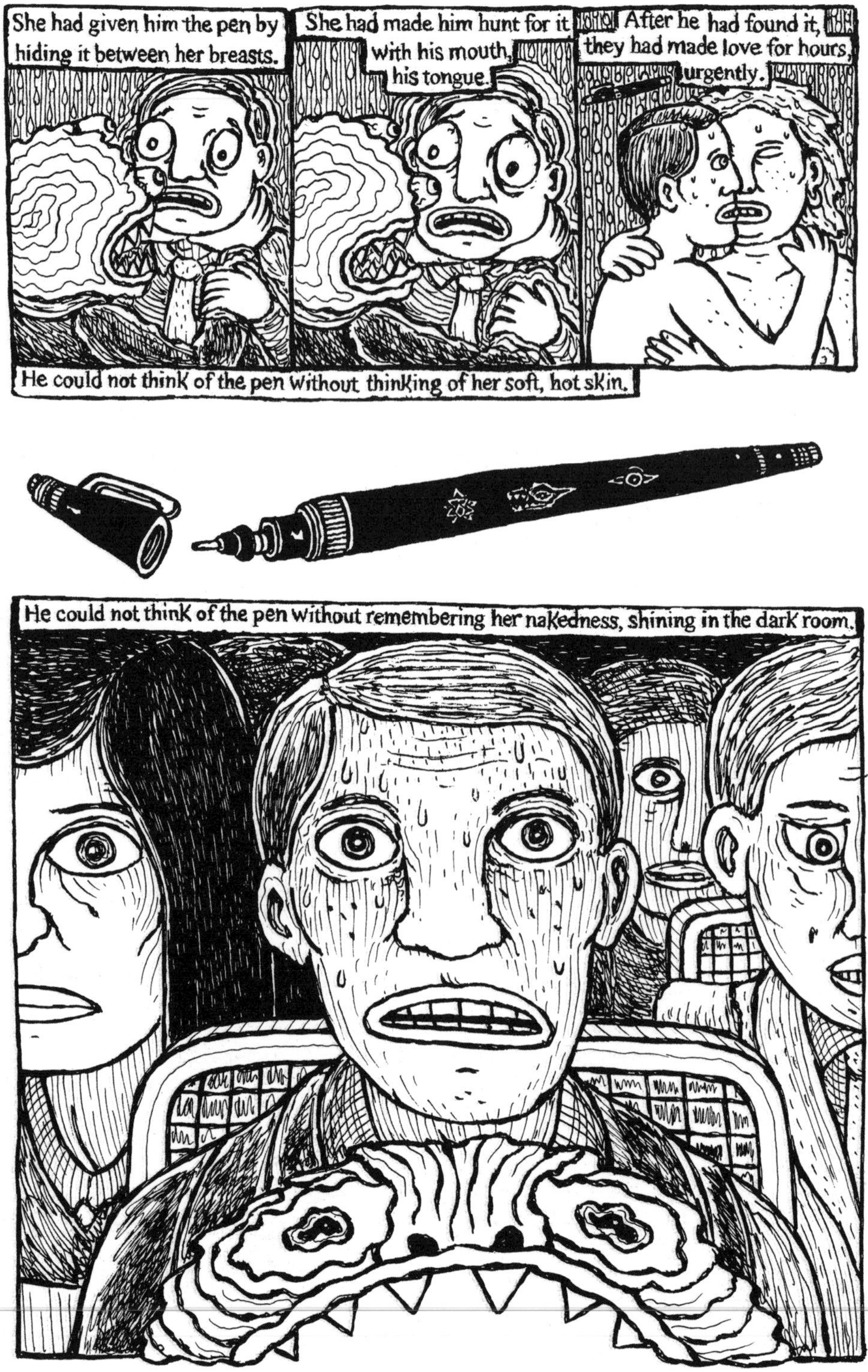
She had given him the pen by hiding it between her breasts.
She had made him hunt for it with his mouth, his tongue.
After he had found it, they had made love for hours, urgently.
He could not think of the pen without thinking of her soft, hot skin.
He could not think of the pen without remembering her nakedness, shining in the dark room.

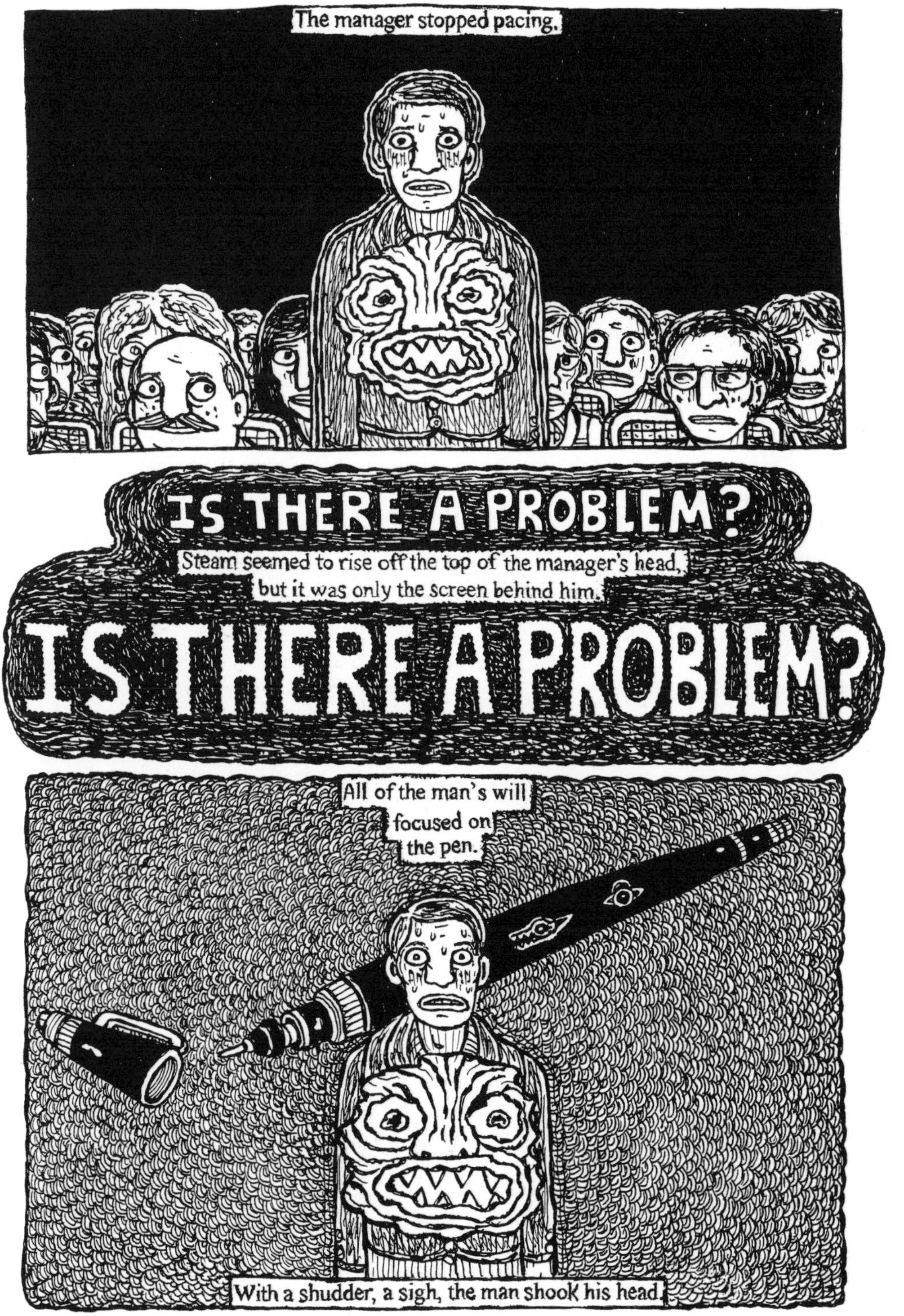
The manager stopped pacing.
IS THERE A PROBLEM?
Steam seemed to rise off the top of the manager's head, but it was only the screen behind him.
IS THERE A PROBLEM?
All of the man's will focused on the pen.
With a shudder, a sigh, the man shook his head.

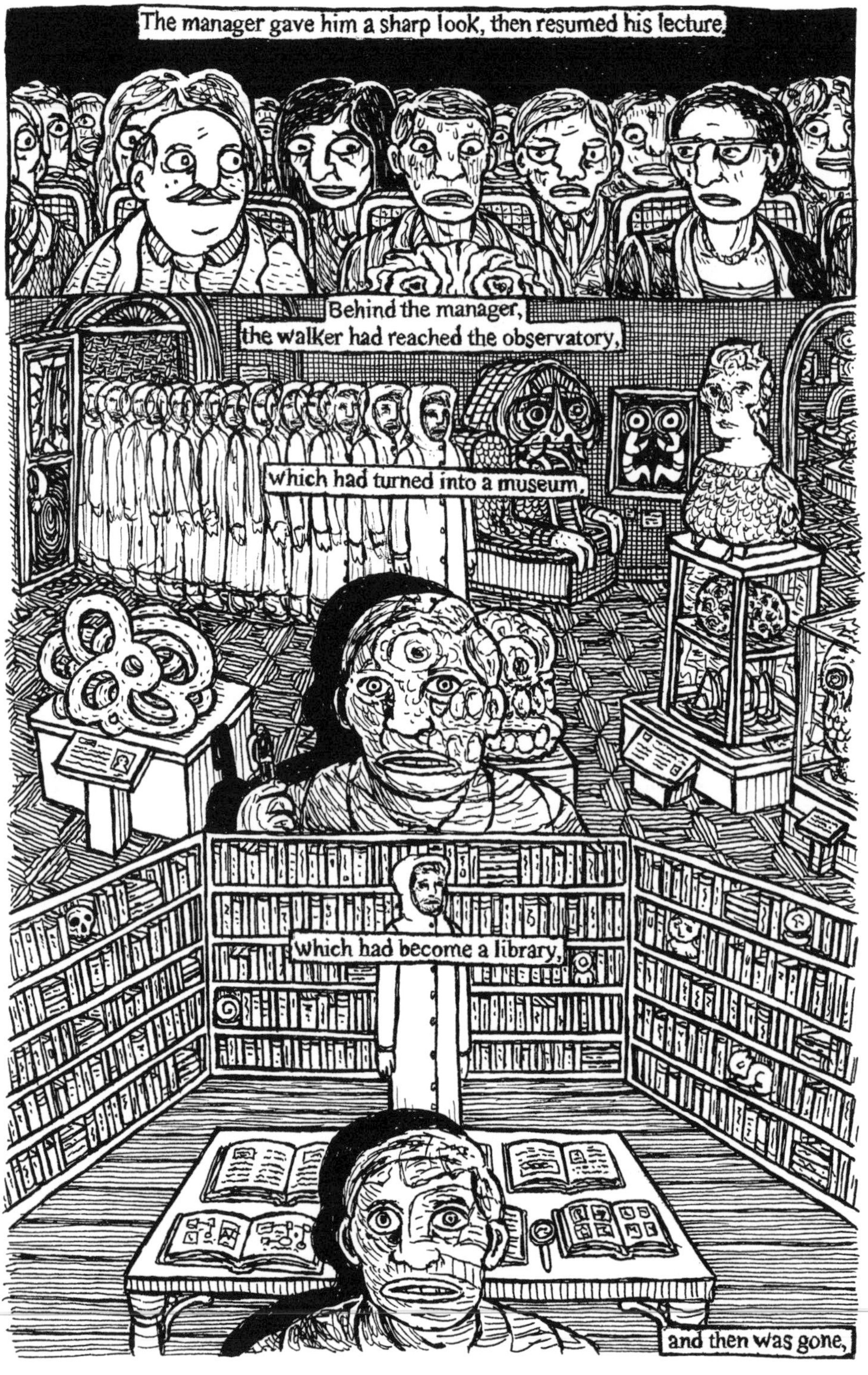
The manager gave him a sharp look, then resumed his lecture.
Behind the manager, the walker had reached the observatory,
which had turned into a museum,
which had become a library,
and then was gone,

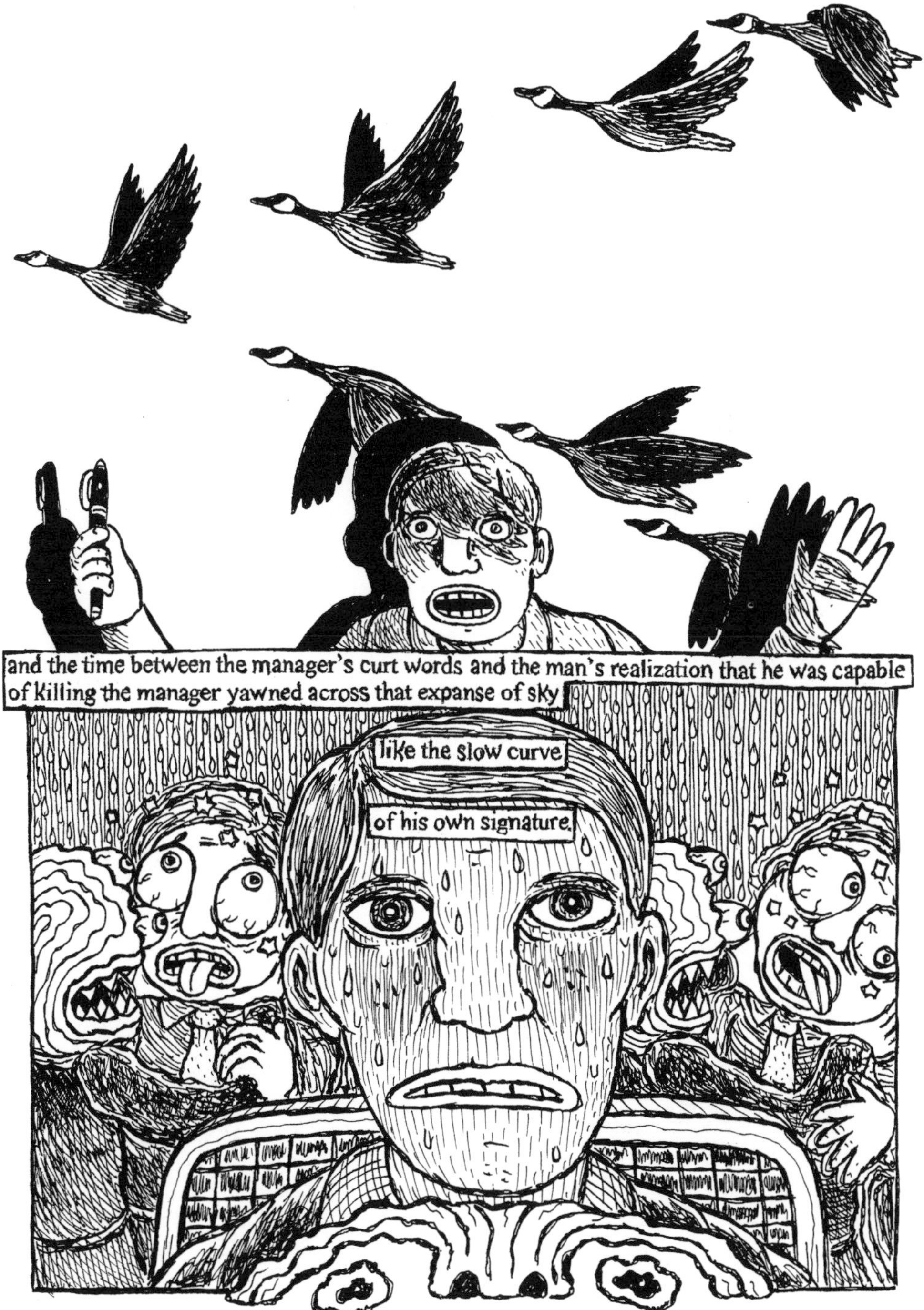
and the time between the manager's curt words and the man's realization that he was capable of killing the manager yawned across that expanse of sky
like the slow curve
of his own signature.

Sometimes

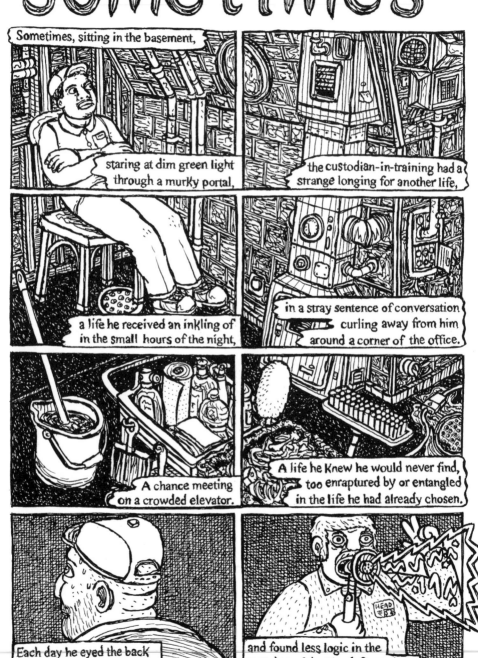

Sometimes, sitting in the basement,

staring at dim green light through a murky portal,

the custodian-in-training had a strange longing for another life,

a life he received an inkling of in the small hours of the night,

in a stray sentence of conversation curling away from him around a corner of the office.

A chance meeting on a crowded elevator.

A life he knew he would never find, too enraptured by or entangled in the life he had already chosen.

Each day he eyed the back of his trainer with suspicion

and found less logic in the speeches of the Head Custodian.

conquest

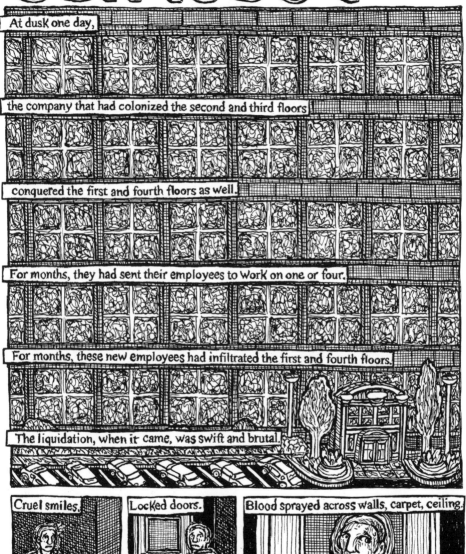

At dusk one day,

the company that had colonized the second and third floors

conquered the first and fourth floors as well.

For months, they had sent their employees to work on one or four.

For months, these new employees had infiltrated the first and fourth floors.

The liquidation, when it came, was swift and brutal.

Cruel smiles.

Locked doors.

Blood sprayed across walls, carpet, ceiling.

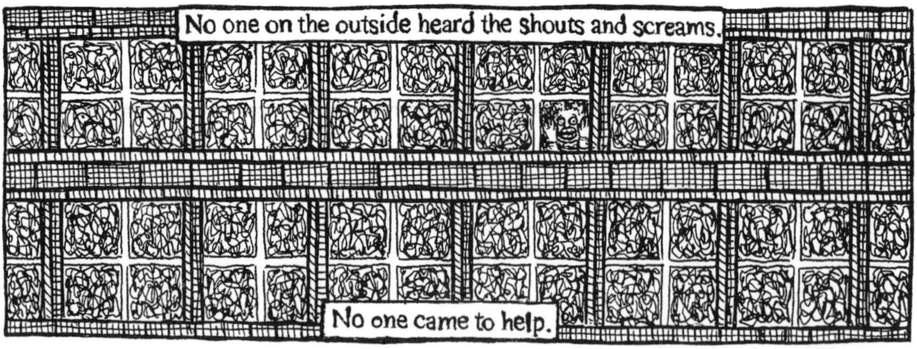
No one on the outside heard the shouts and screams.
No one came to help.

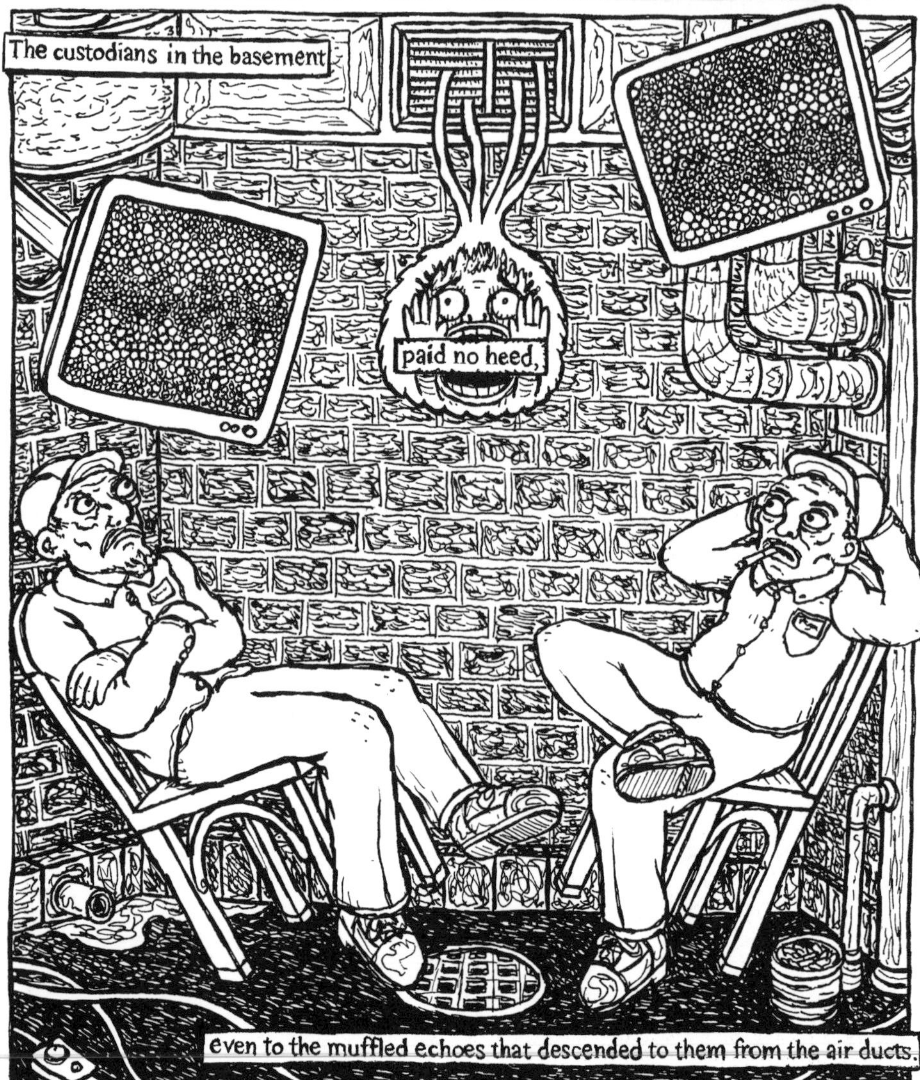
The custodians in the basement
paid no heed,
even to the muffled echoes that descended to them from the air ducts.

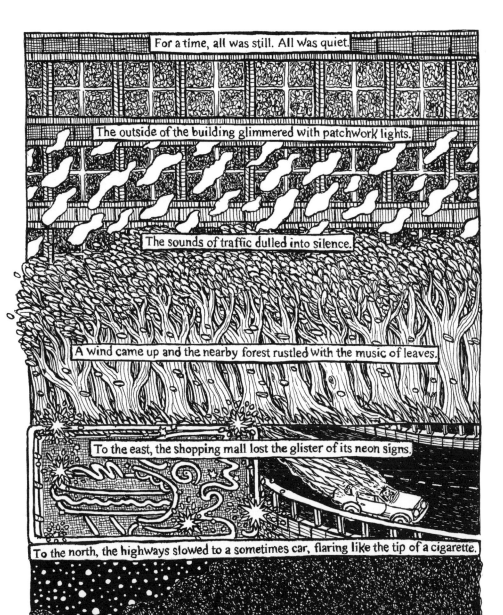

For a time, all was still. All was quiet.

The outside of the building glimmered with patchwork lights.

The sounds of traffic dulled into silence.

A wind came up and the nearby forest rustled with the music of leaves.

To the east, the shopping mall lost the glister of its neon signs.

To the north, the highways slowed to a sometimes car, flaring like the tip of a cigarette.

To the south, the sudden stars cut off abruptly,

victims of the gloom that hid the south from all but the most piercing gaze.

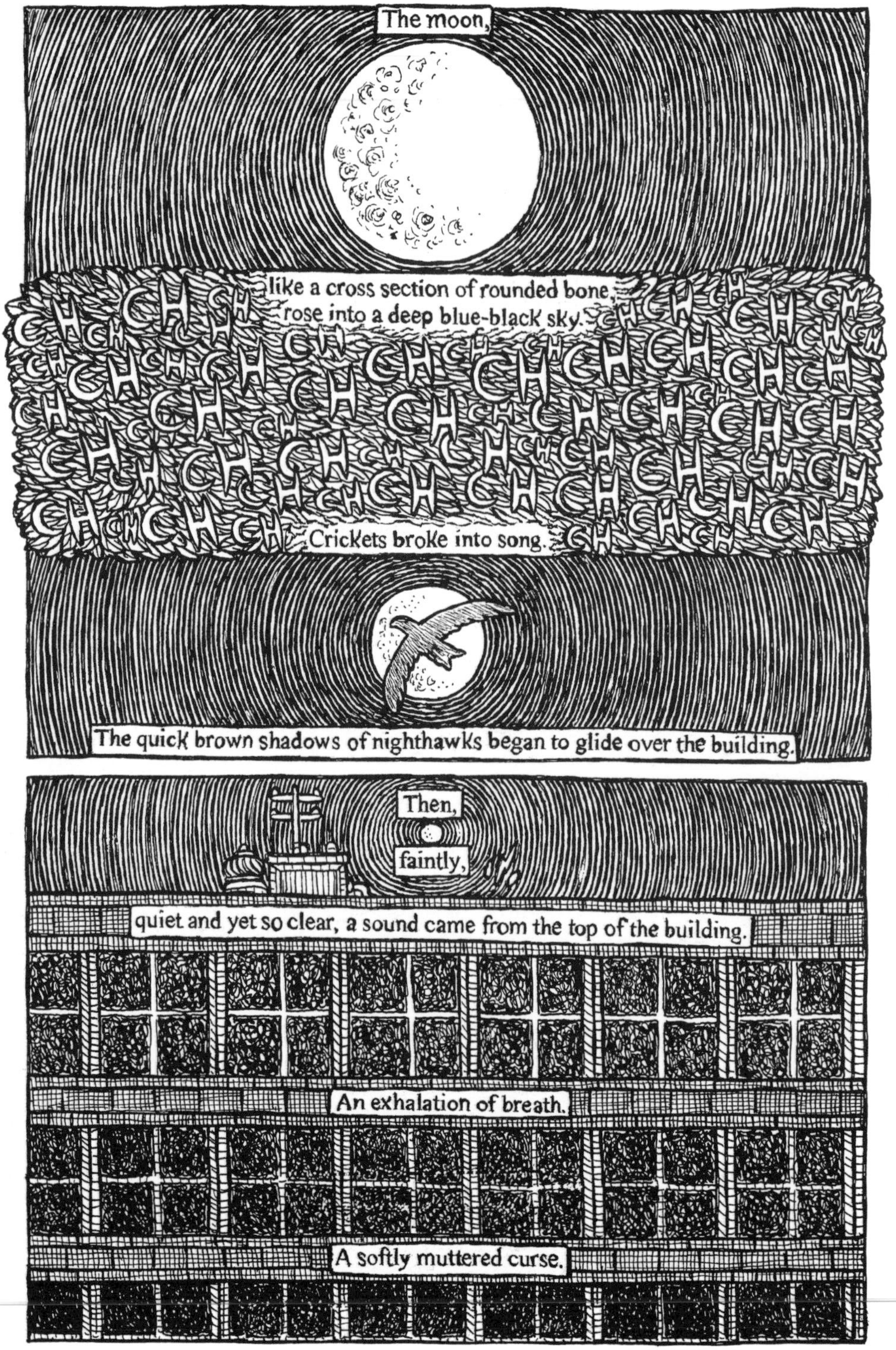

The moon,
like a cross section of rounded bone, rose into a deep blue-black sky.
CH CH CH CH
Crickets broke into song.
The quick brown shadows of nighthawks began to glide over the building.
Then,
faintly,
quiet and yet so clear, a sound came from the top of the building.
An exhalation of breath.
A softly muttered curse.

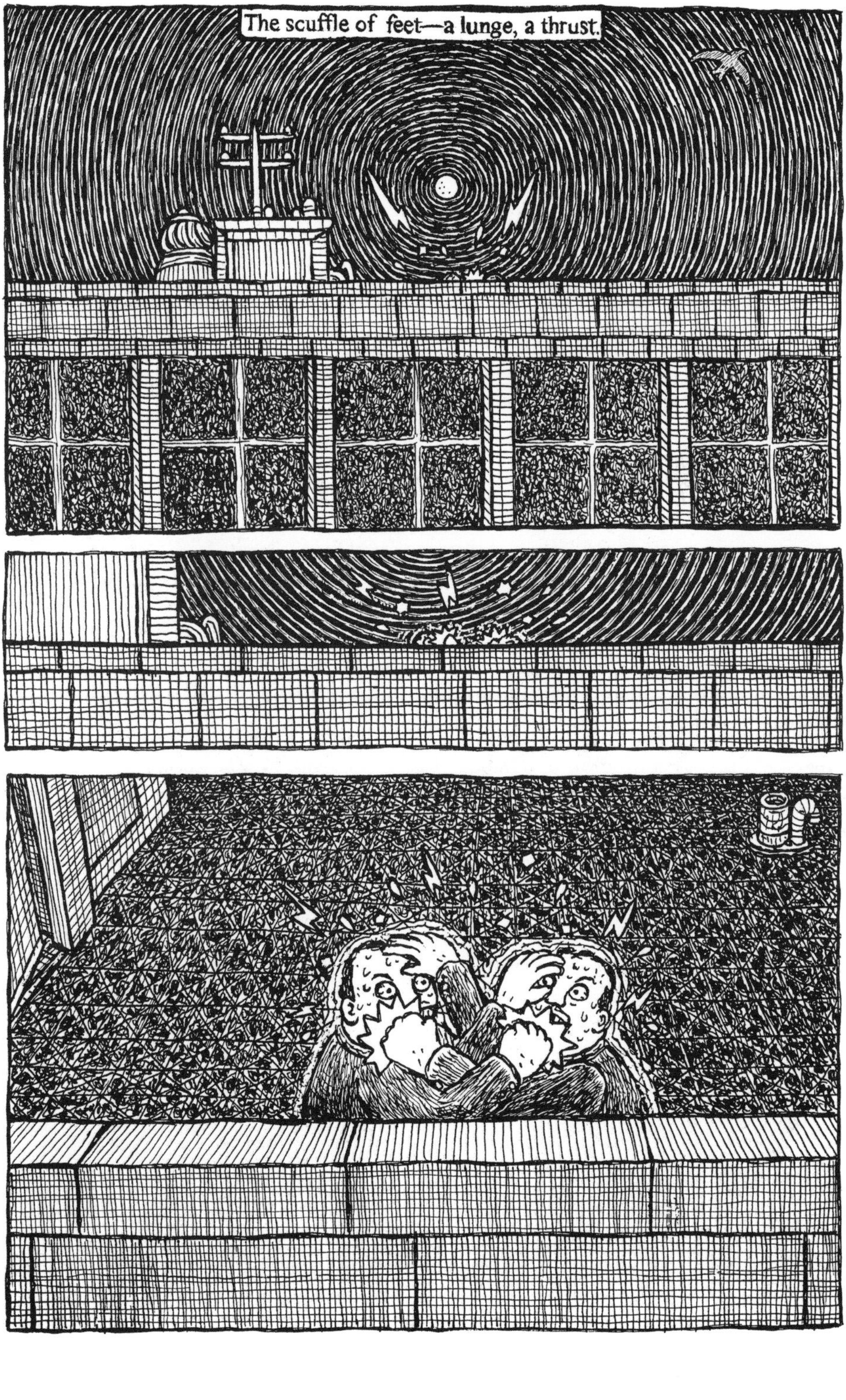
The scuffle of feet—a lunge, a thrust.

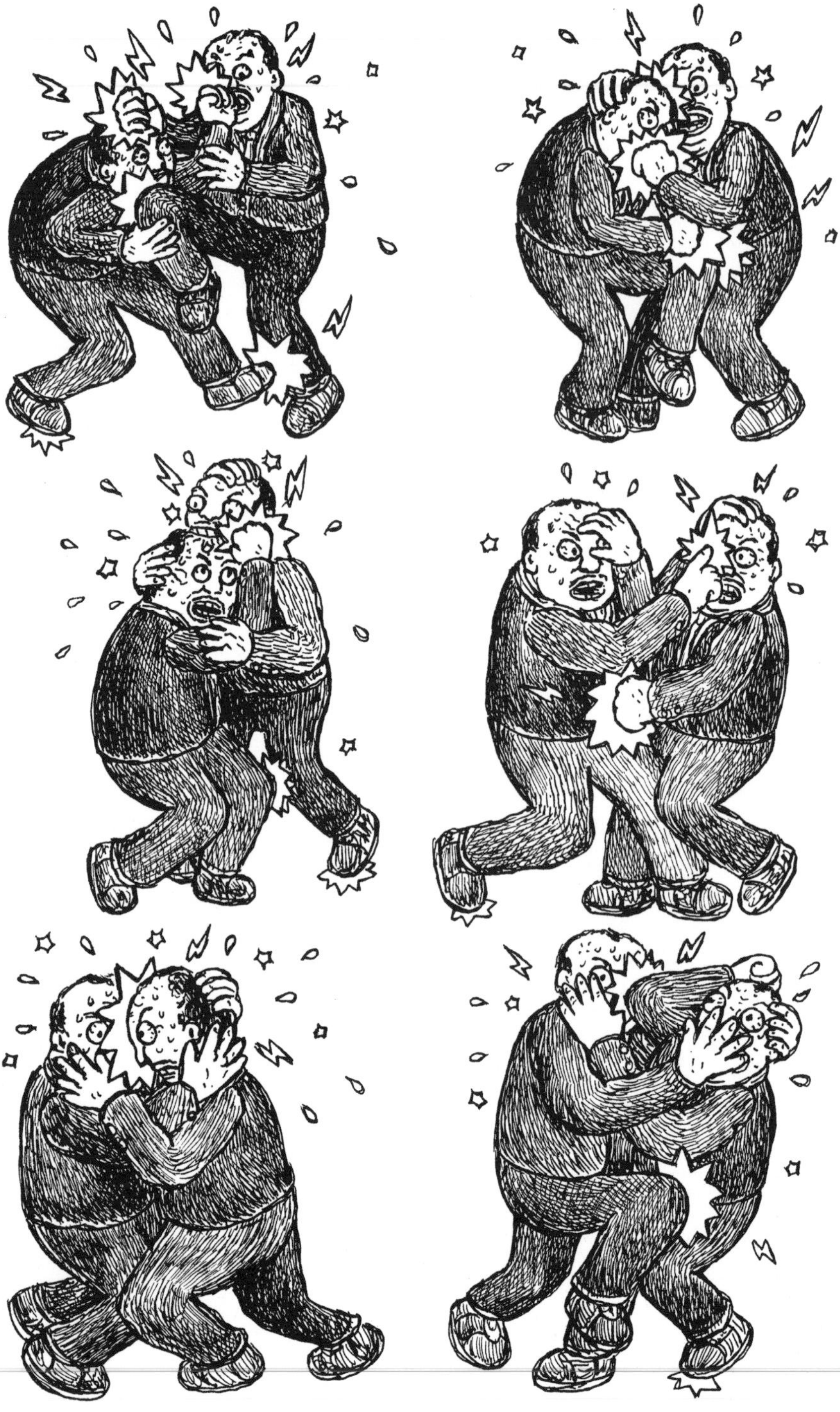

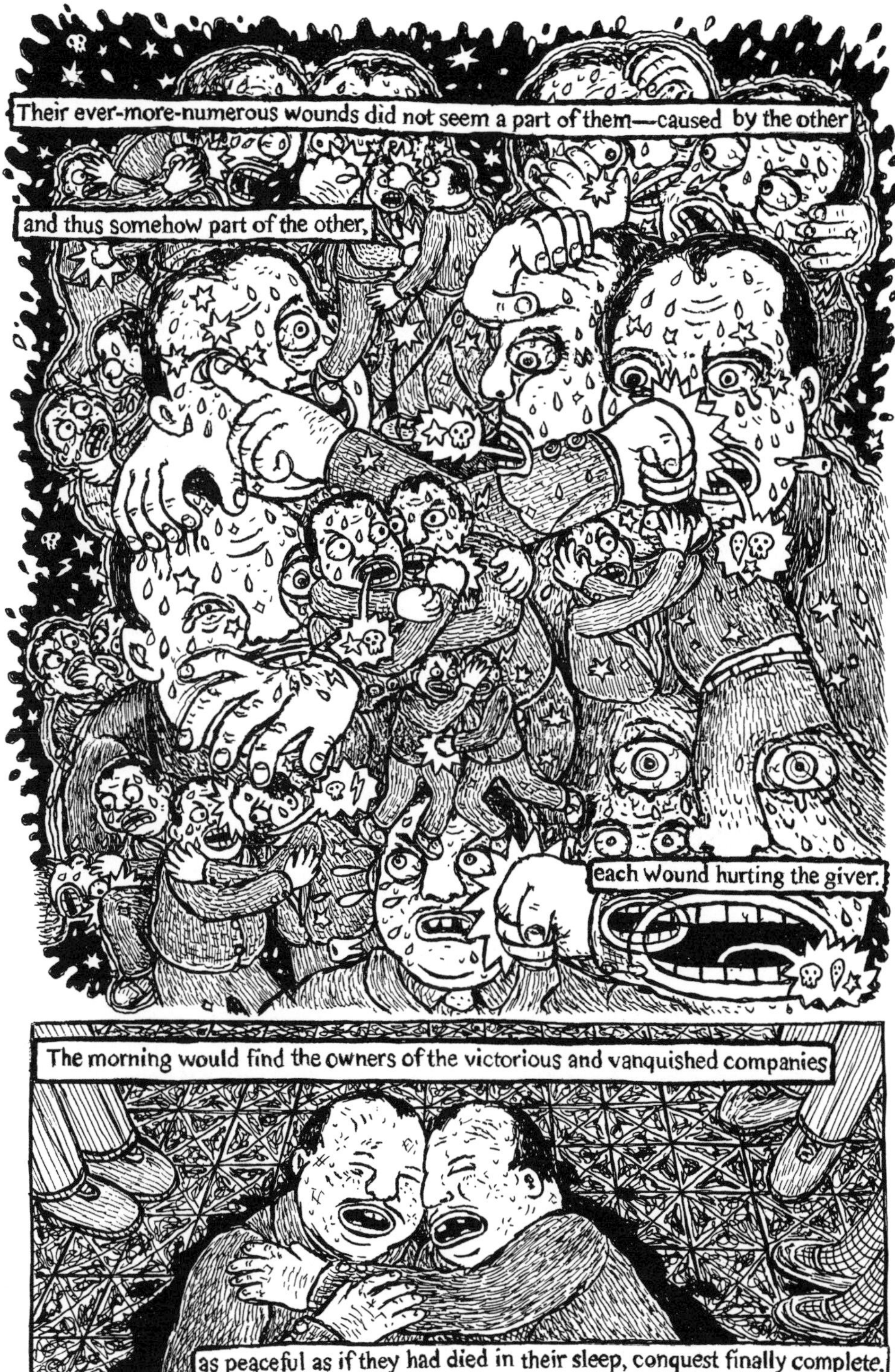
Their ever-more-numerous wounds did not seem a part of them—caused by the other
and thus somehow part of the other,
each wound hurting the giver.
The morning would find the owners of the victorious and vanquished companies
as peaceful as if they had died in their sleep, conquest finally complete.

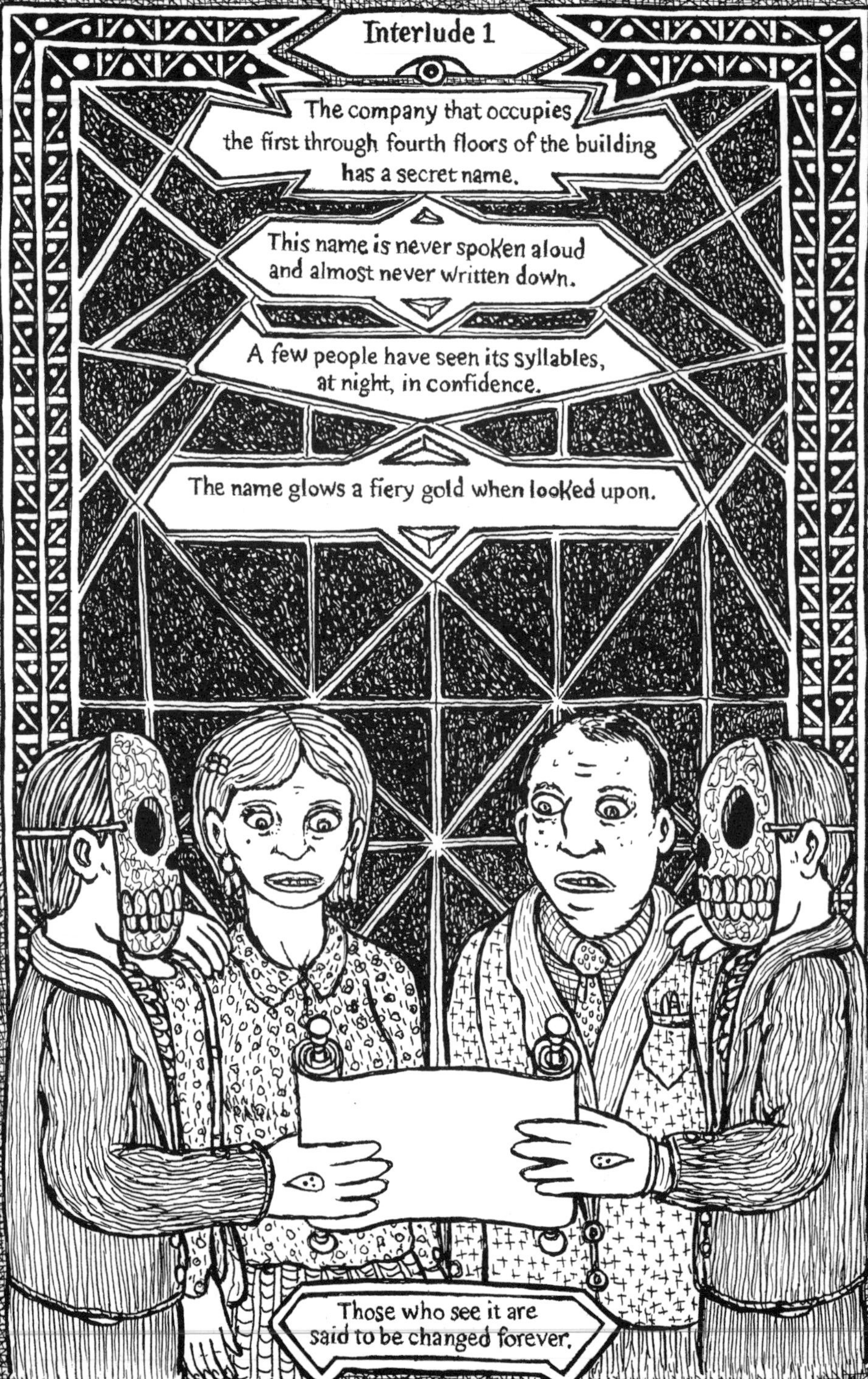
Interlude 1
The company that occupies the first through fourth floors of the building has a secret name.
This name is never spoken aloud and almost never written down.
A few people have seen its syllables, at night, in confidence.
The name glows a fiery gold when looked upon.
Those who see it are said to be changed forever.

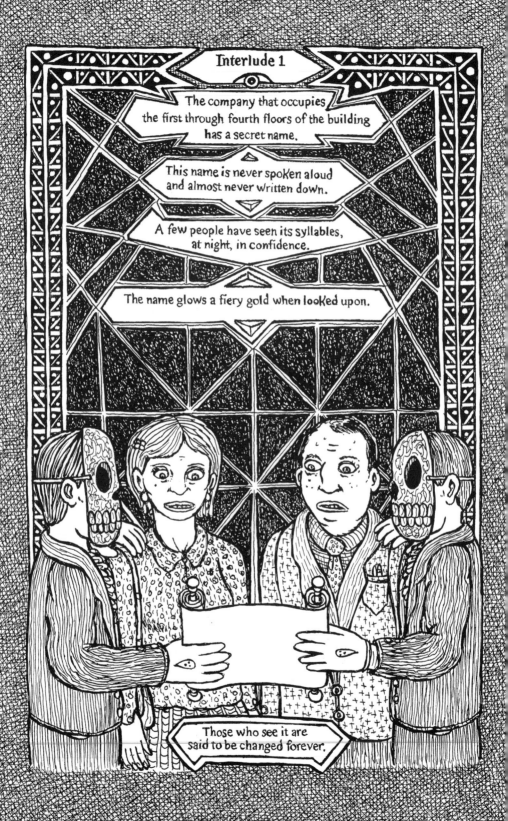

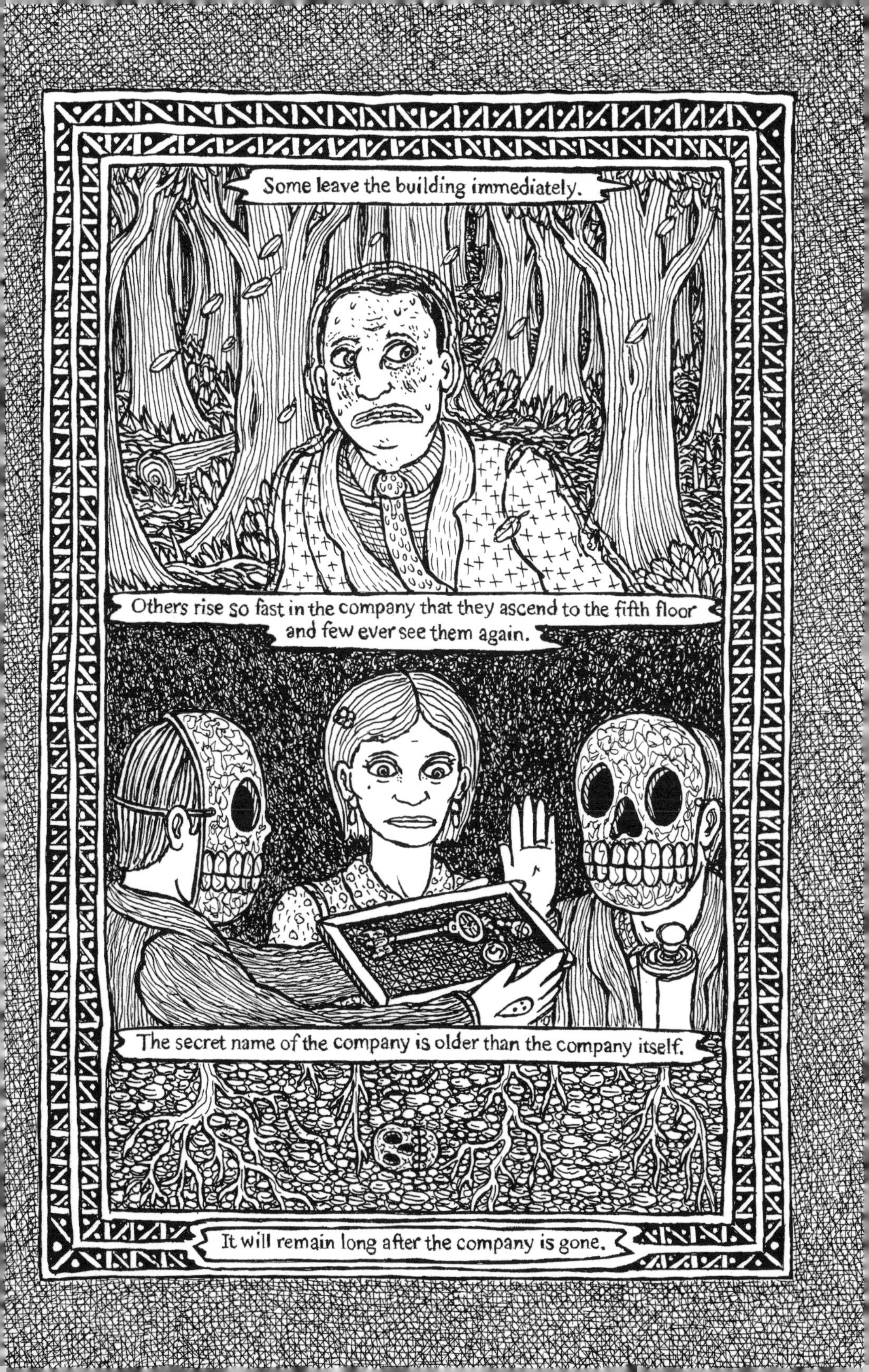
Some leave the building immediately.
Others rise so fast in the company that they ascend to the fifth floor and few ever see them again.
The secret name of the company is older than the company itself.
It will remain long after the company is gone.

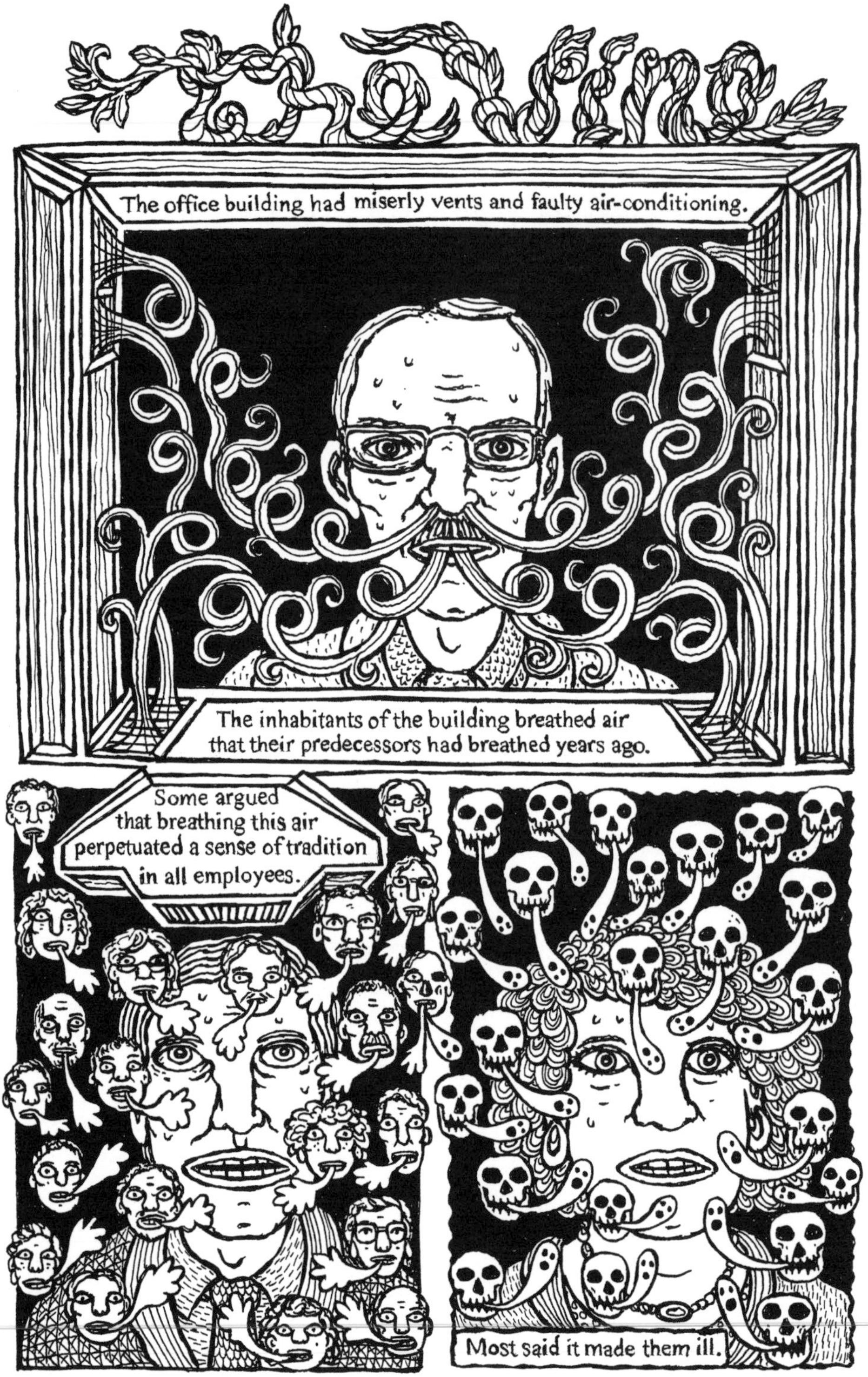
The office building had miserly vents and faulty air-conditioning.
The inhabitants of the building breathed air that their predecessors had breathed years ago.
Some argued that breathing this air perpetuated a sense of tradition in all employees.
Most said it made them ill.

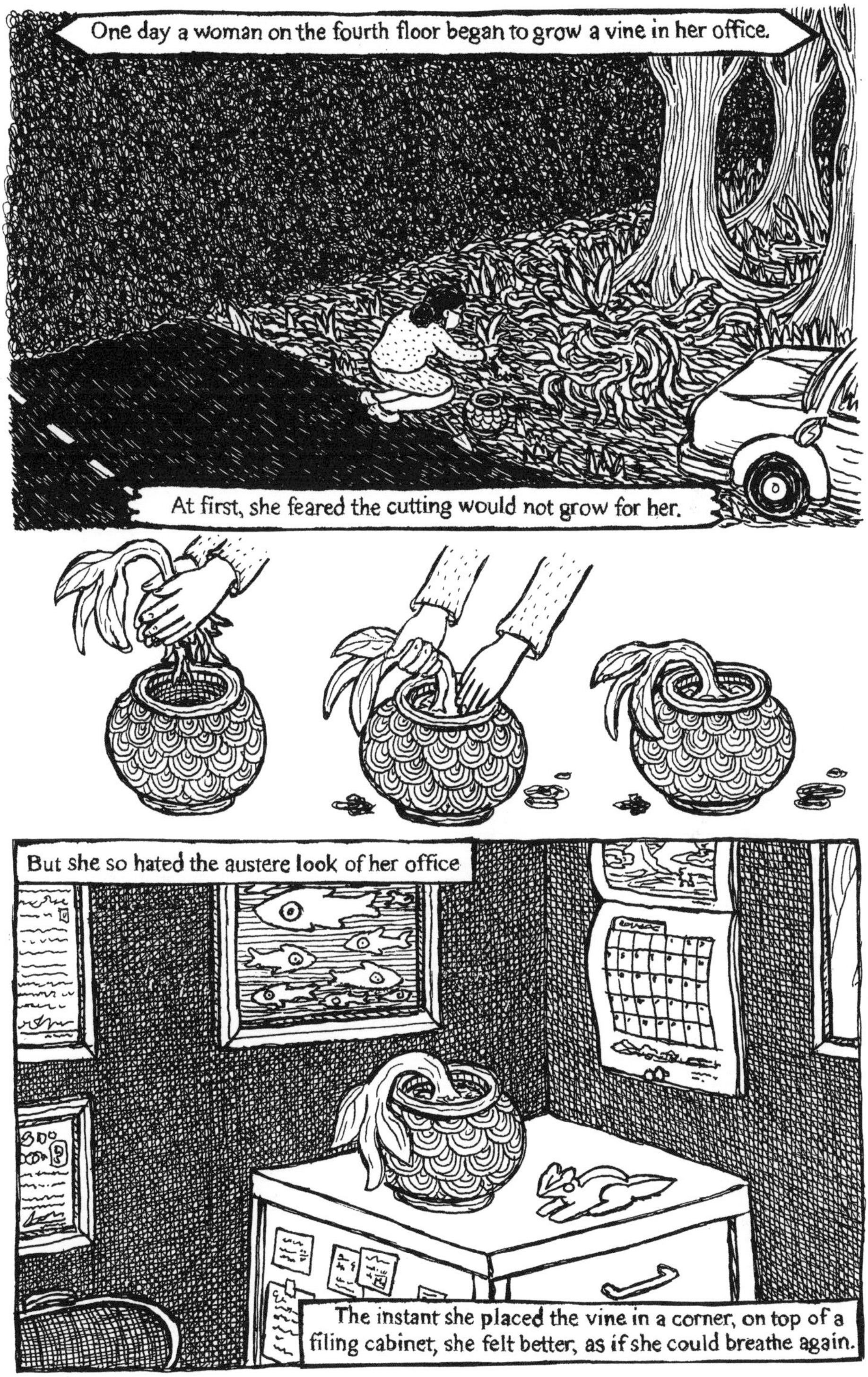
One day a woman on the fourth floor began to grow a vine in her office.
At first, she feared the cutting would not grow for her.
But she so hated the austere look of her office
The instant she placed the vine in a corner, on top of a filing cabinet, she felt better, as if she could breathe again.

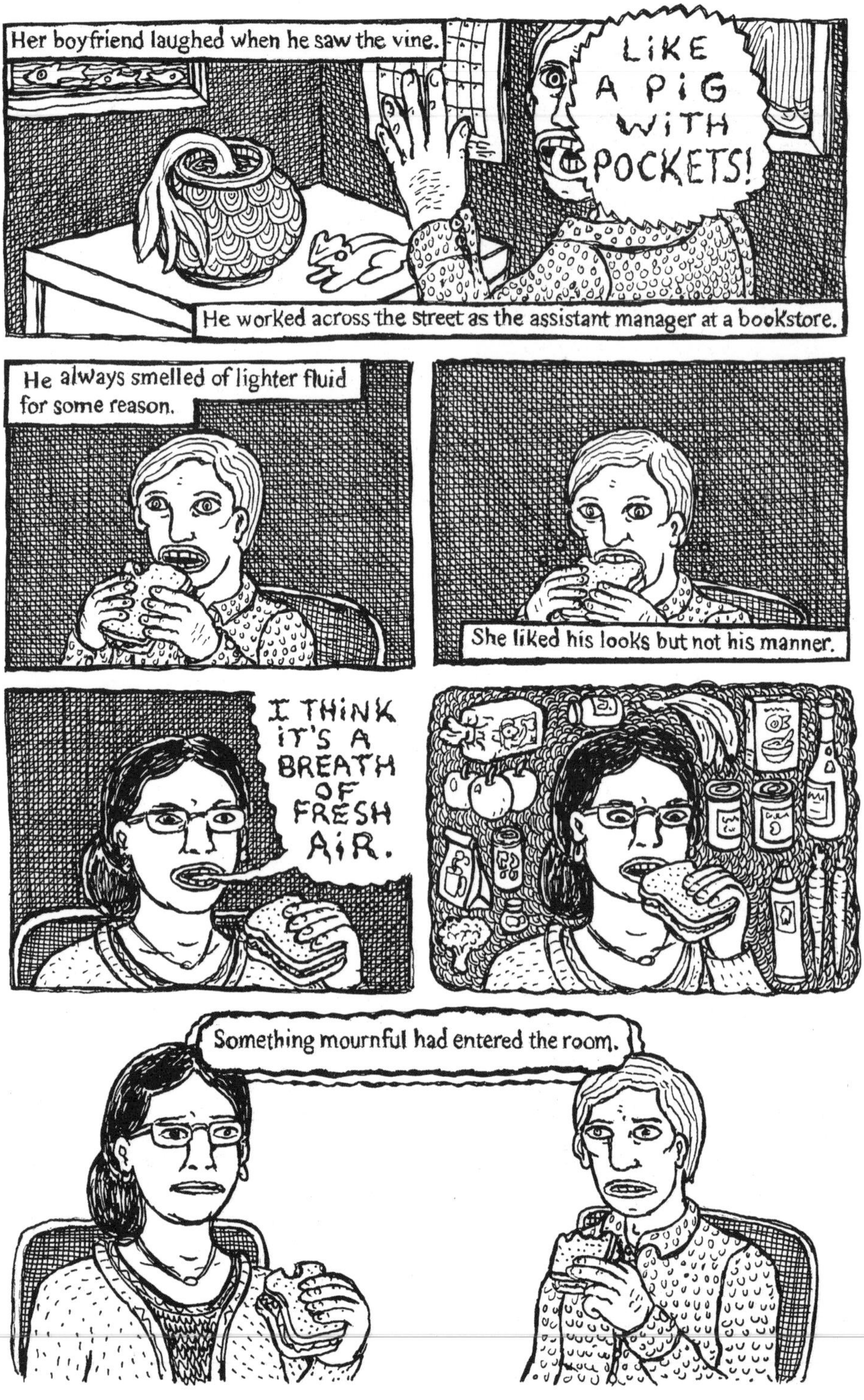
Her boyfriend laughed when he saw the vine.
LIKE A PIG WITH POCKETS!
He worked across the street as the assistant manager at a bookstore.
He always smelled of lighter fluid for some reason.
She liked his looks but not his manner.
I THINK IT'S A BREATH OF FRESH AIR.
Something mournful had entered the room.

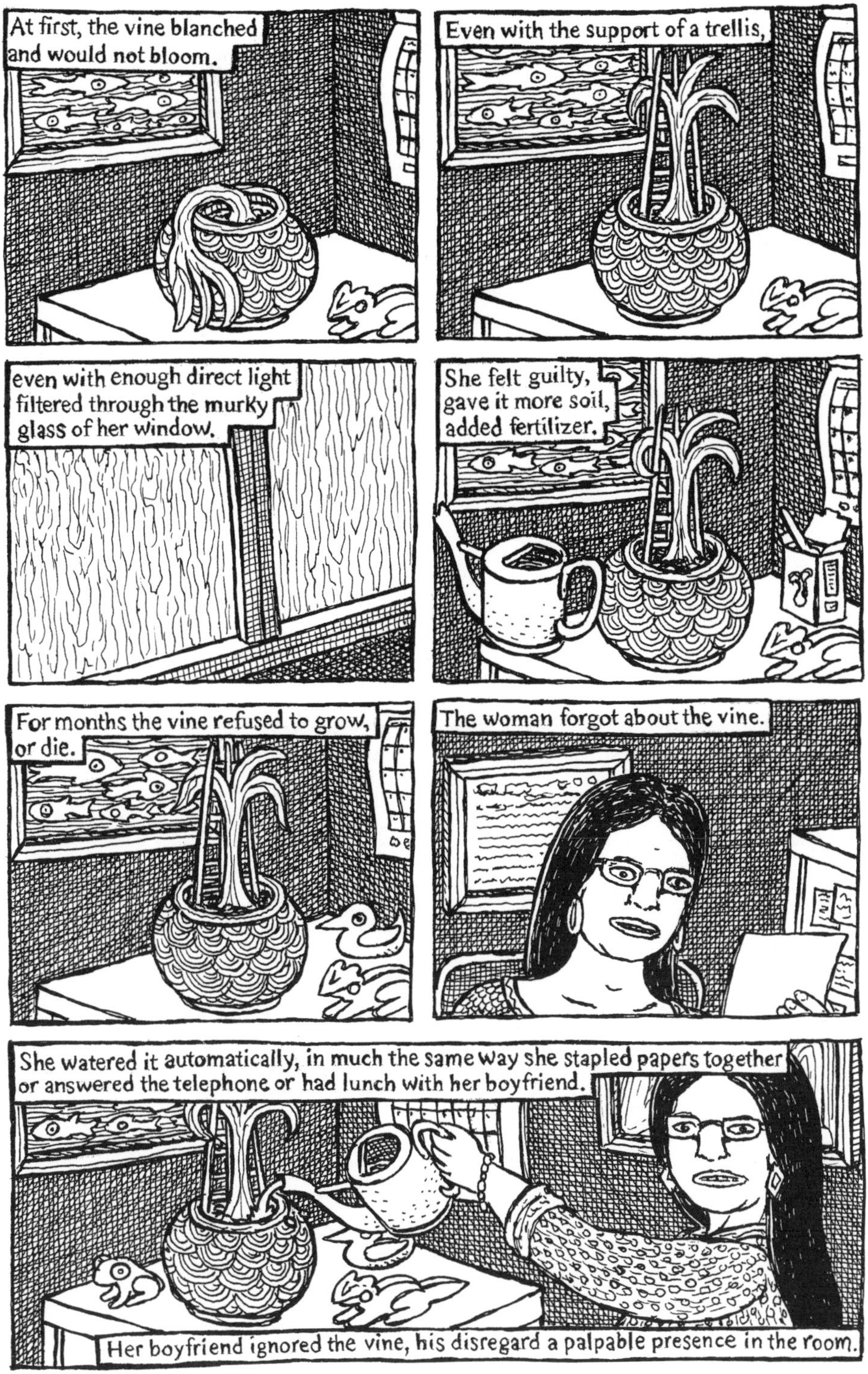
At first, the vine blanched and would not bloom.
Even with the support of a trellis,
even with enough direct light filtered through the murky glass of her window.
She felt guilty, gave it more soil, added fertilizer.
For months the vine refused to grow, or die.
The woman forgot about the vine.
She watered it automatically, in much the same way she stapled papers together or answered the telephone or had lunch with her boyfriend.
Her boyfriend ignored the vine, his disregard a palpable presence in the room.

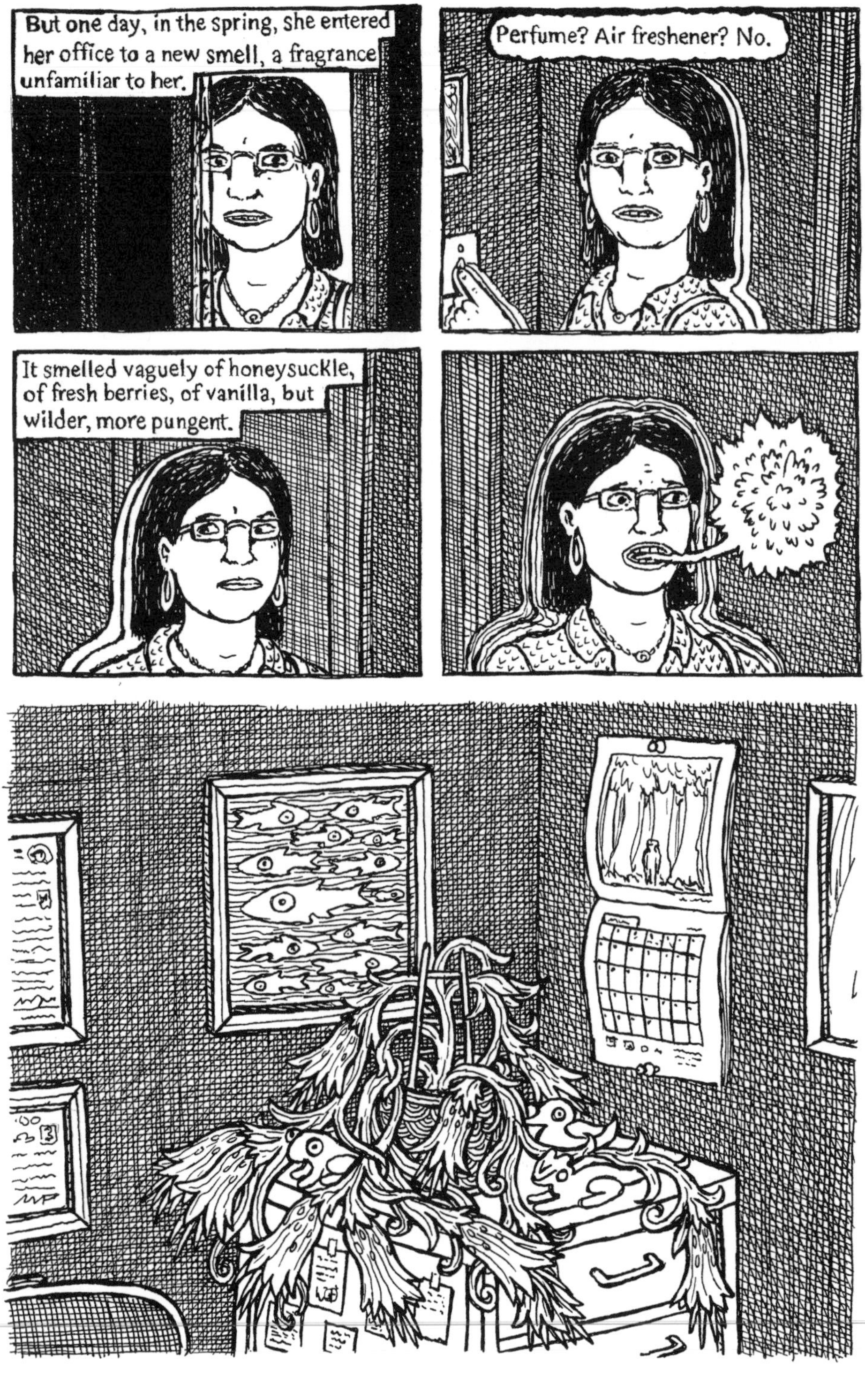
But one day, in the spring, she entered her office to a new smell, a fragrance unfamiliar to her.
Perfume? Air freshener? No.
It smelled vaguely of honeysuckle, of fresh berries, of vanilla, but wilder, more pungent.

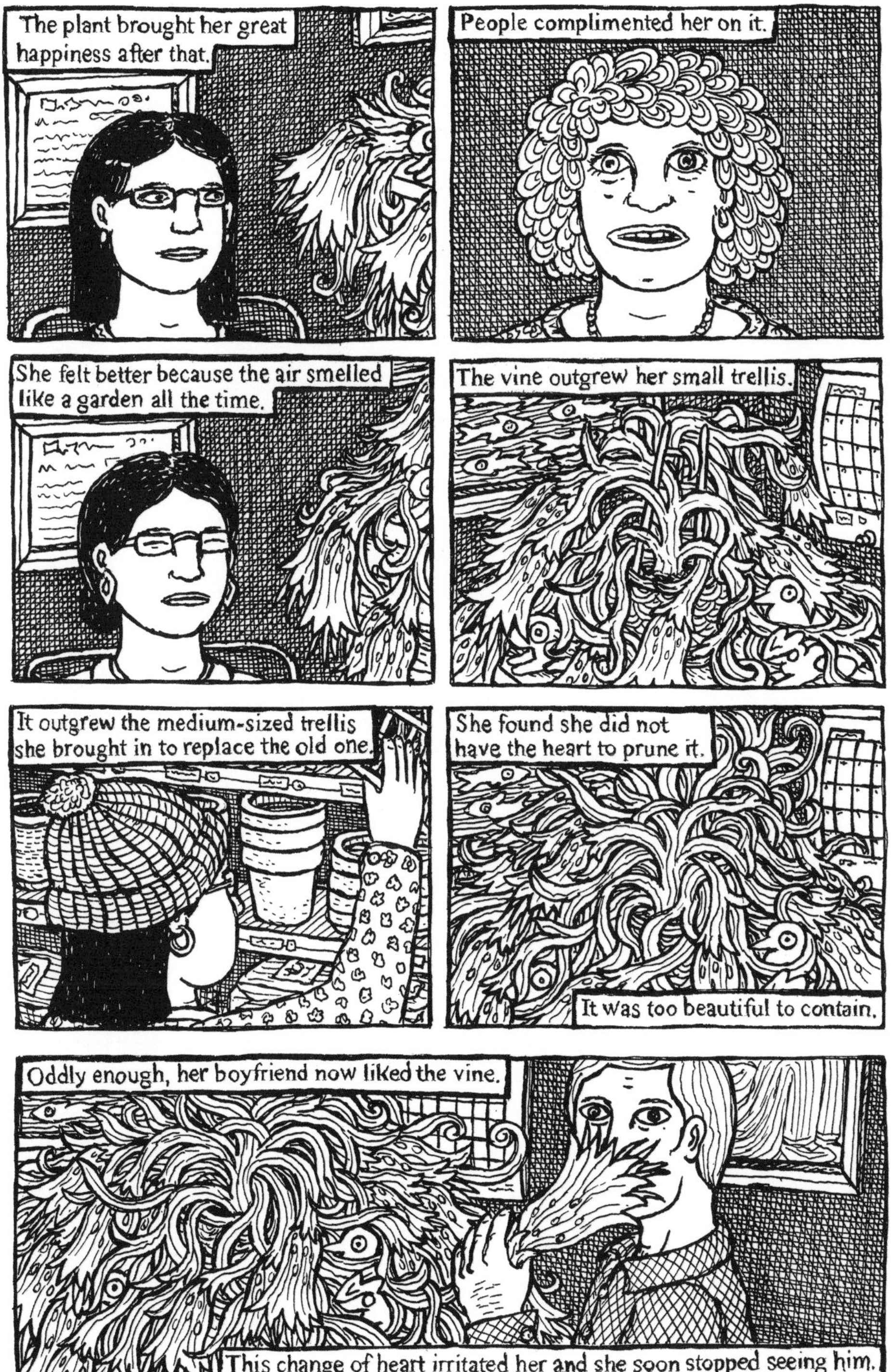
The plant brought her great happiness after that.
People complimented her on it.
She felt better because the air smelled like a garden all the time.
The vine outgrew her small trellis.
It outgrew the medium-sized trellis she brought in to replace the old one.
She found she did not have the heart to prune it.
It was too beautiful to contain.
Oddly enough, her boyfriend now liked the vine.
This change of heart irritated her and she soon stopped seeing him.

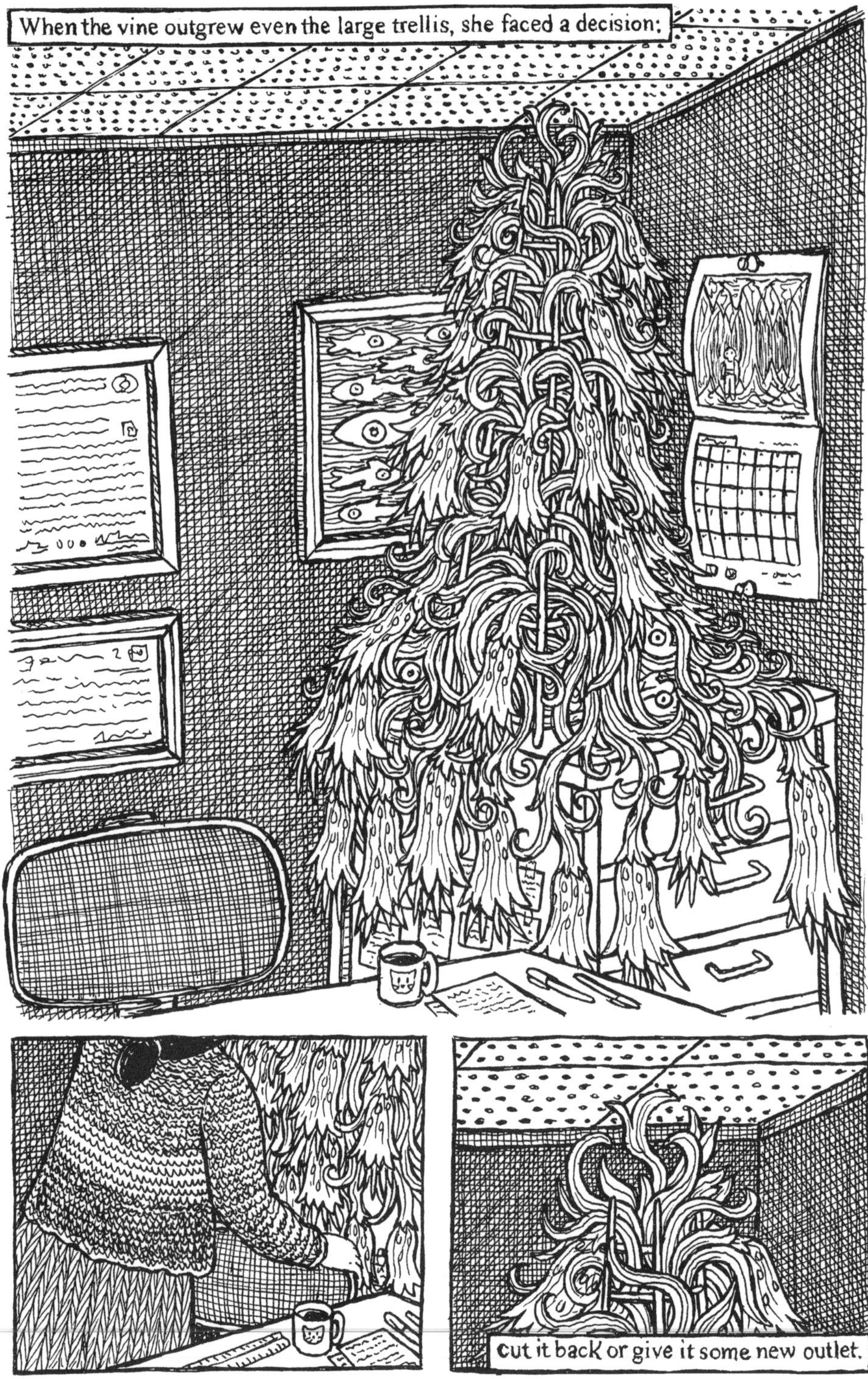
When the vine outgrew even the large trellis, she faced a decision:
cut it back or give it some new outlet.

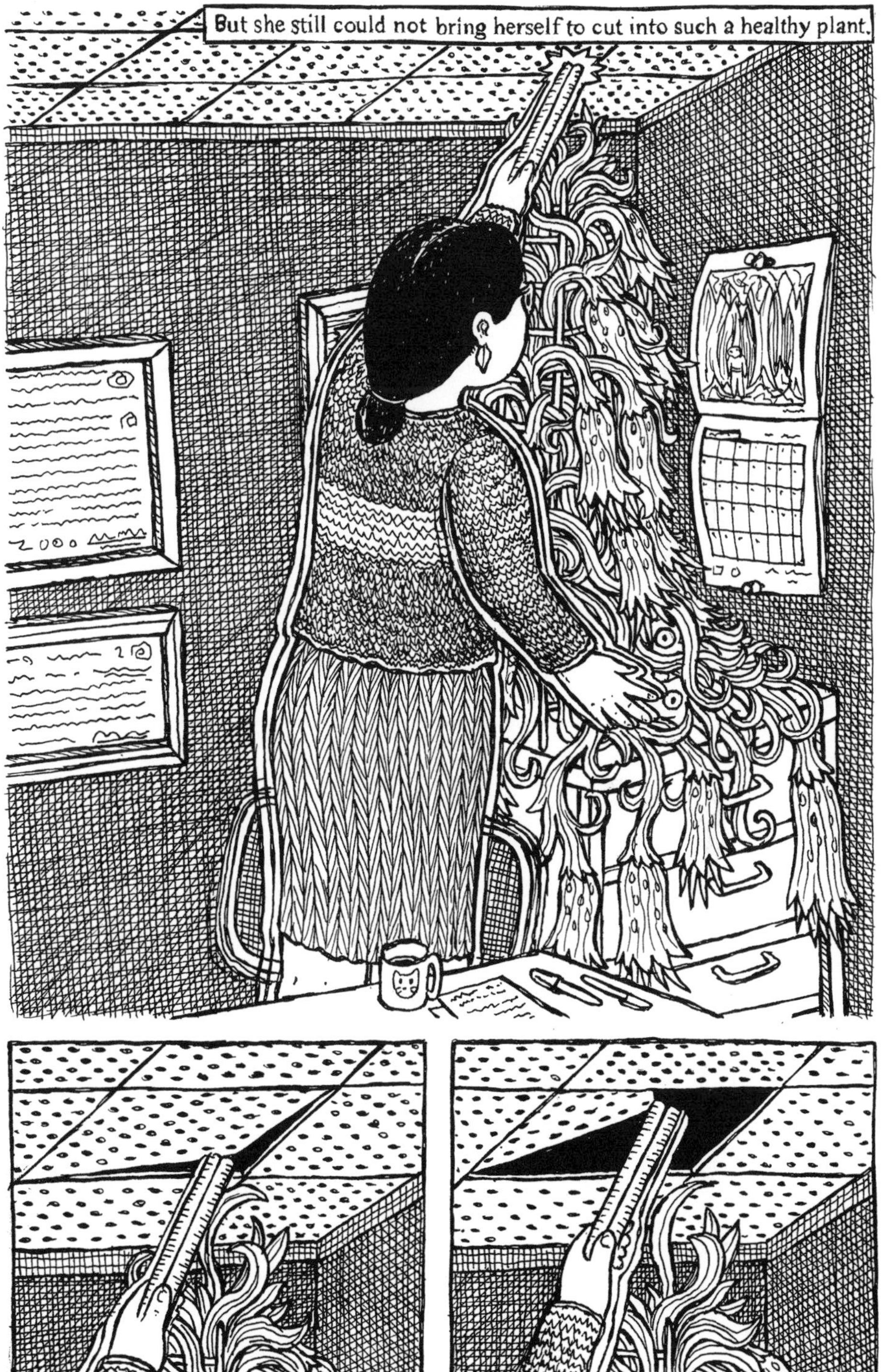
But she still could not bring herself to cut into such a healthy plant.

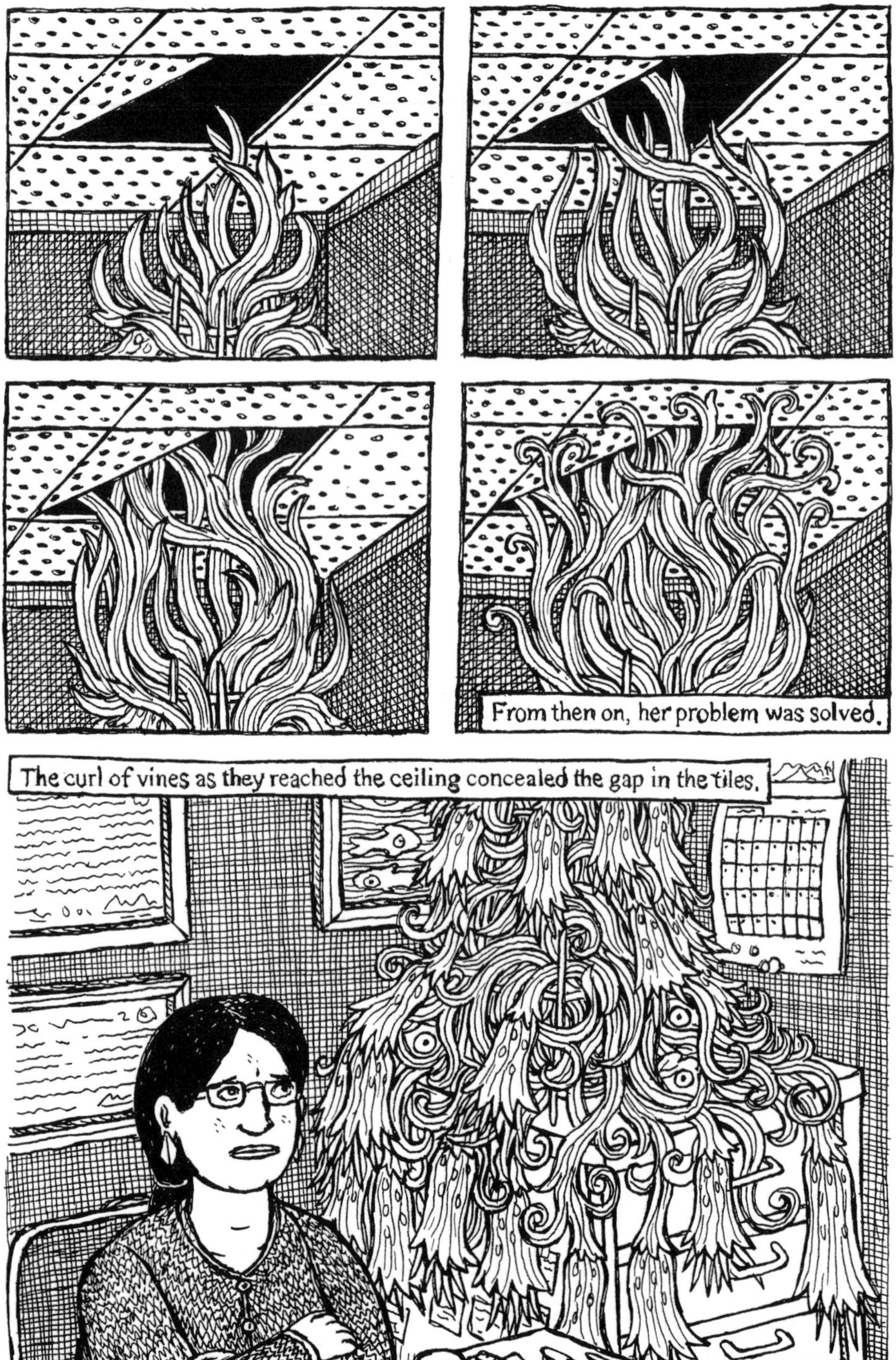
From then on, her problem was solved.
The curl of vines as they reached the ceiling concealed the gap in the tiles.
No one noticed.

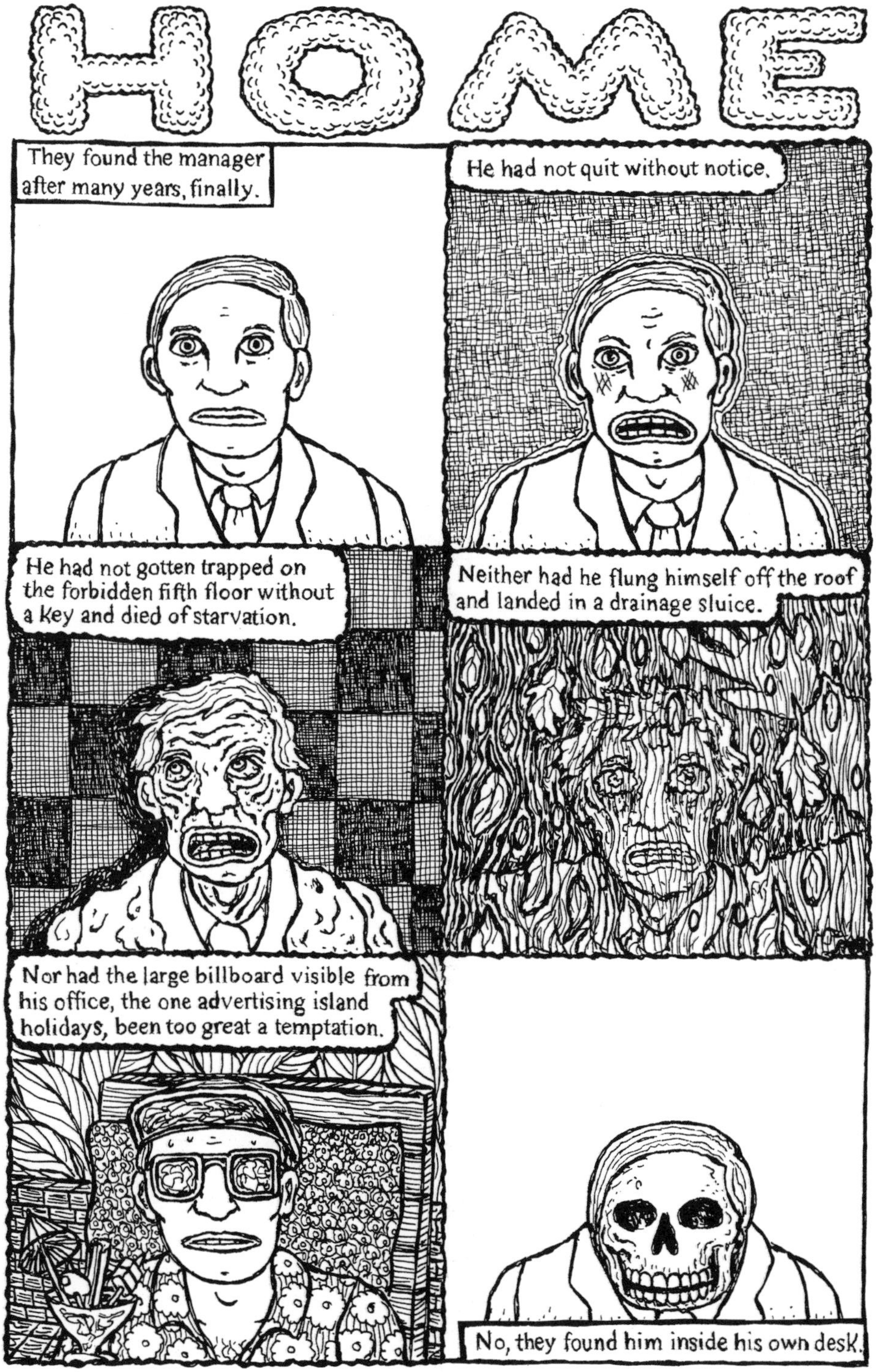
HOME
They found the manager after many years, finally.
He had not quit without notice.
He had not gotten trapped on the forbidden fifth floor without a key and died of starvation.
Neither had he flung himself off the roof and landed in a drainage sluice.
Nor had the large billboard visible from his office, the one advertising island holidays, been too great a temptation.
No, they found him inside his own desk.

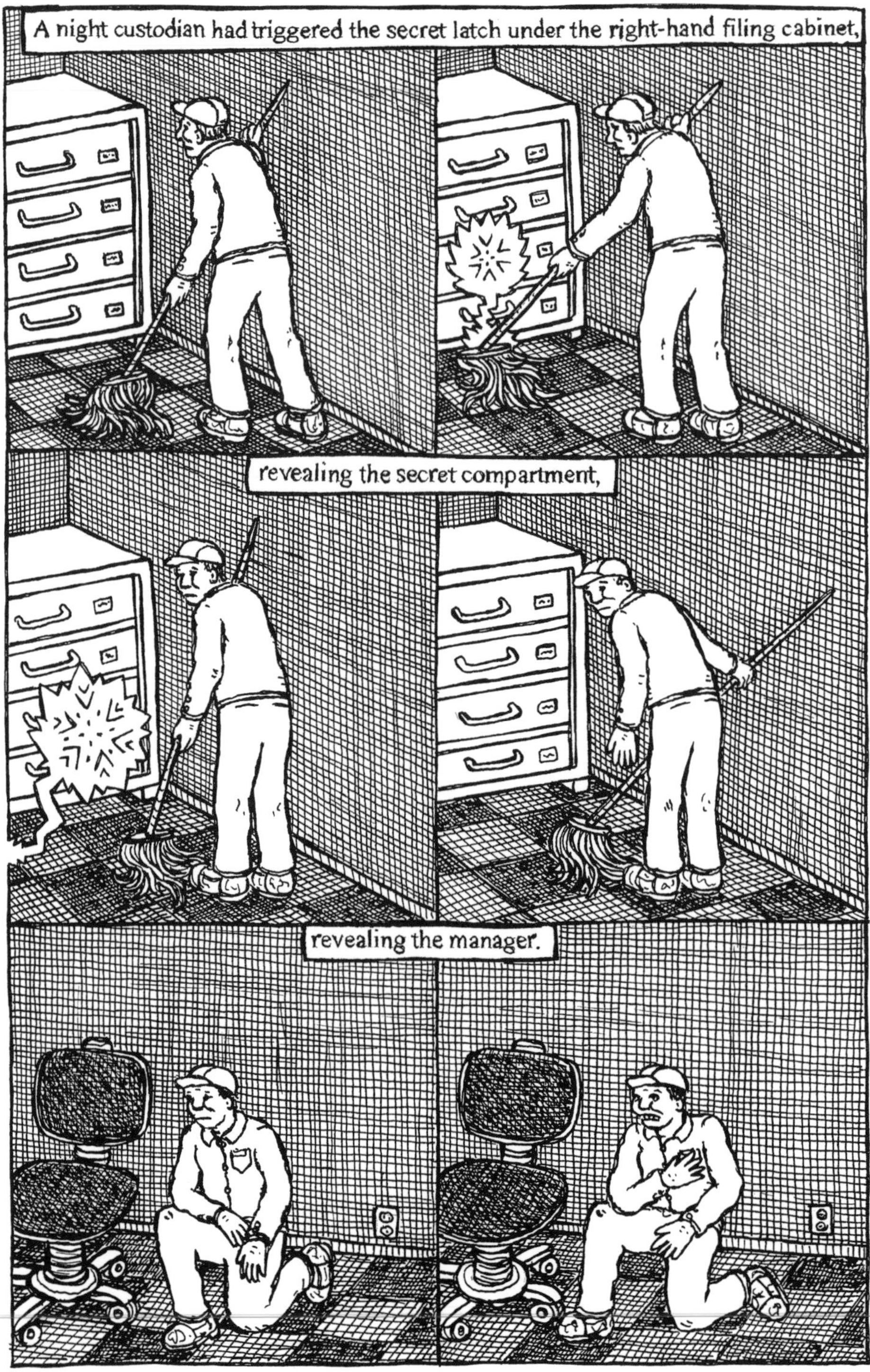
A night custodian had triggered the secret latch under the right-hand filing cabinet,
revealing the secret compartment,
revealing the manager.

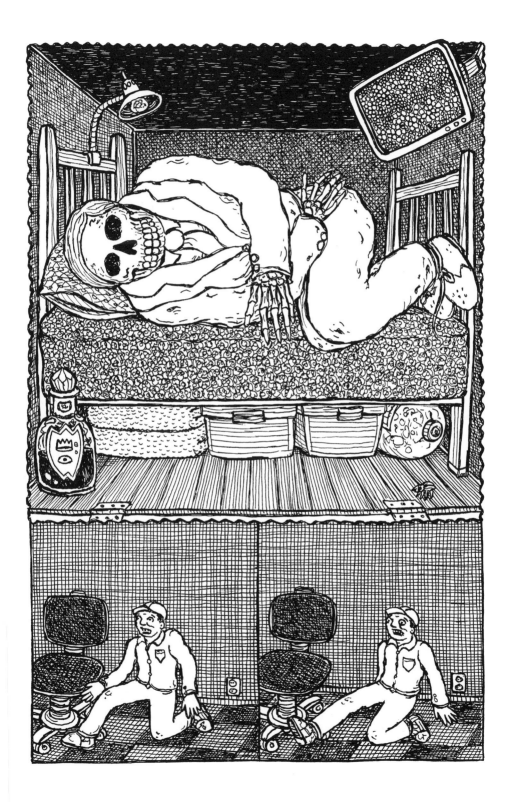

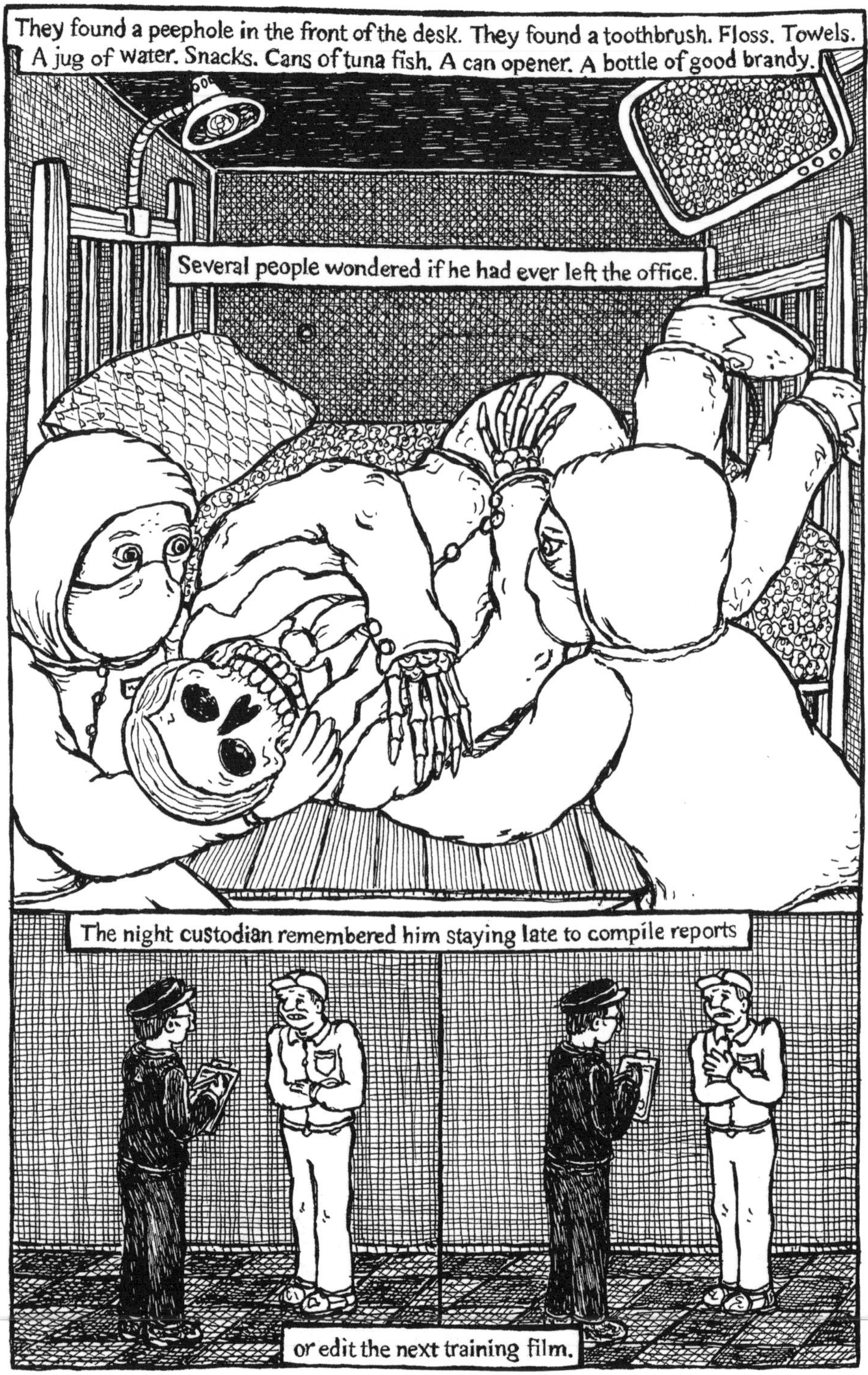
They found a peephole in the front of the desk. They found a toothbrush. Floss. Towels. A jug of water. Snacks. Cans of tuna fish. A can opener. A bottle of good brandy.
Several people wondered if he had ever left the office.
The night custodian remembered him staying late to compile reports
or edit the next training film.

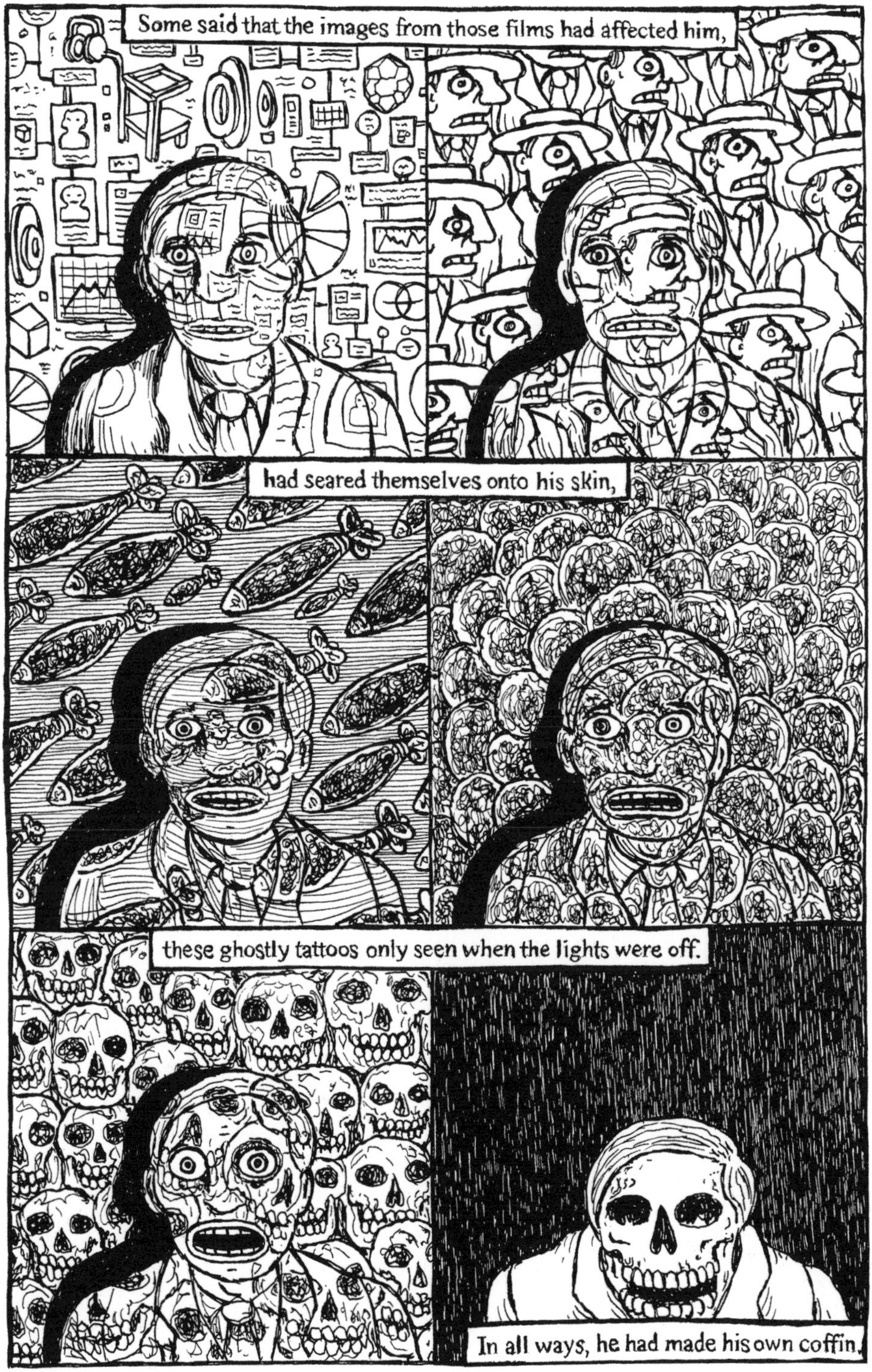
Some said that the images from those films had affected him,
had seared themselves onto his skin,
these ghostly tattoos only seen when the lights were off.
In all ways, he had made his own coffin.

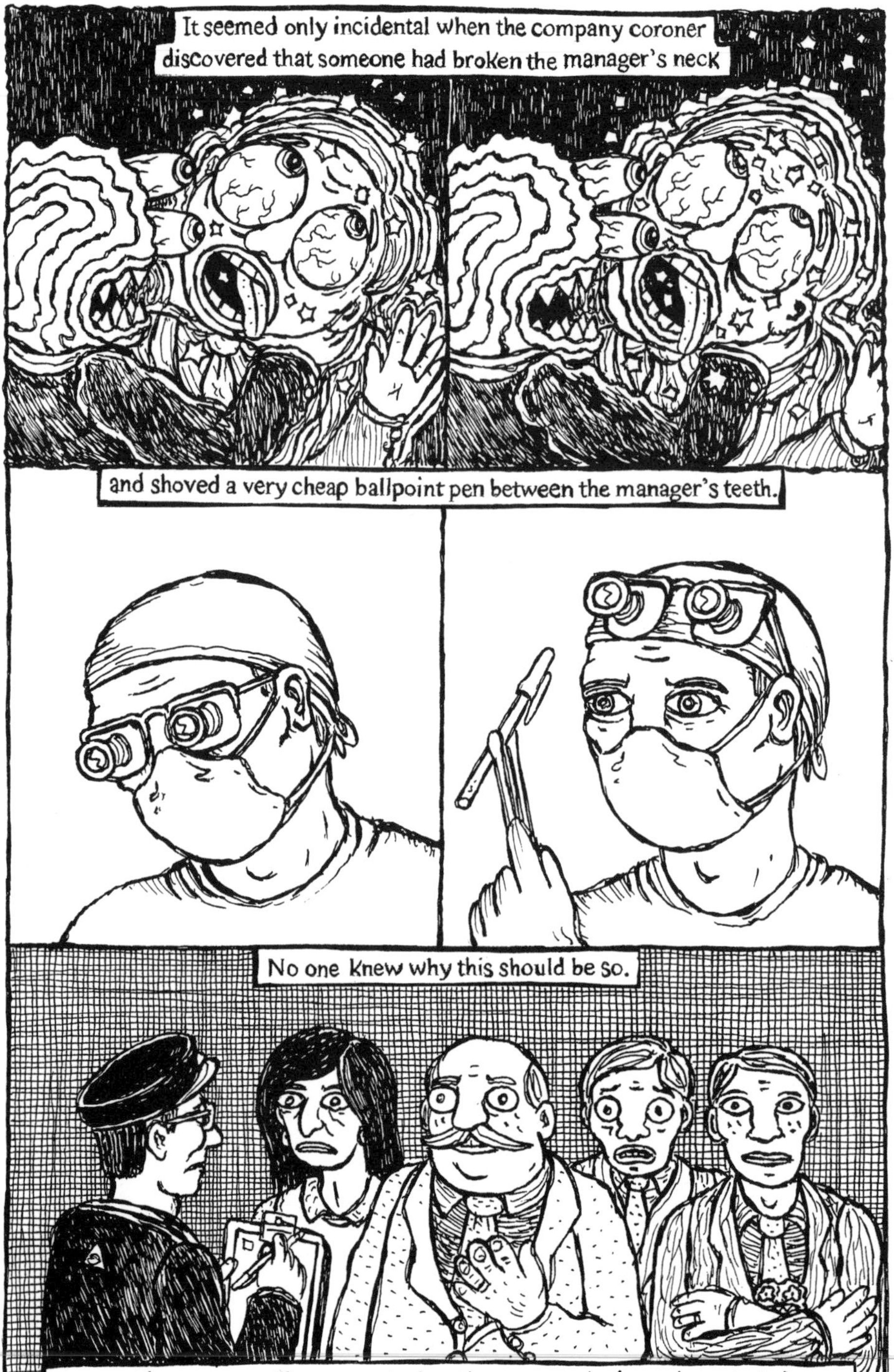
It seemed only incidental when the company coroner discovered that someone had broken the manager's neck
and shoved a very cheap ballpoint pen between the manager's teeth.
No one knew why this should be so.
Nor could anyone recall a moment when the manager had ever been truly happy.

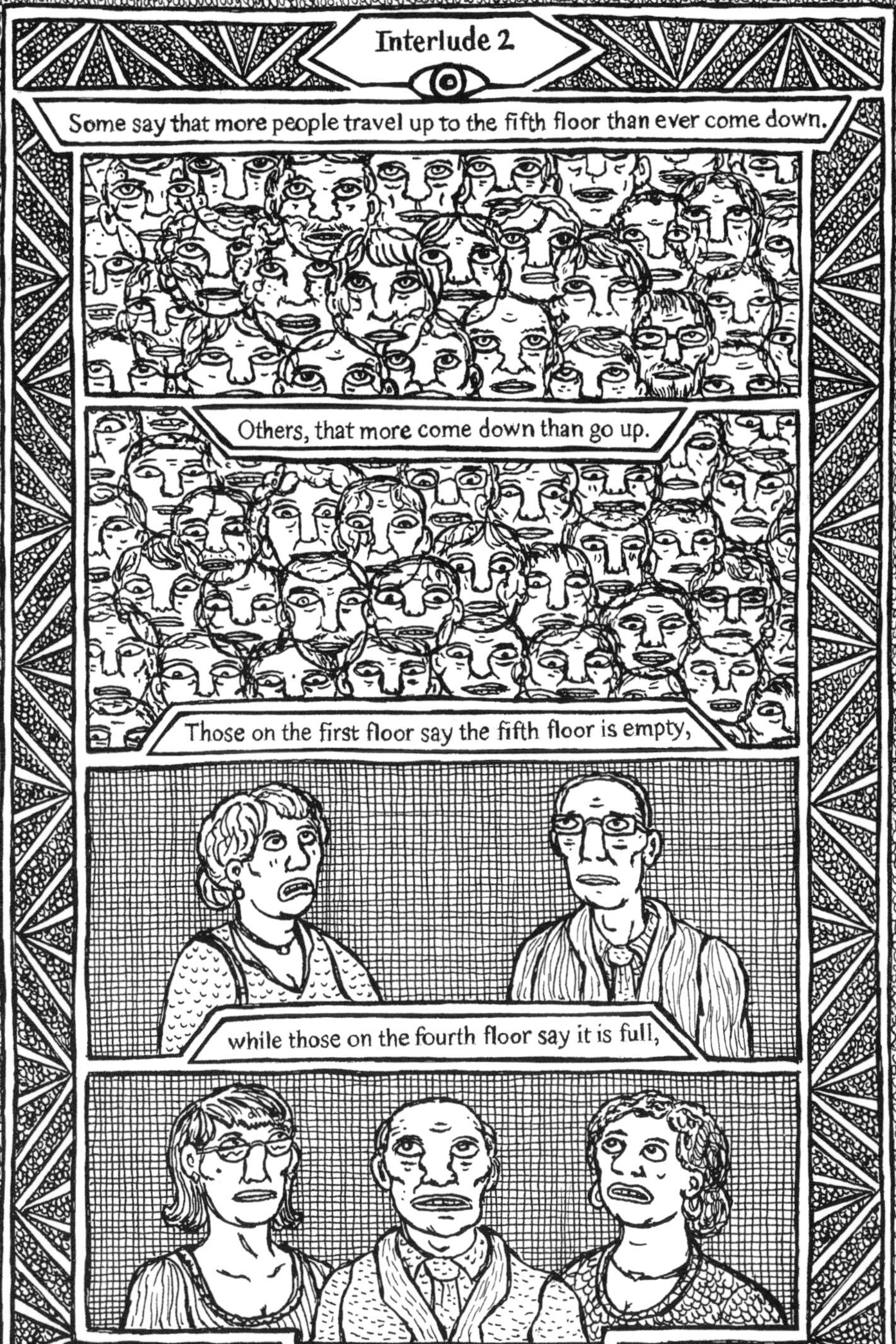
Interlude 2
Some say that more people travel up to the fifth floor than ever come down.
Others, that more come down than go up.
Those on the first floor say the fifth floor is empty,
while those on the fourth floor say it is full,
but will not say full of what.

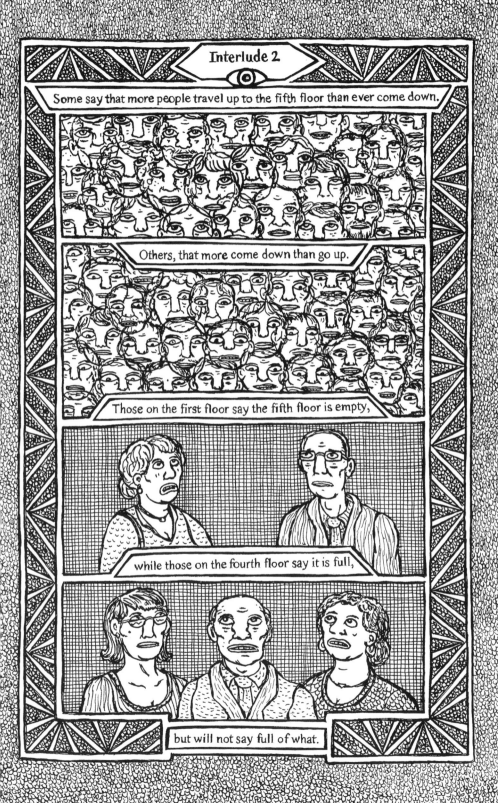

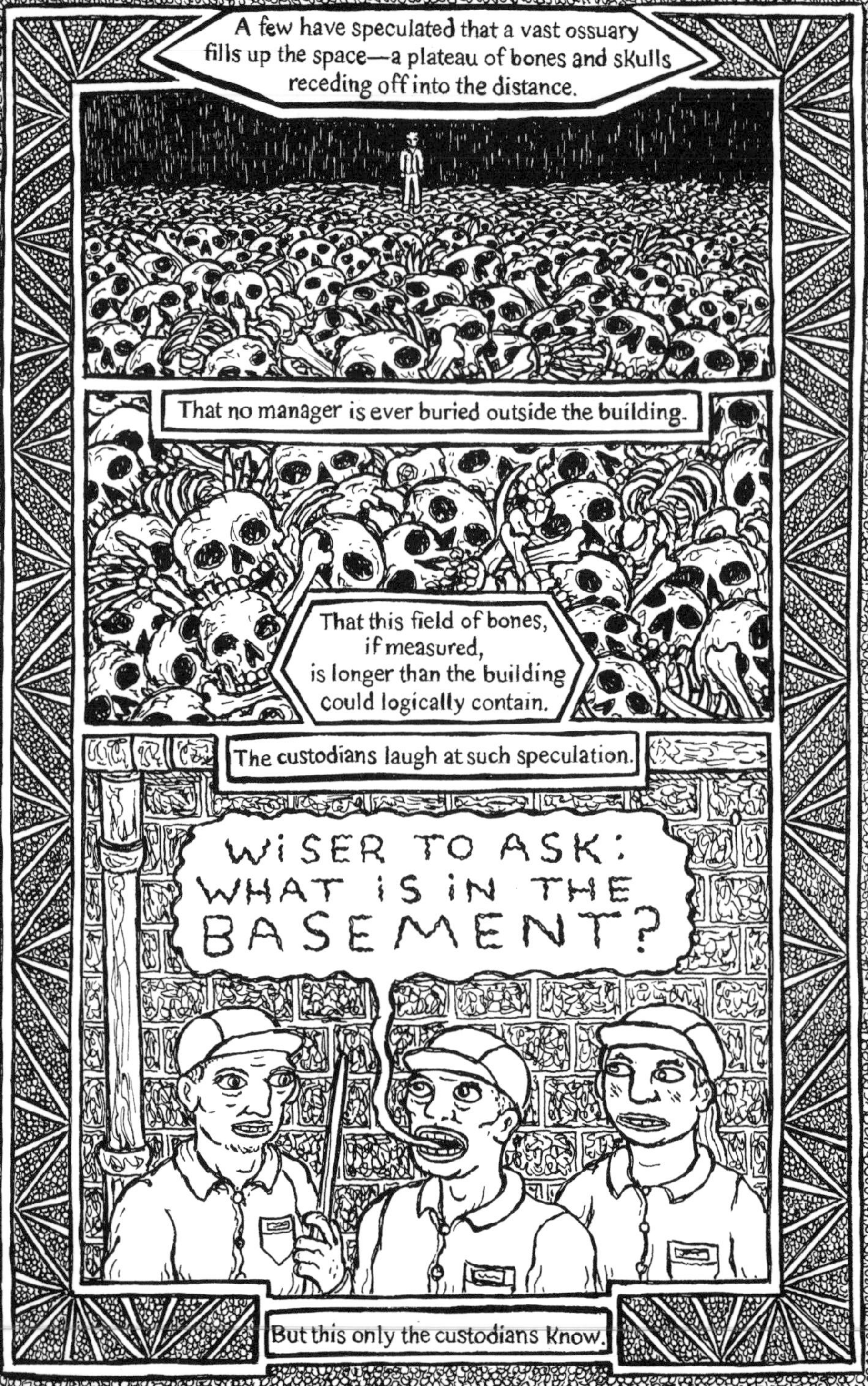

A few have speculated that a vast ossuary fills up the space—a plateau of bones and skulls receding off into the distance.
That no manager is ever buried outside the building.
That this field of bones, if measured, is longer than the building could logically contain.
The custodians laugh at such speculation.
WISER TO ASK: WHAT IS IN THE BASEMENT?
But this only the custodians know.

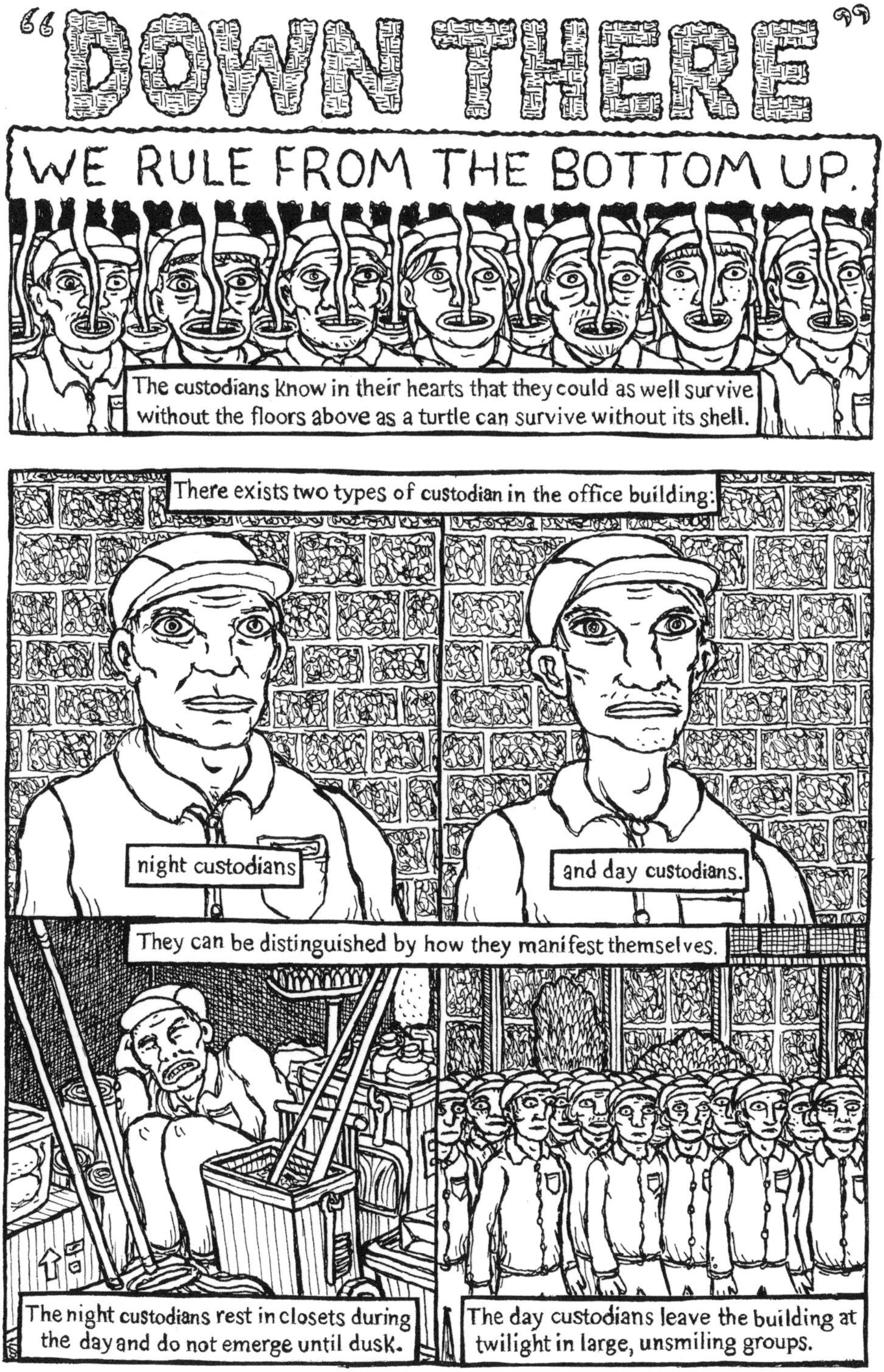
"DOWN THERE"
WE RULE FROM THE BOTTOM UP.
The custodians know in their hearts that they could as well survive without the floors above as a turtle can survive without its shell.
There exists two types of custodian in the office building:
night custodians
and day custodians.
They can be distinguished by how they manifest themselves.
The night custodians rest in closets during the day and do not emerge until dusk.
The day custodians leave the building at twilight in large, unsmiling groups.

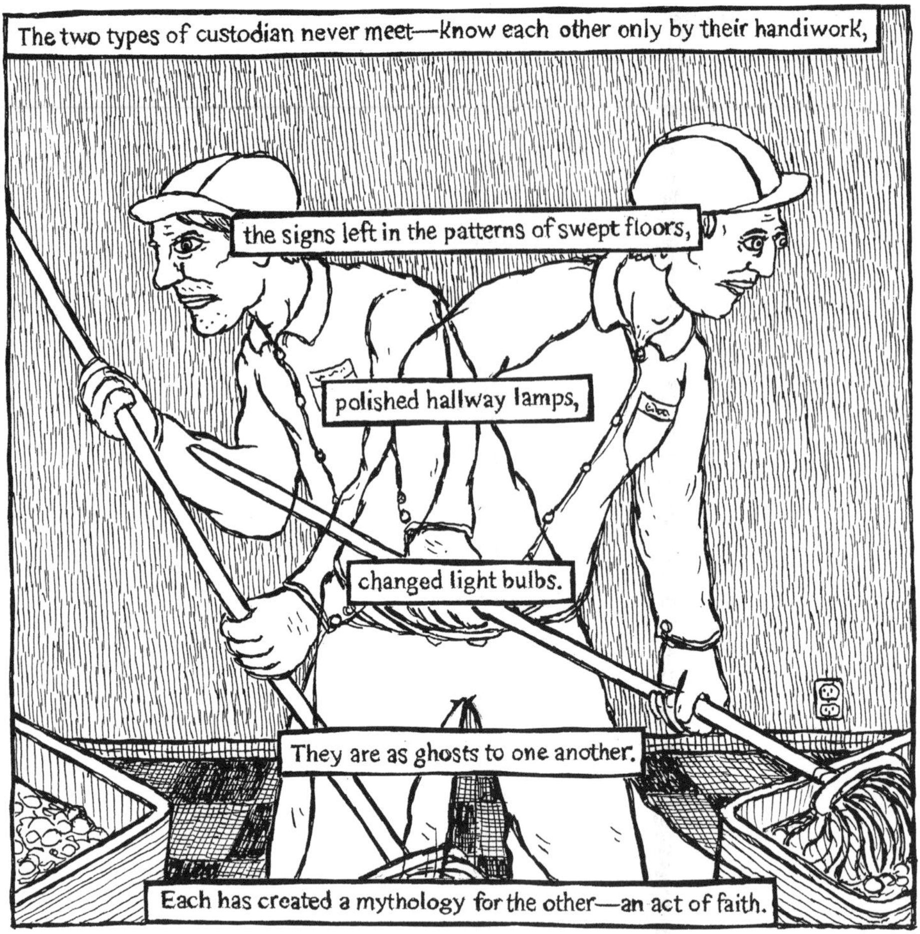
The two types of custodian never meet—know each other only by their handiwork,
the signs left in the patterns of swept floors,
polished hallway lamps,
changed light bulbs.
They are as ghosts to one another.
Each has created a mythology for the other—an act of faith.

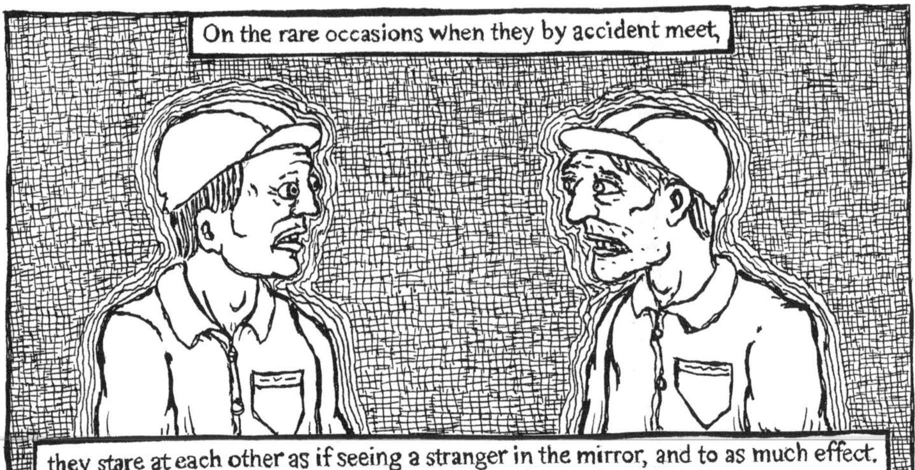
On the rare occasions when they by accident meet,
they stare at each other as if seeing a stranger in the mirror, and to as much effect.

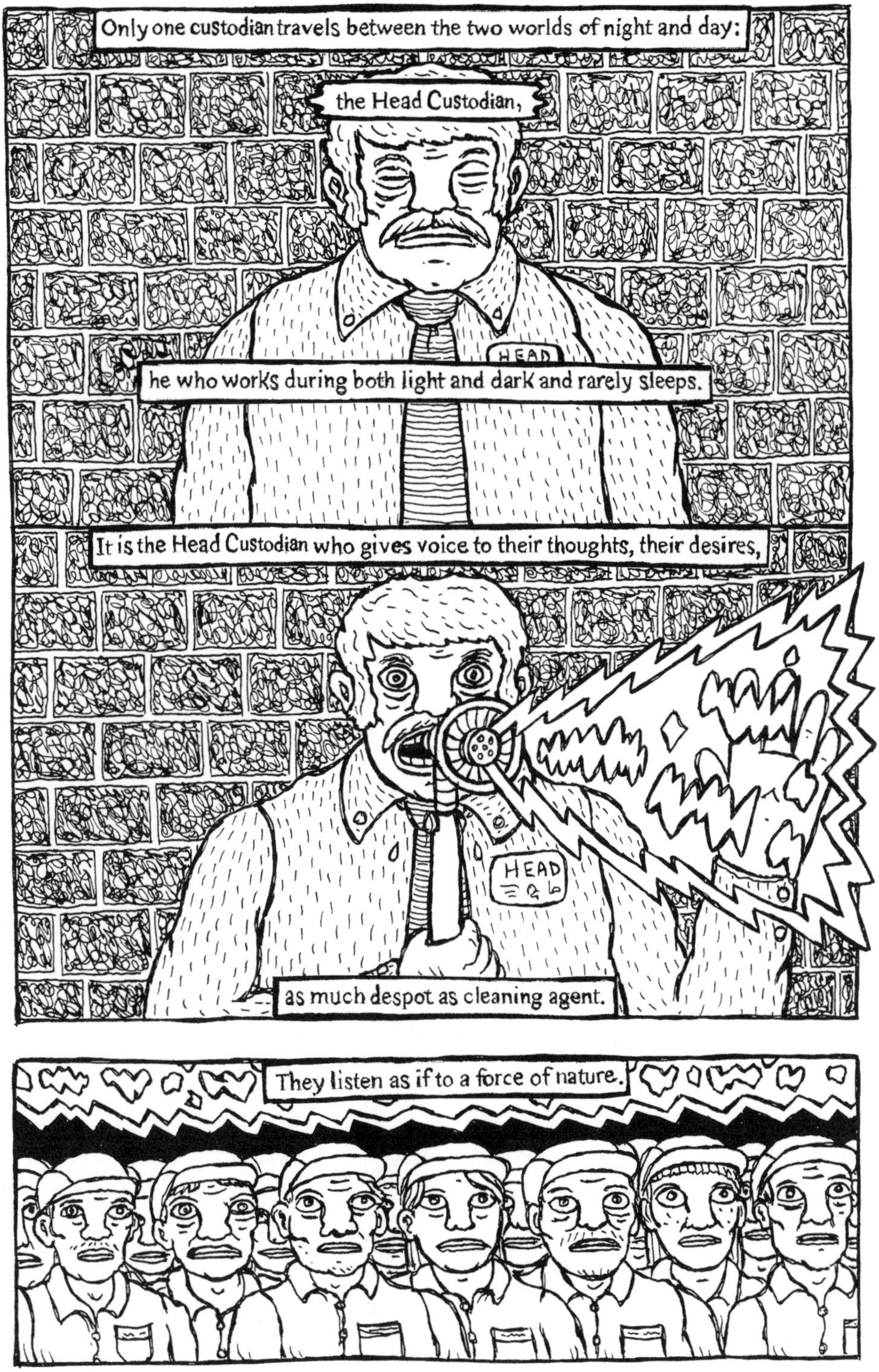
Only one custodian travels between the two worlds of night and day:
the Head Custodian,
HEAD
he who works during both light and dark and rarely sleeps.
It is the Head Custodian who gives voice to their thoughts, their desires,
HEAD
as much despot as cleaning agent.
They listen as if to a force of nature.

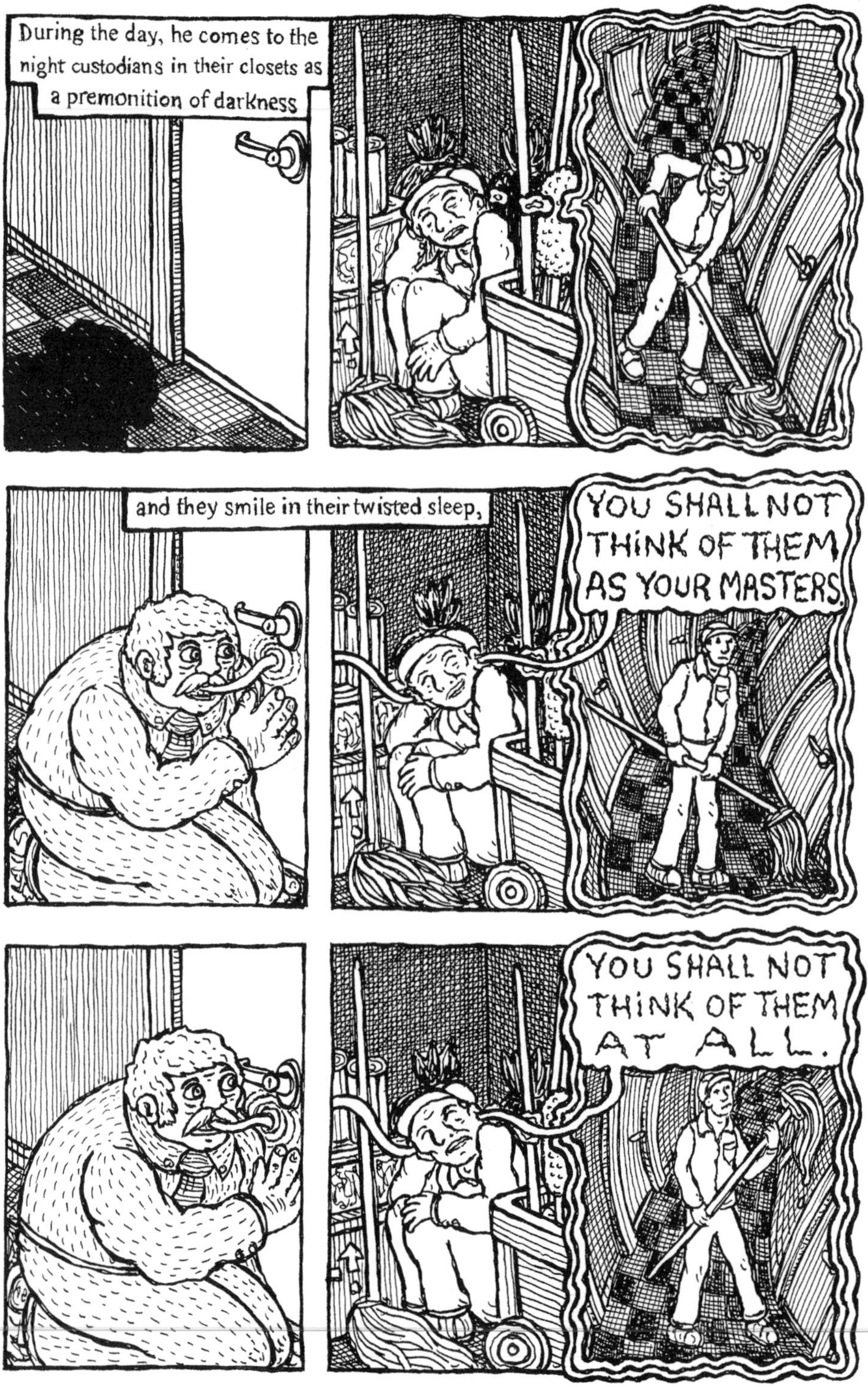
During the day, he comes to the night custodians in their closets as a premonition of darkness
and they smile in their twisted sleep,
YOU SHALL NOT THINK OF THEM AS YOUR MASTERS.
YOU SHALL NOT THINK OF THEM AT ALL.

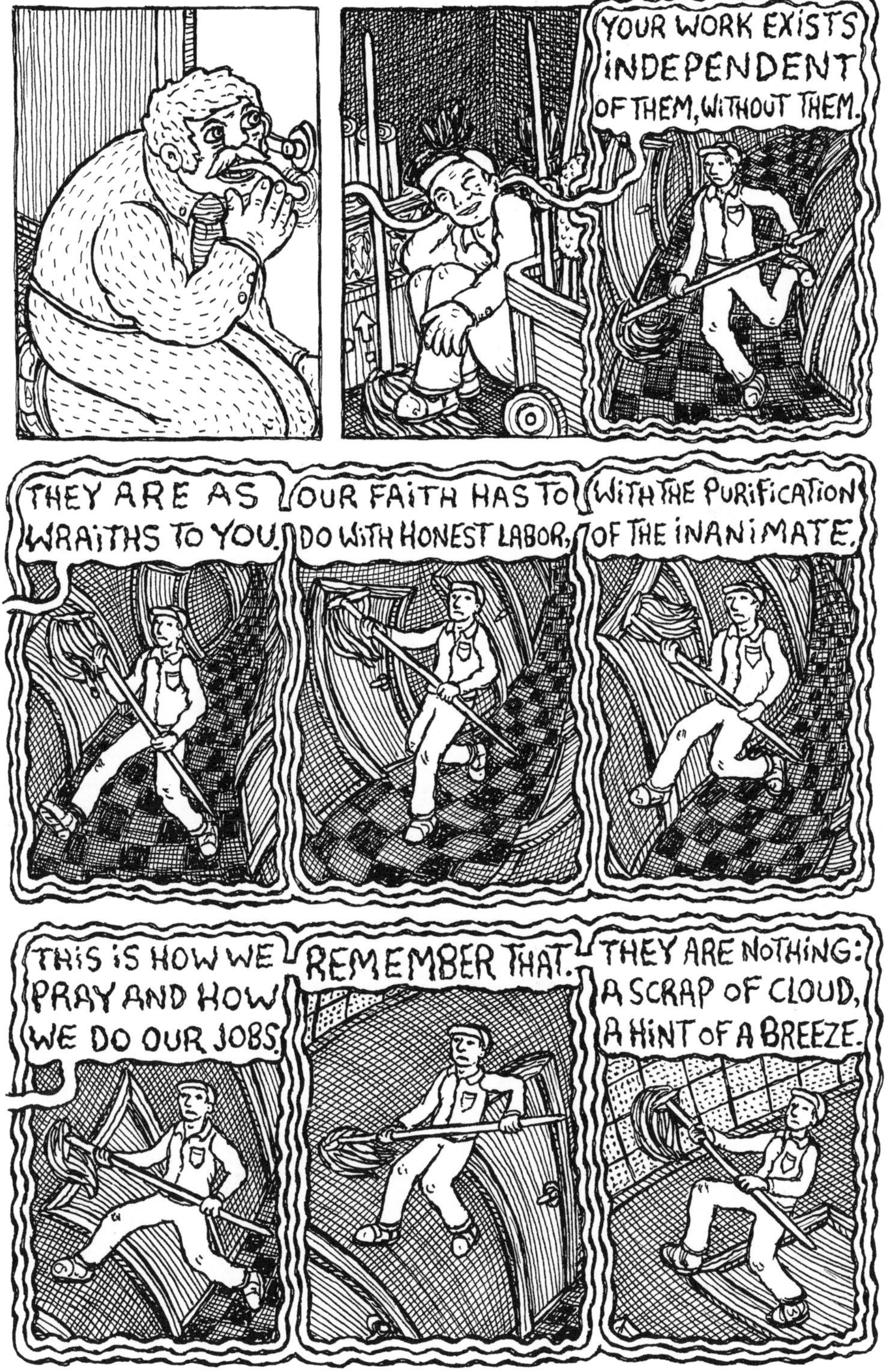
YOUR WORK EXISTS INDEPENDENT OF THEM, WITHOUT THEM.
THEY ARE AS WRAITHS TO YOU.
OUR FAITH HAS TO DO WITH HONEST LABOR,
WITH THE PURIFICATION OF THE INANIMATE.
THIS IS HOW WE PRAY AND HOW WE DO OUR JOBS.
REMEMBER THAT.
THEY ARE NOTHING: A SCRAP OF CLOUD, A HINT OF A BREEZE.

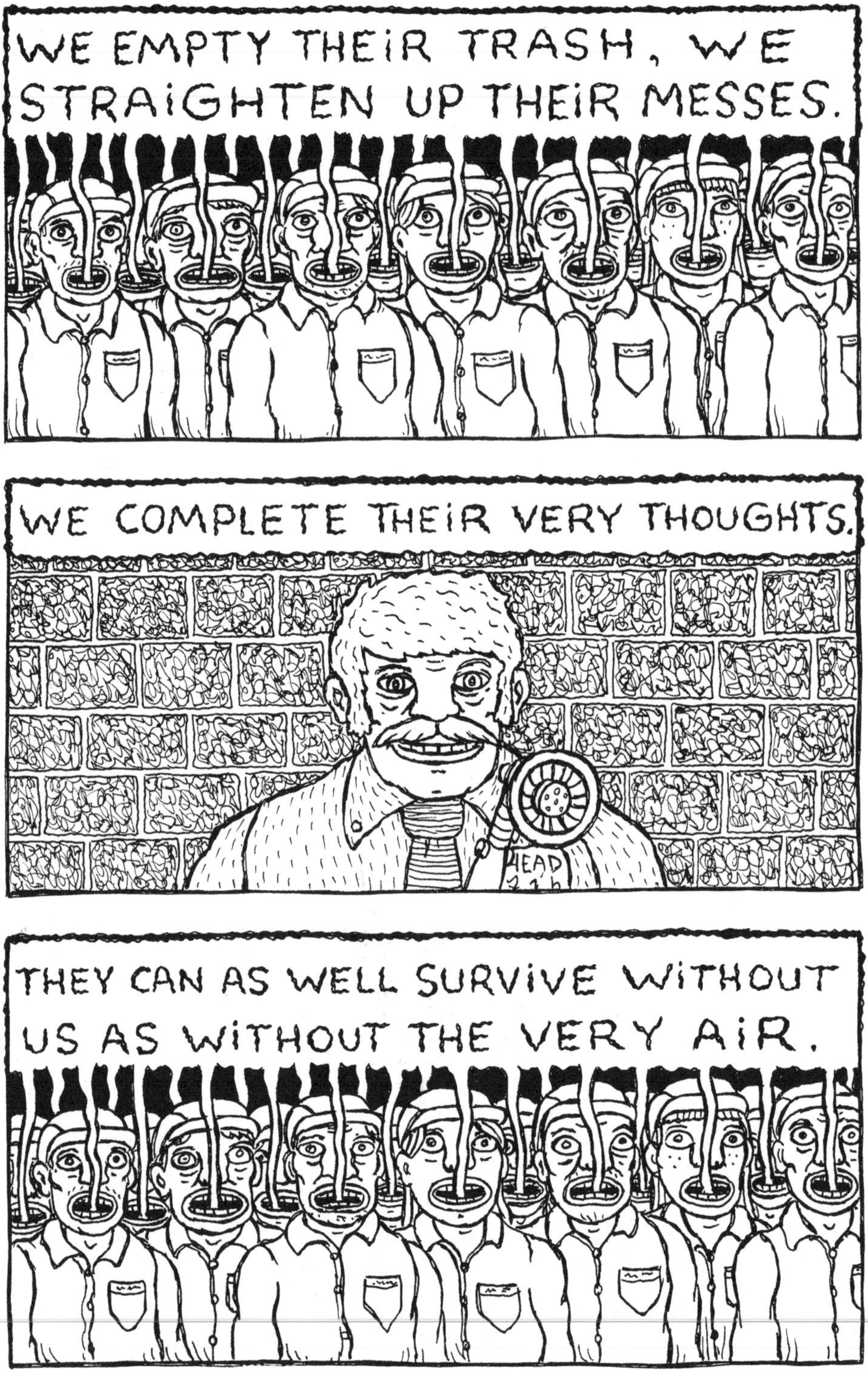
WE EMPTY THEIR TRASH, WE STRAIGHTEN UP THEIR MESSES.
WE COMPLETE THEIR VERY THOUGHTS.
HEAD
THEY CAN AS WELL SURVIVE WITHOUT US AS WITHOUT THE VERY AIR.

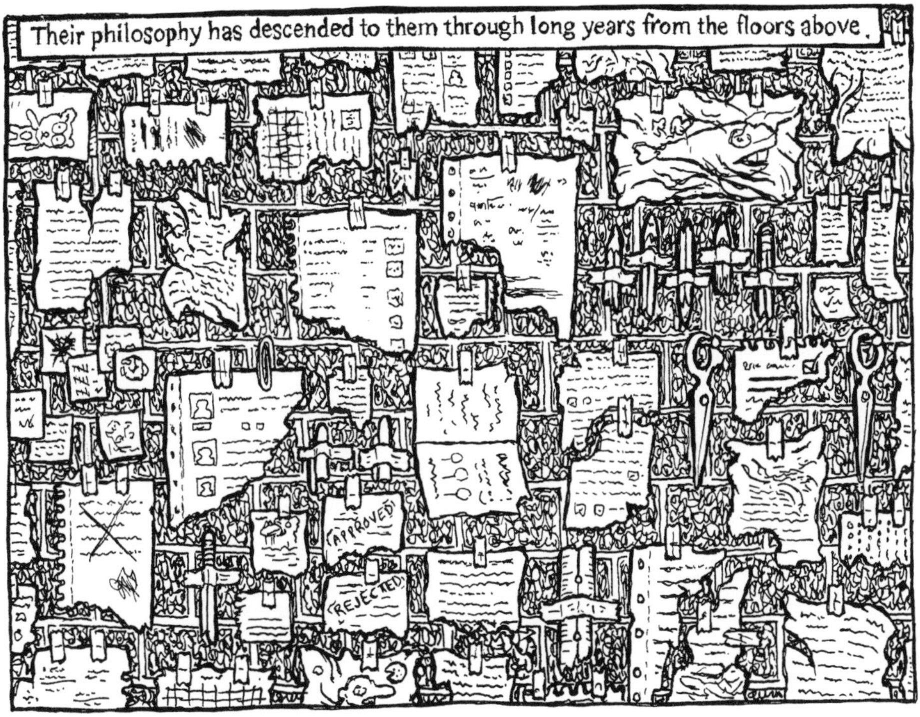
Their philosophy has descended to them through long years from the floors above.
APPROVED
REJECTED

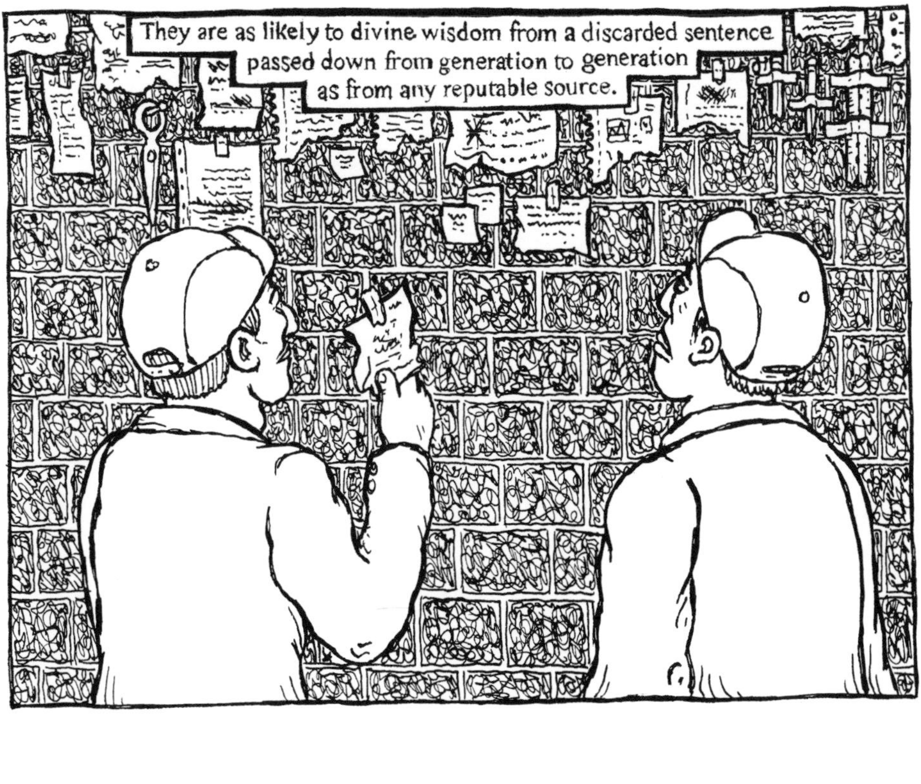
They are as likely to divine wisdom from a discarded sentence passed down from generation to generation as from any reputable source.

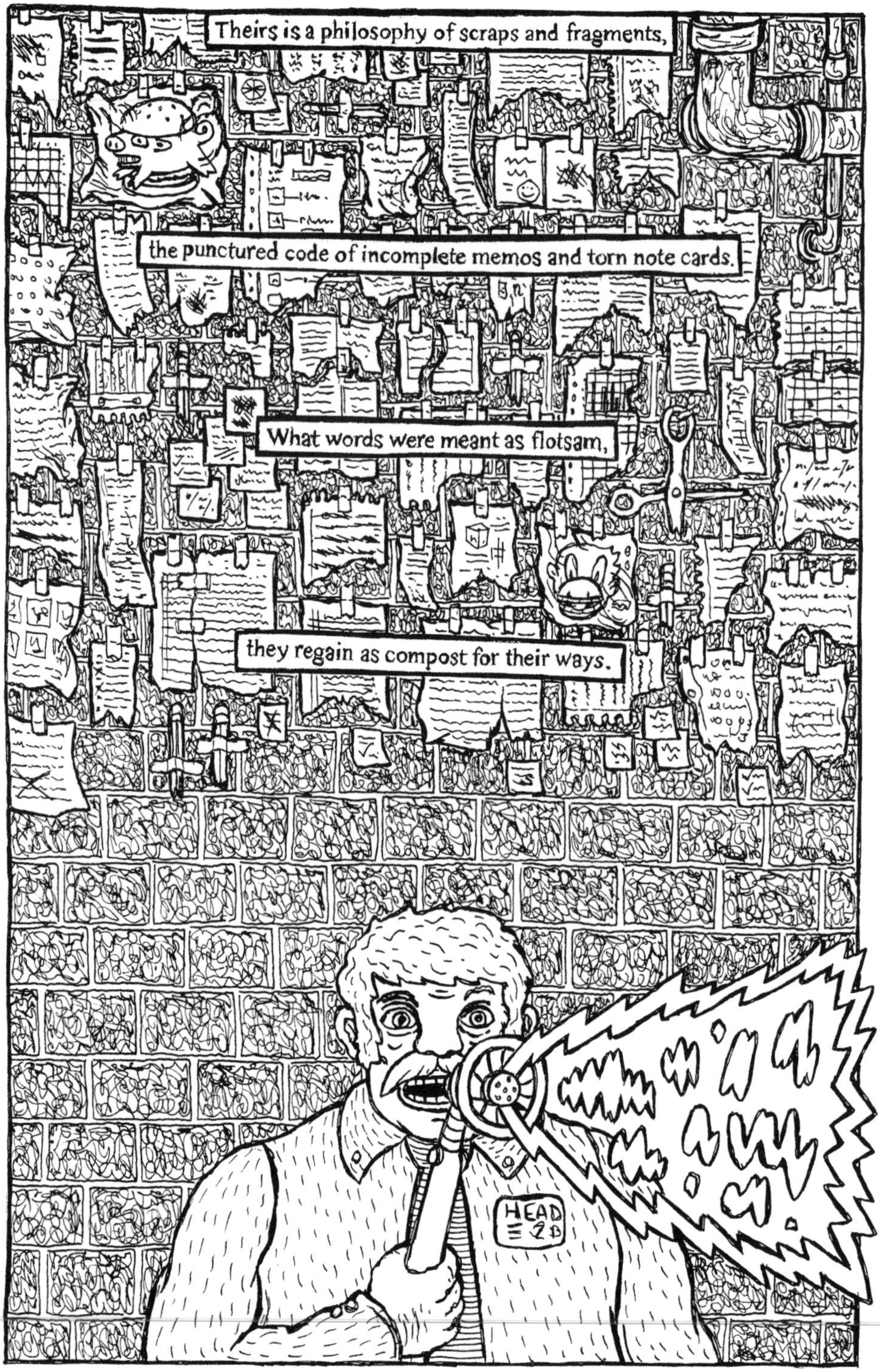
Theirs is a philosophy of scraps and fragments,
the punctured code of incomplete memos and torn note cards.
What words were meant as flotsam,
they regain as compost for their ways.
HEAD

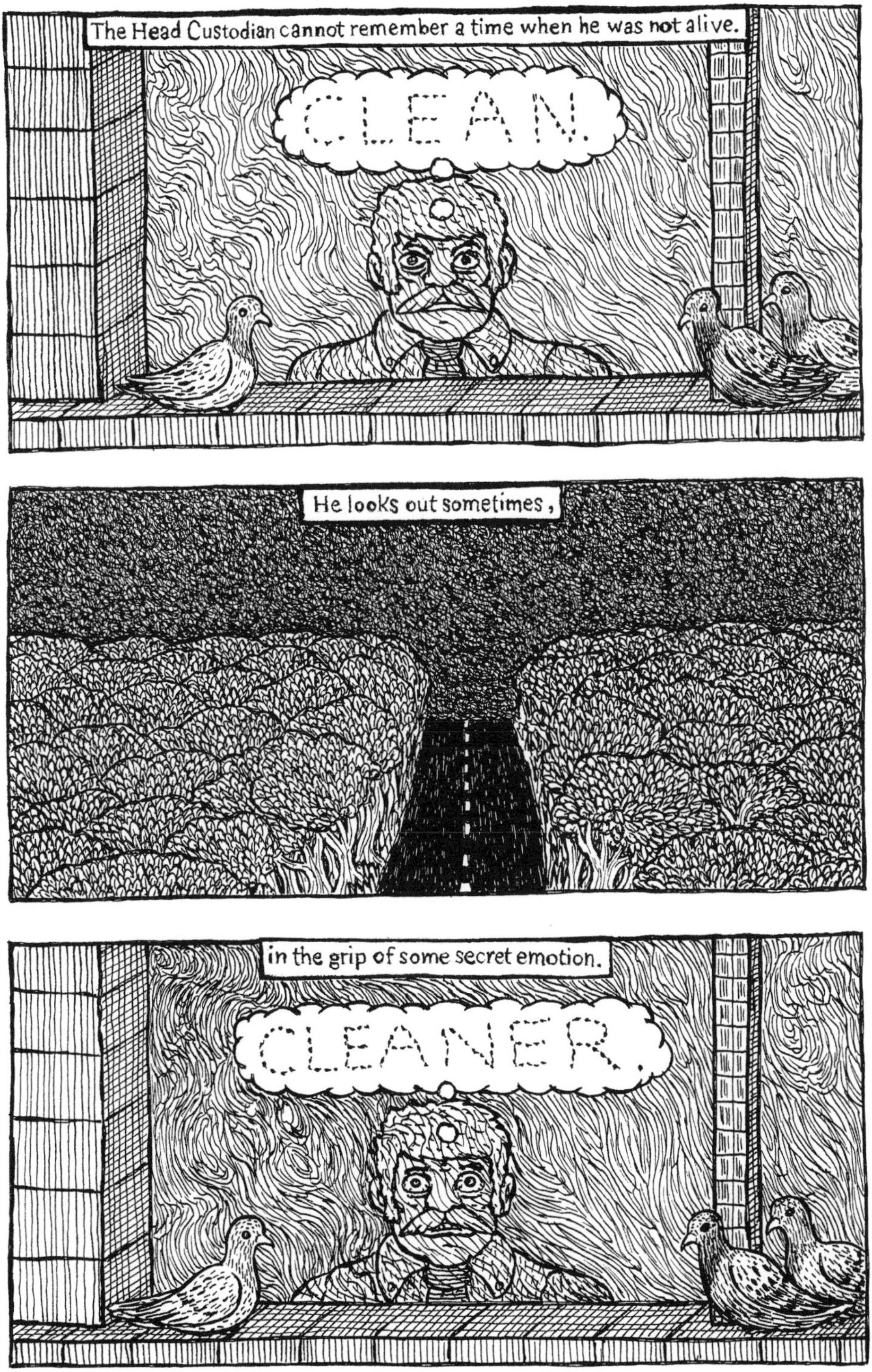
The Head Custodian cannot remember a time when he was not alive.
CLEAN.
He looks out sometimes,
in the grip of some secret emotion.
CLEANER.

Infiltration

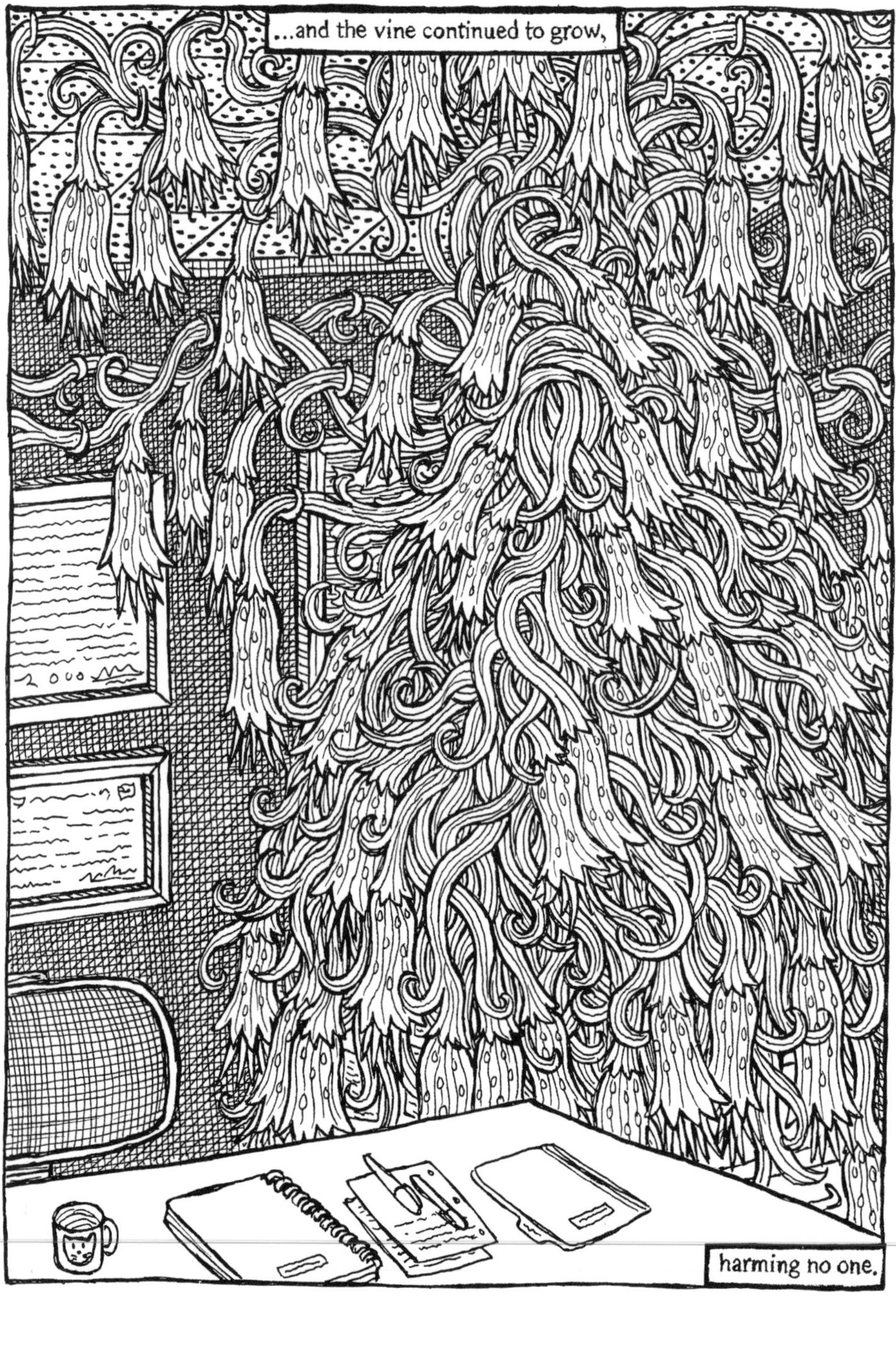
...and the vine continued to grow,
harming no one.

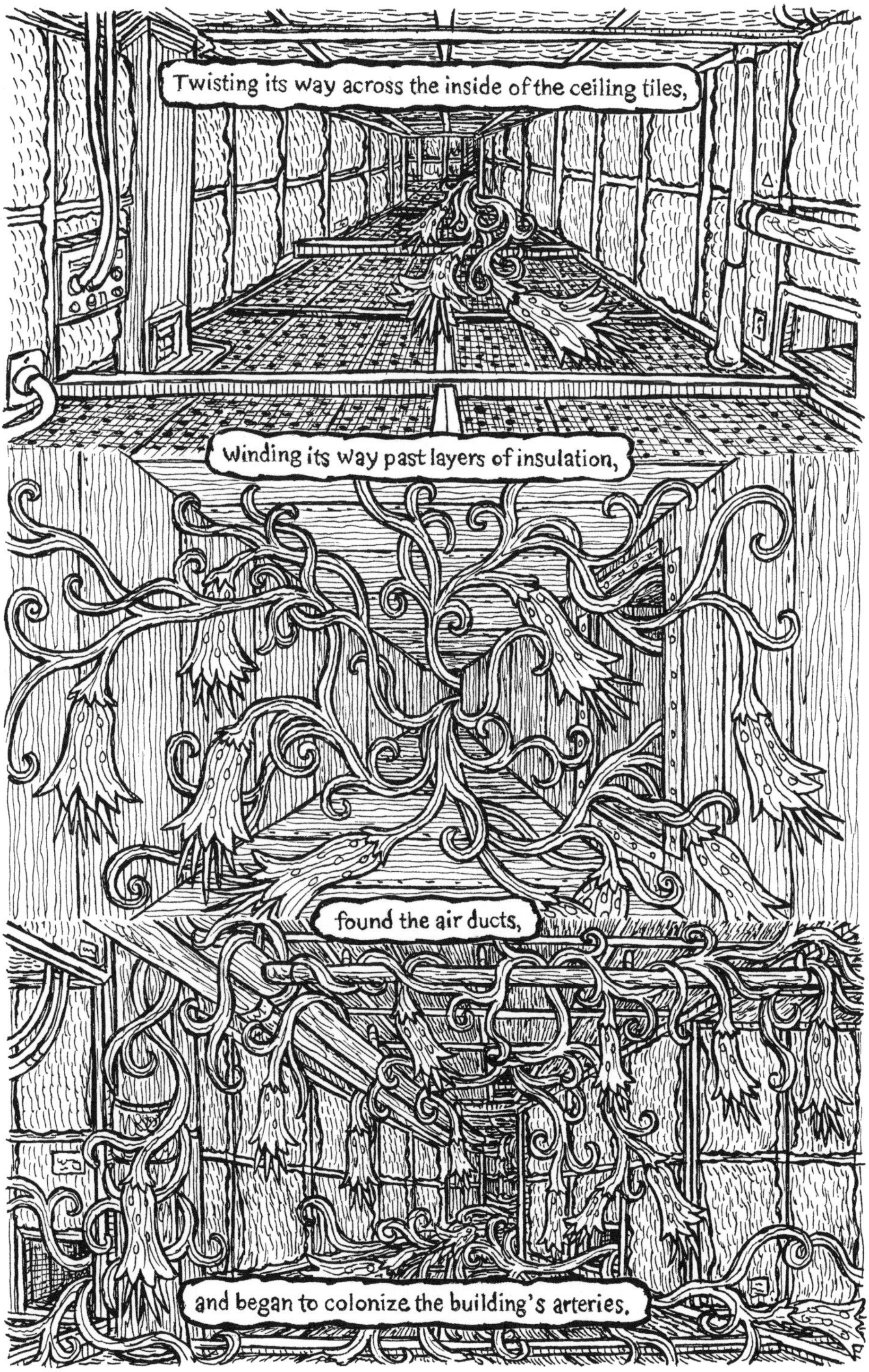
Twisting its way across the inside of the ceiling tiles,
Winding its way past layers of insulation,
found the air ducts,
and began to colonize the building's arteries.

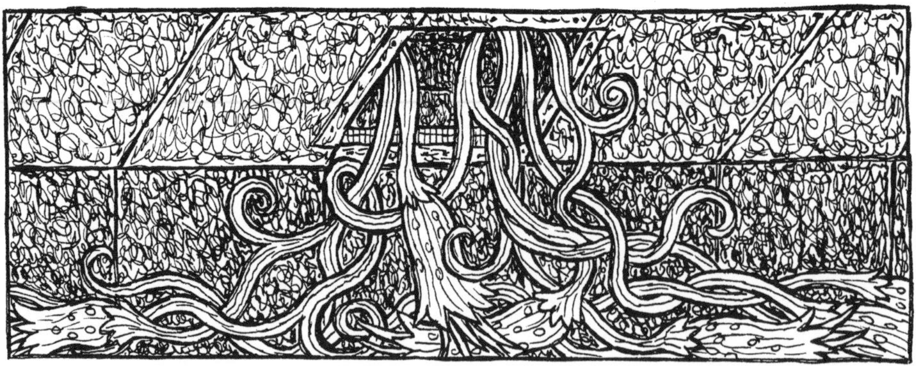

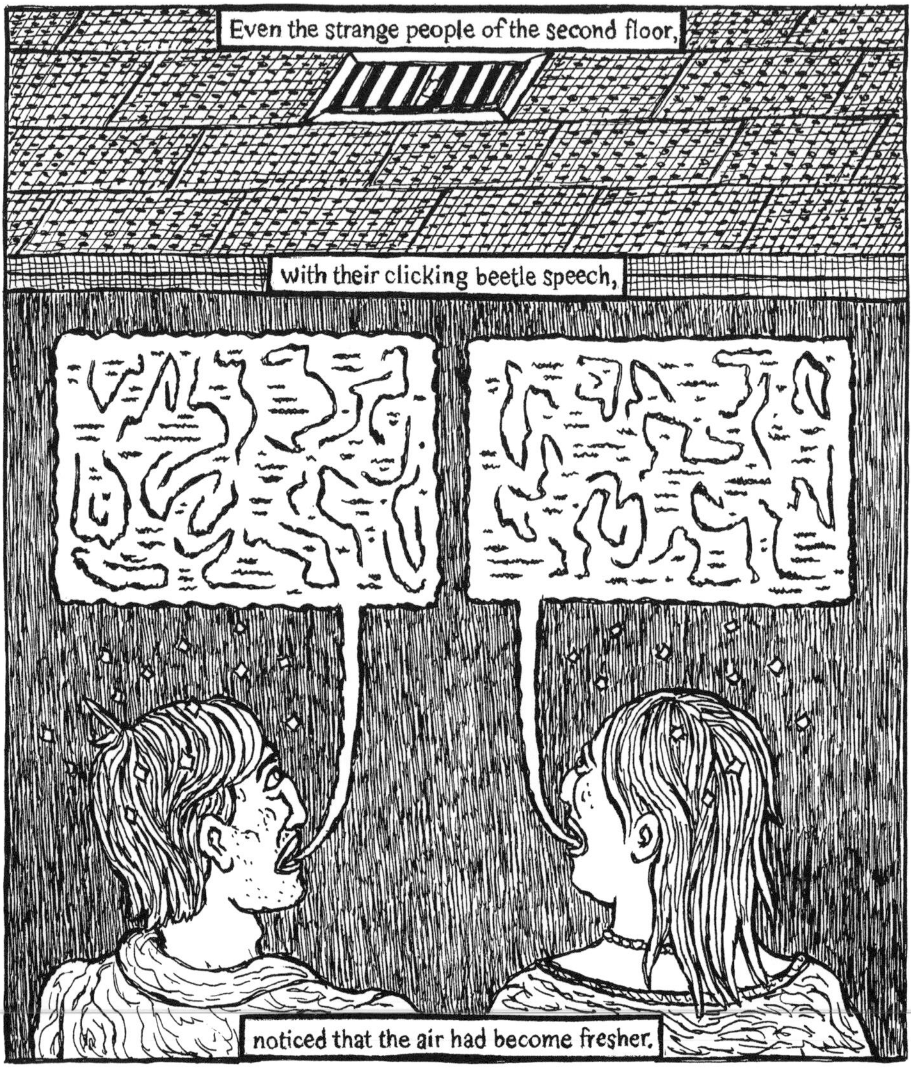
Even the strange people of the second floor,
with their clicking beetle speech,
noticed that the air had become fresher.

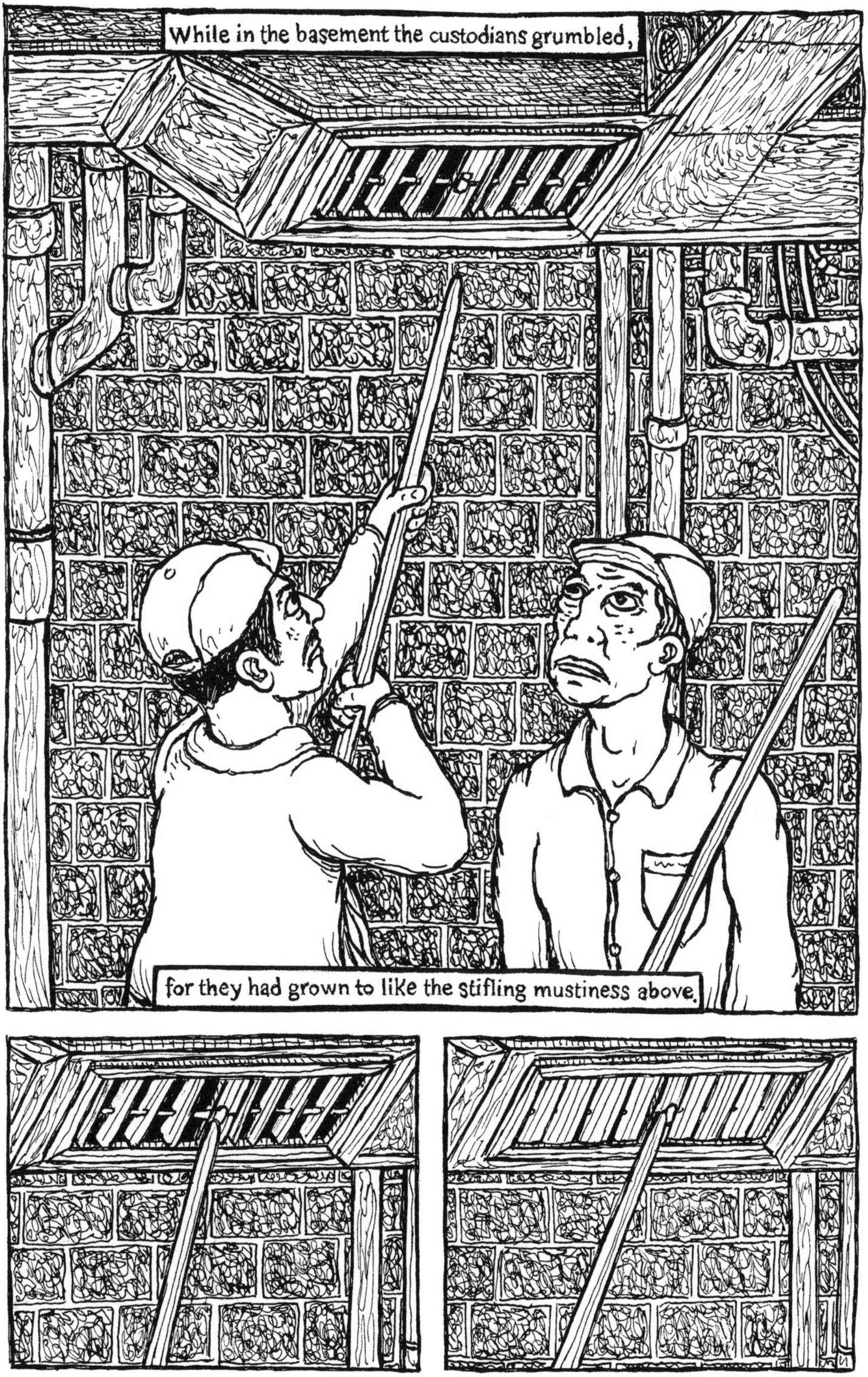
While in the basement the custodians grumbled,
for they had grown to like the stifling mustiness above.

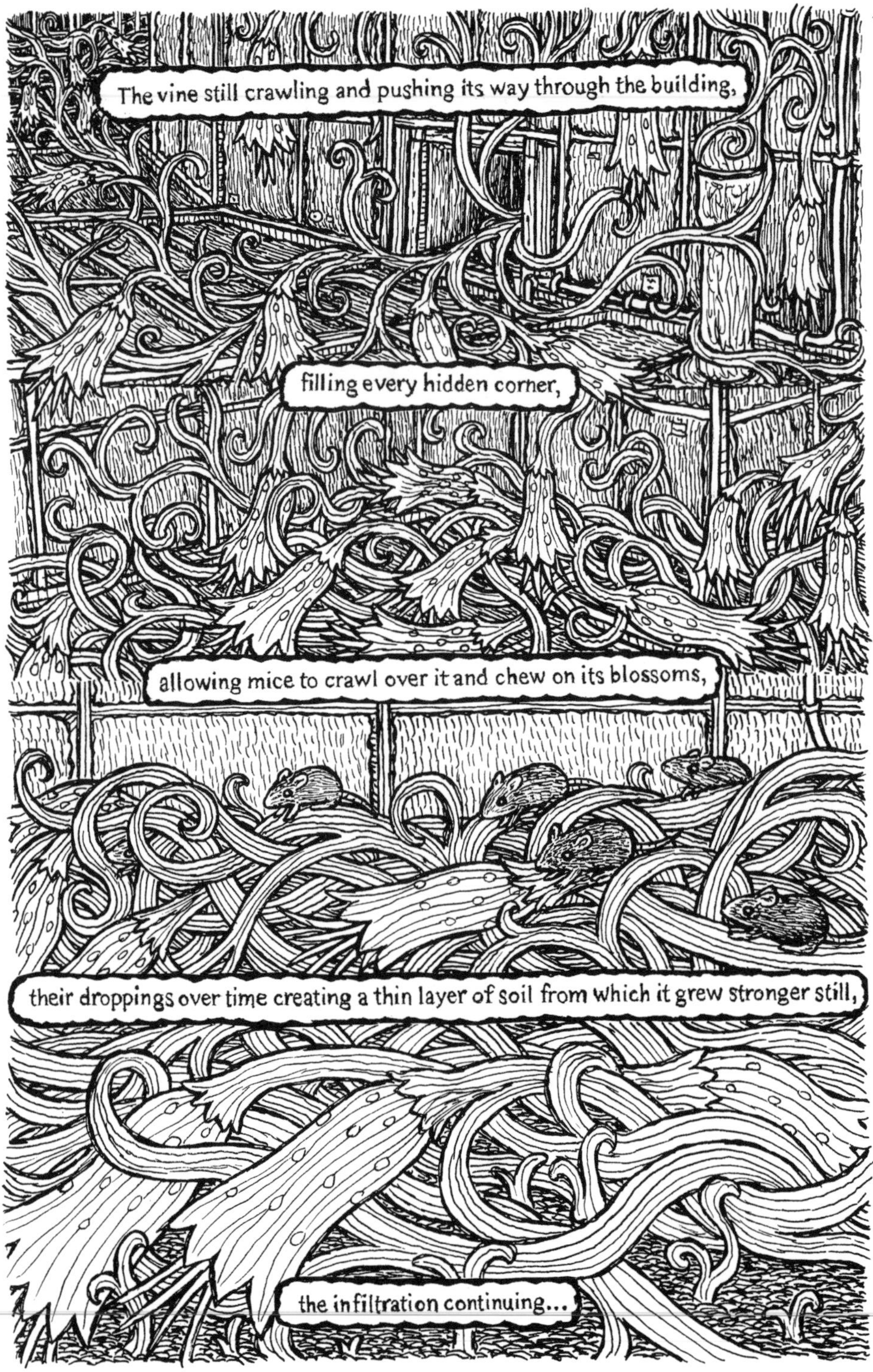
The vine still crawling and pushing its way through the building,
filling every hidden corner,
allowing mice to crawl over it and chew on its blossoms,
their droppings over time creating a thin layer of soil from which it grew stronger still,
the infiltration continuing...

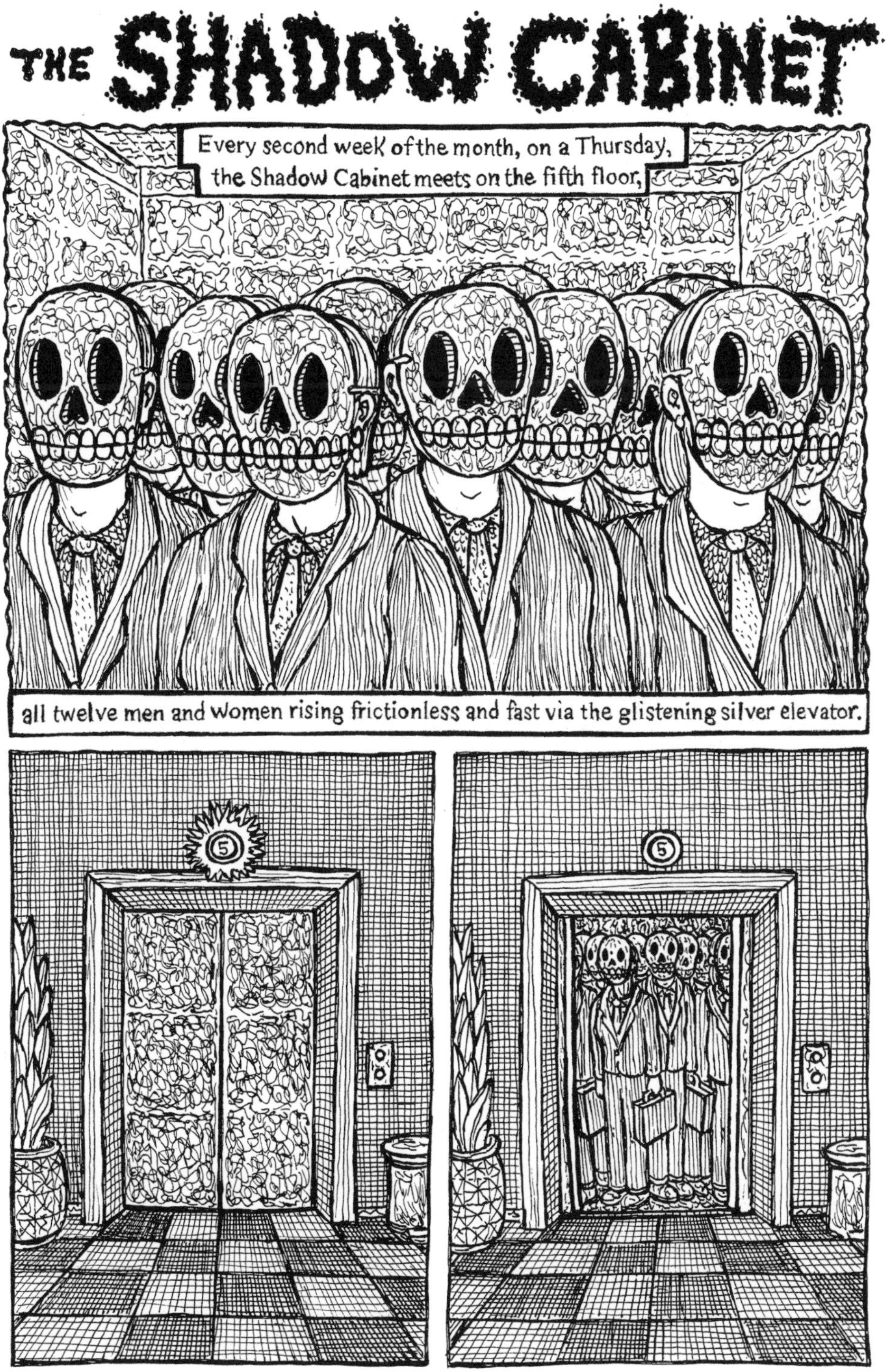
THE SHADOW CABINET
Every second week of the month, on a Thursday, the Shadow Cabinet meets on the fifth floor,
all twelve men and women rising frictionless and fast via the glistening silver elevator.
5
5

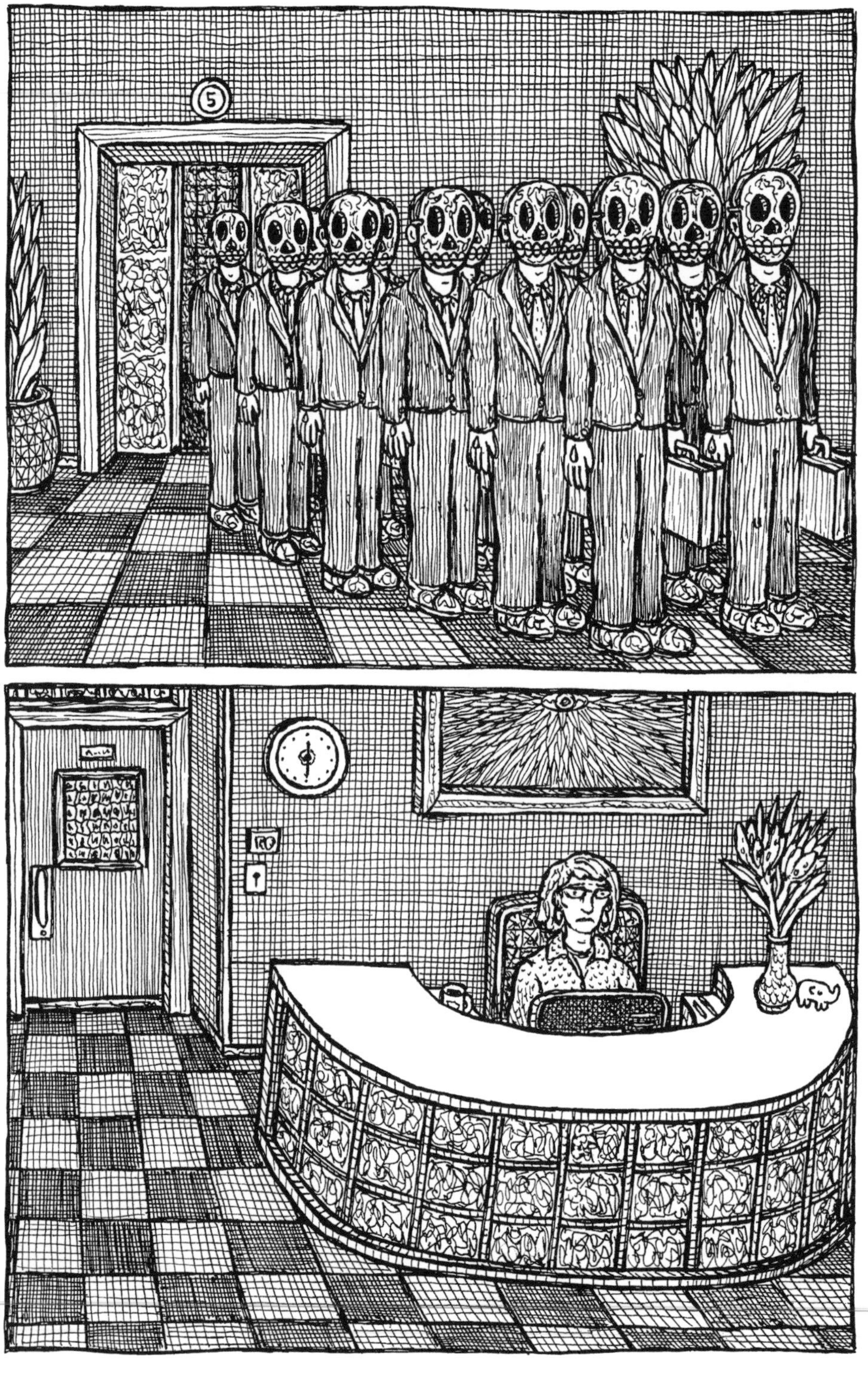
5

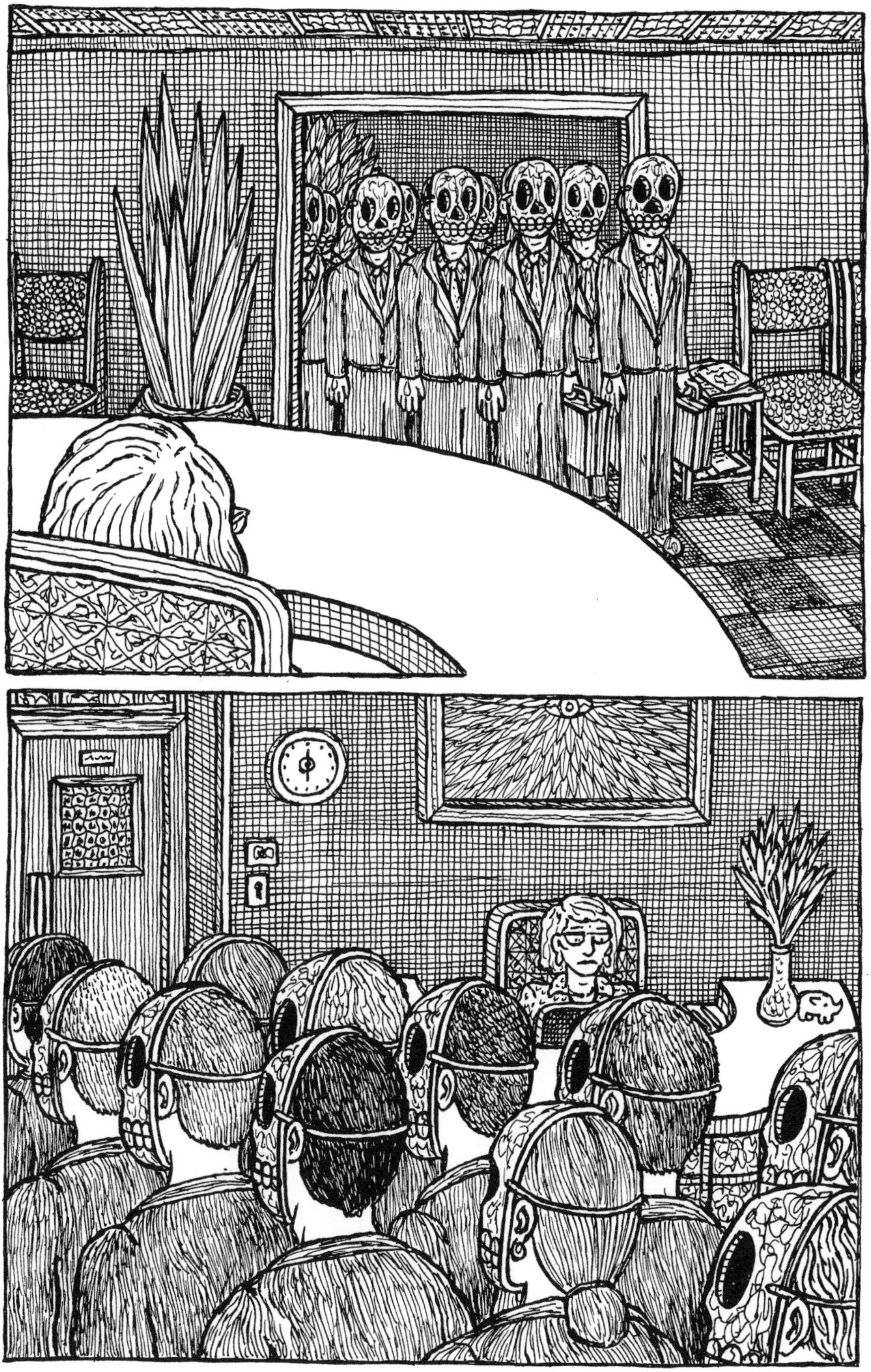

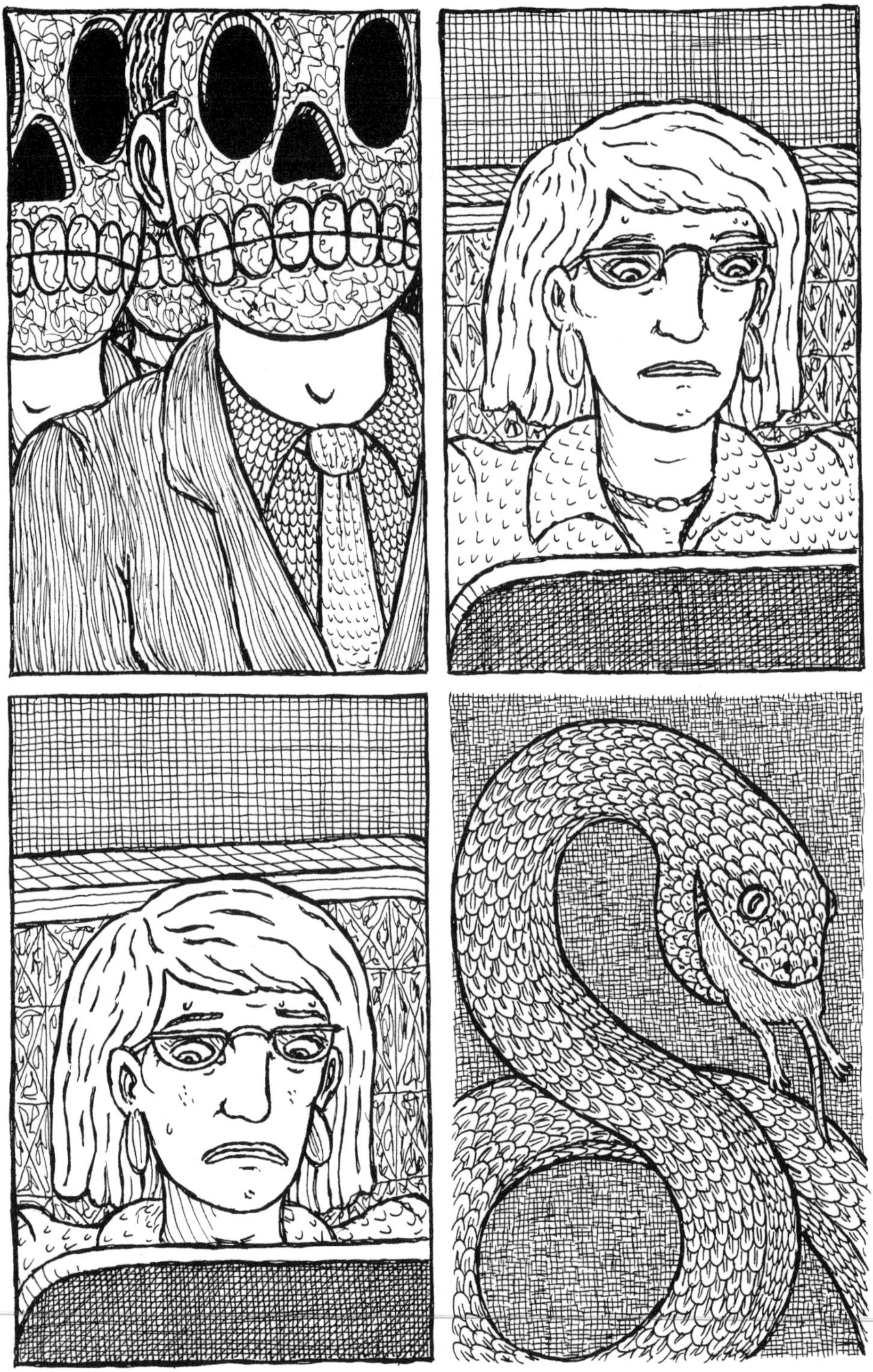

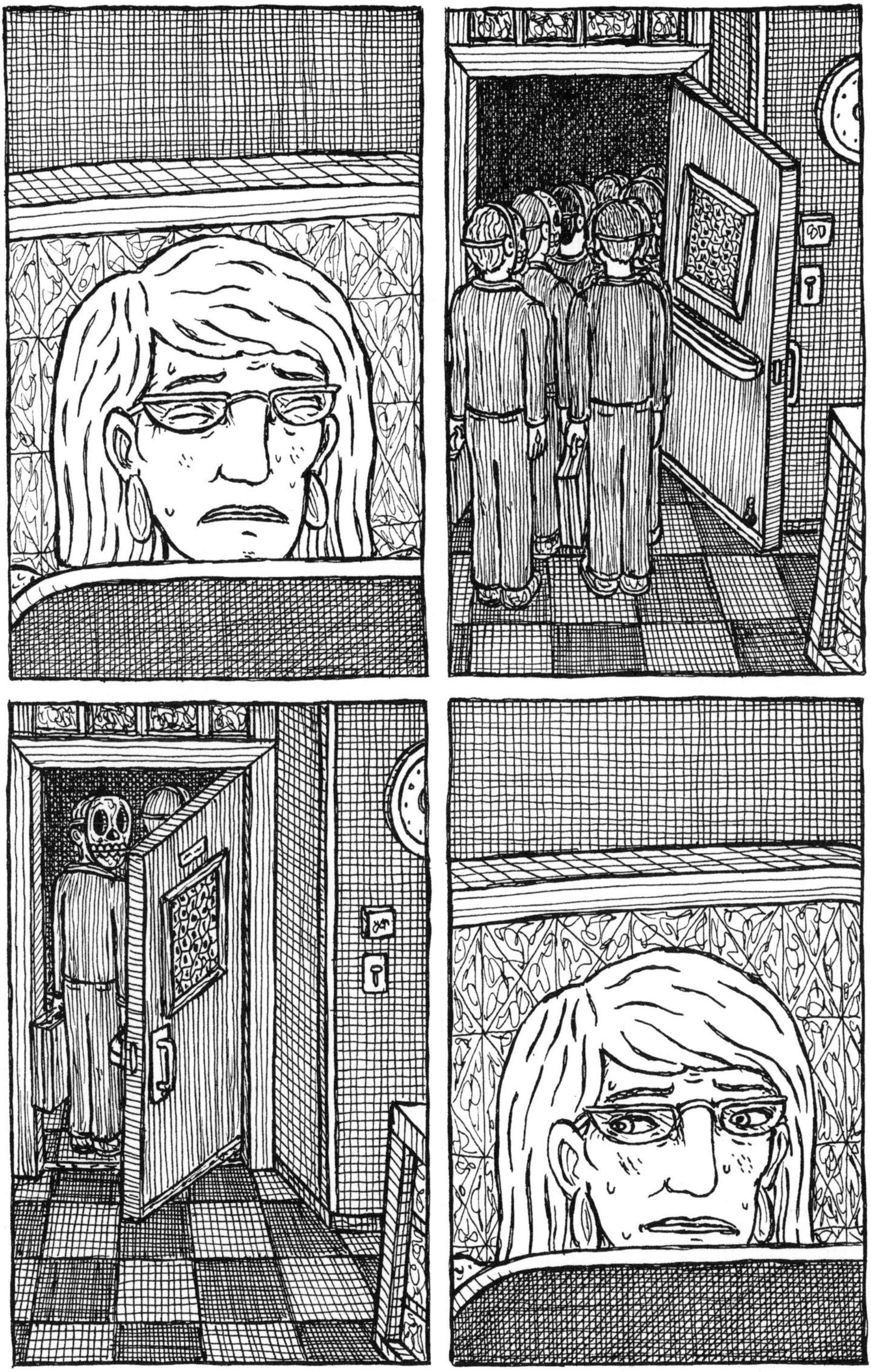

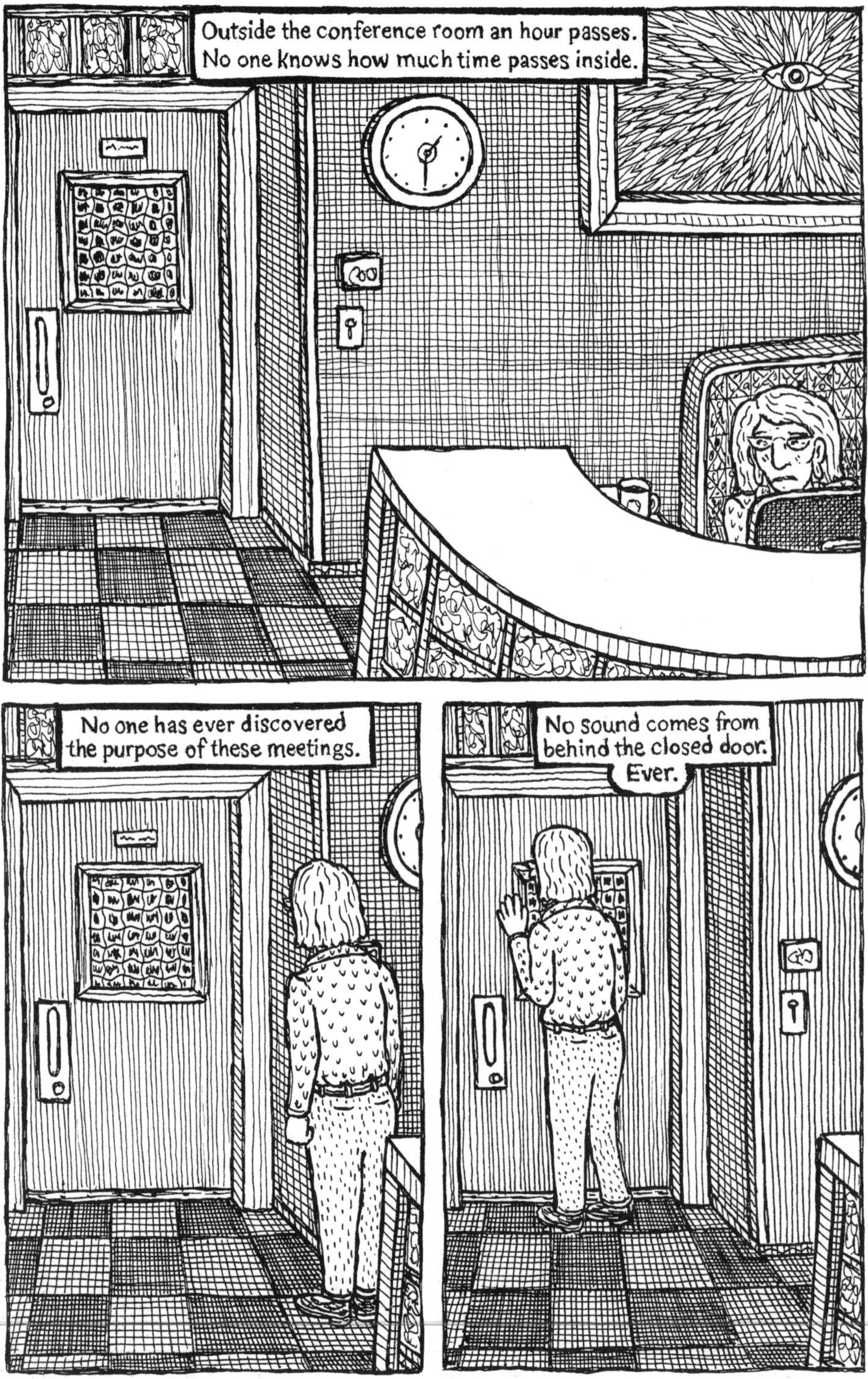
Outside the conference room an hour passes. No one knows how much time passes inside.
No one has ever discovered the purpose of these meetings.
No sound comes from behind the closed door.
Ever.

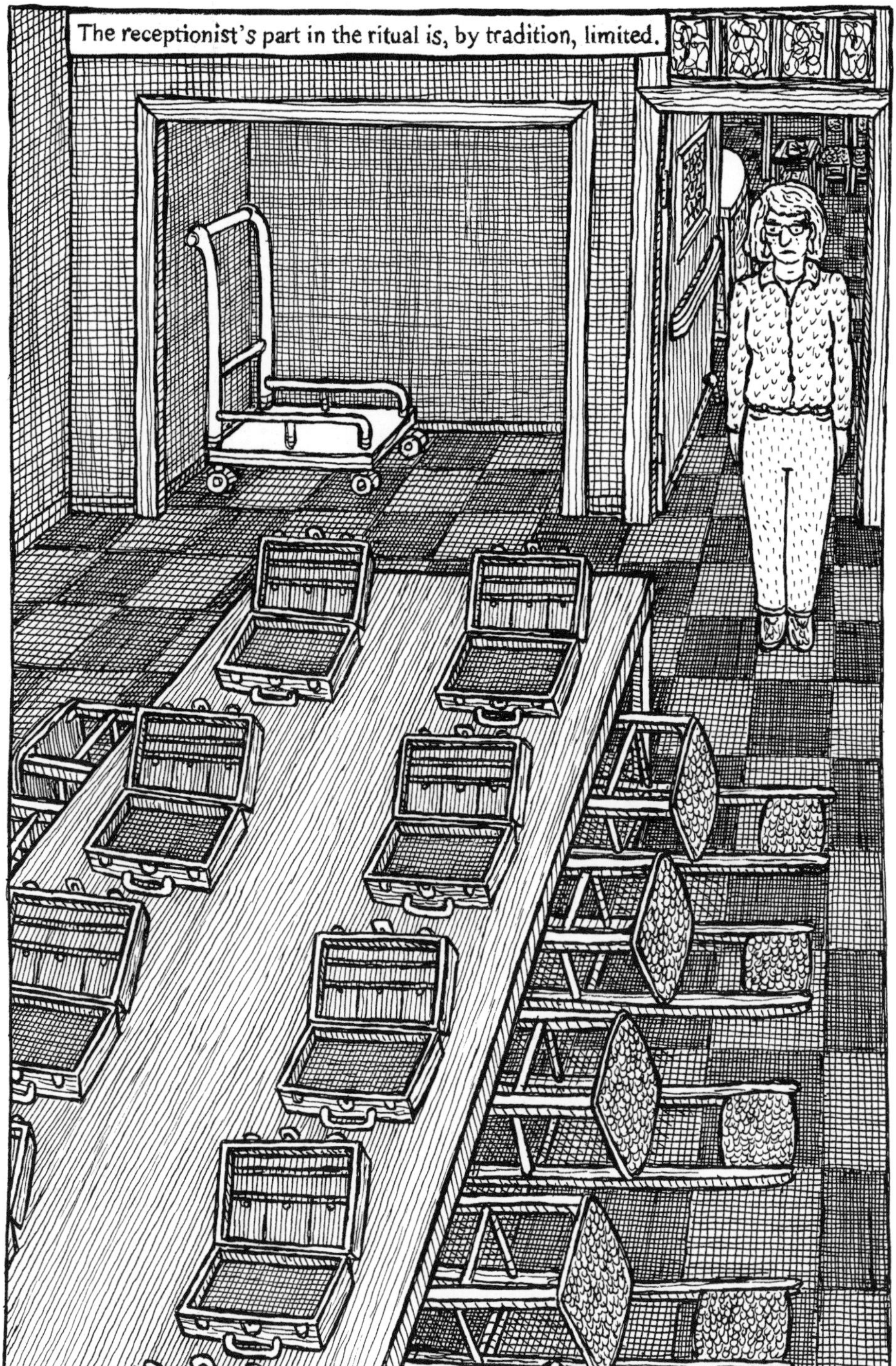
The receptionist's part in the ritual is, by tradition, limited.

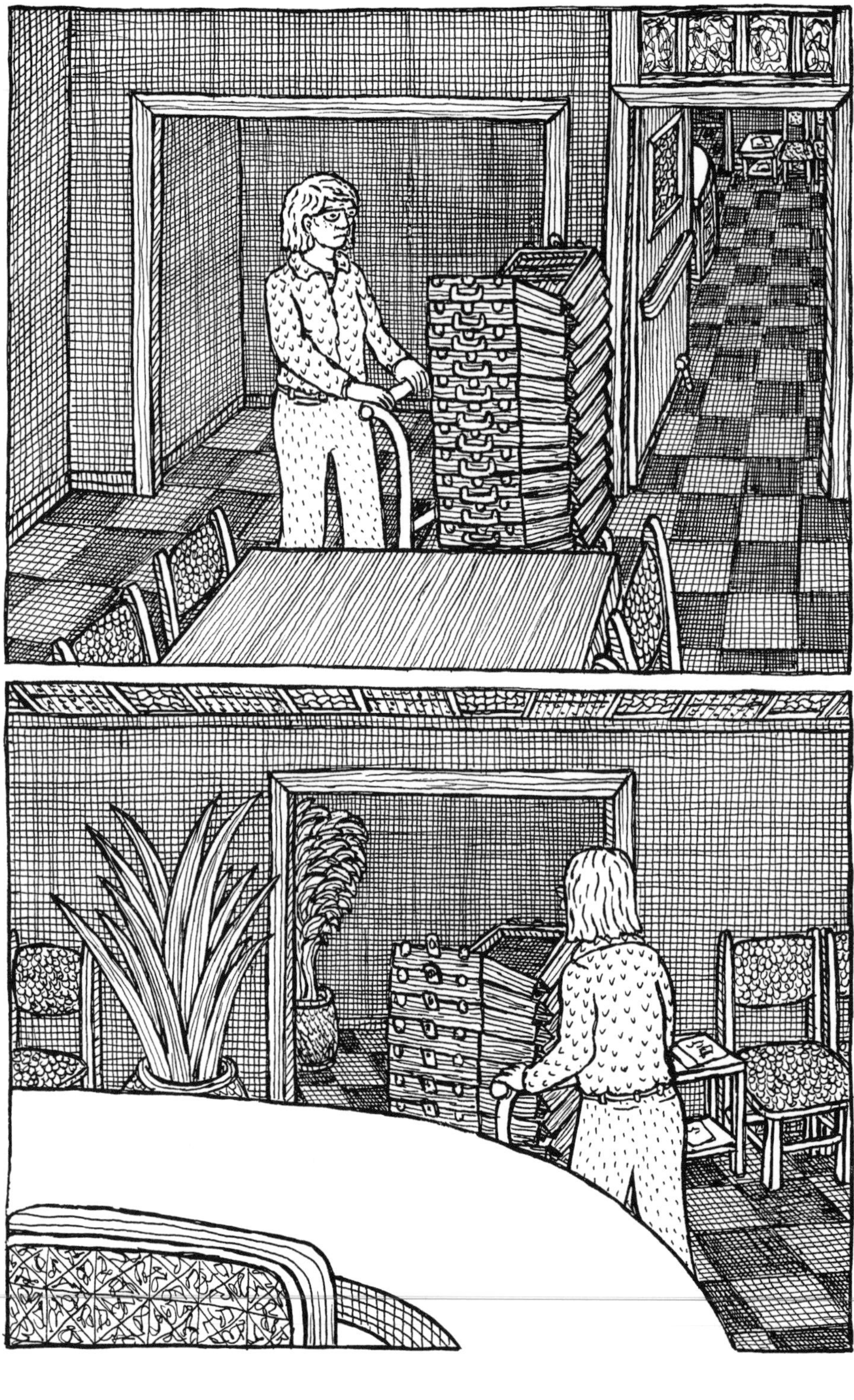

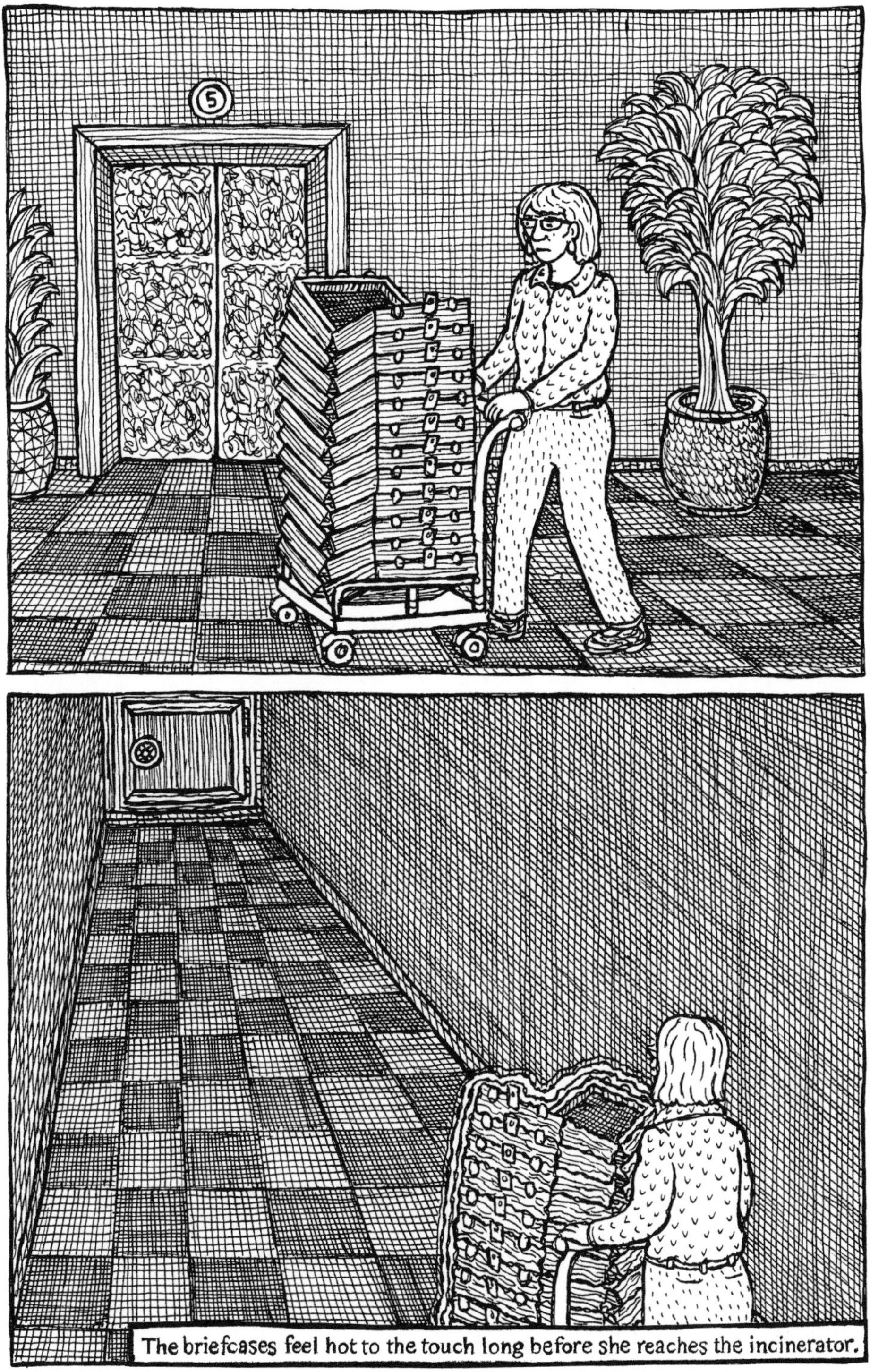
5
The briefcases feel hot to the touch long before she reaches the incinerator.

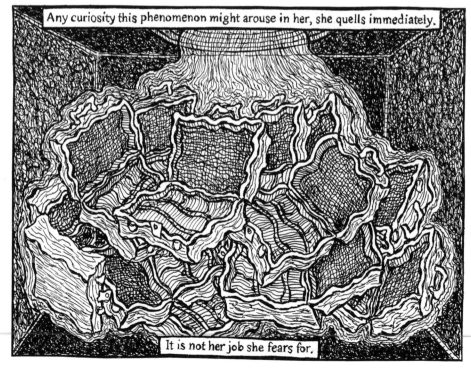

Any curiosity this phenomenon might arouse in her, she quells immediately.

It is not her job she fears for.

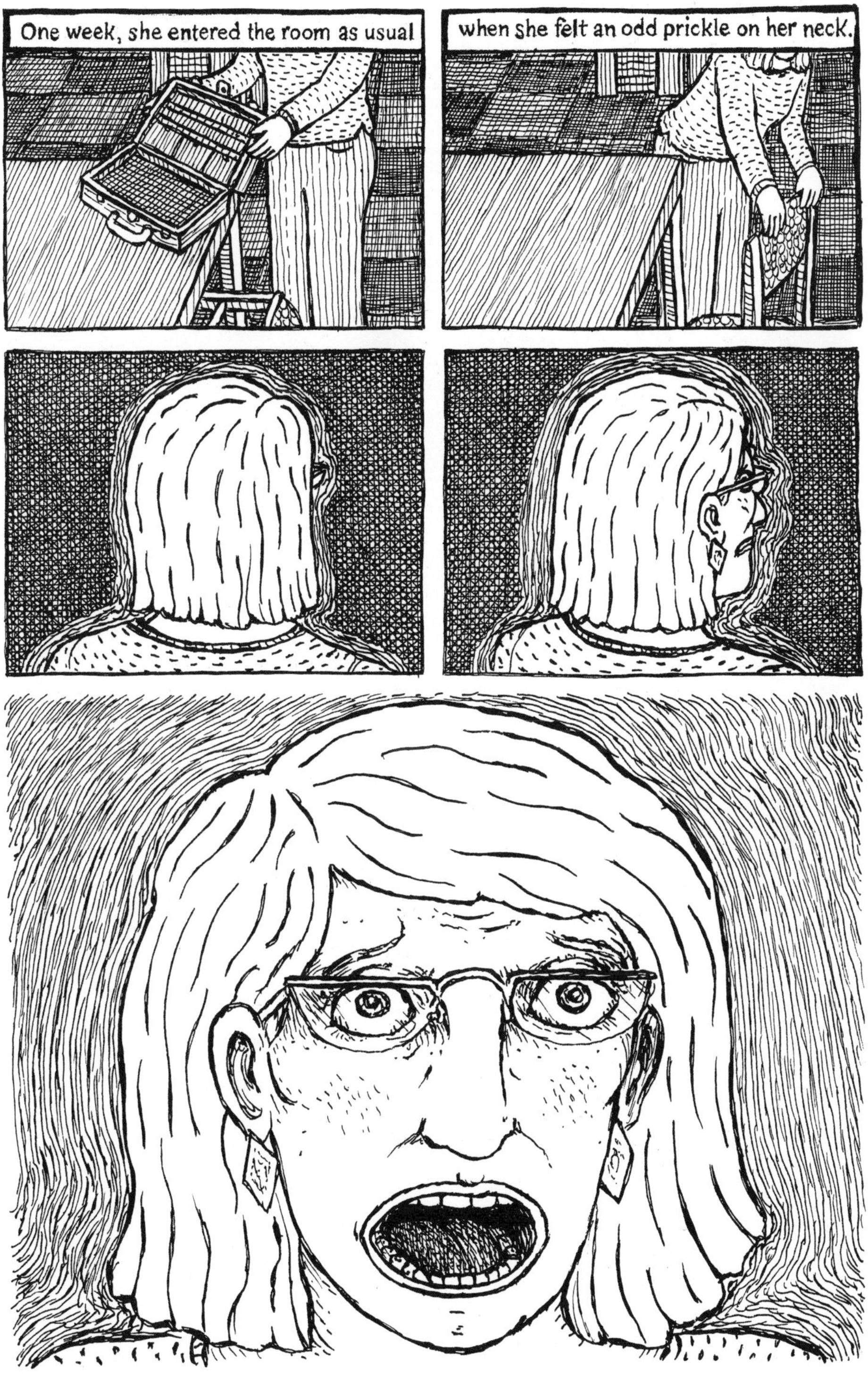
One week, she entered the room as usual
when she felt an odd prickle on her neck.

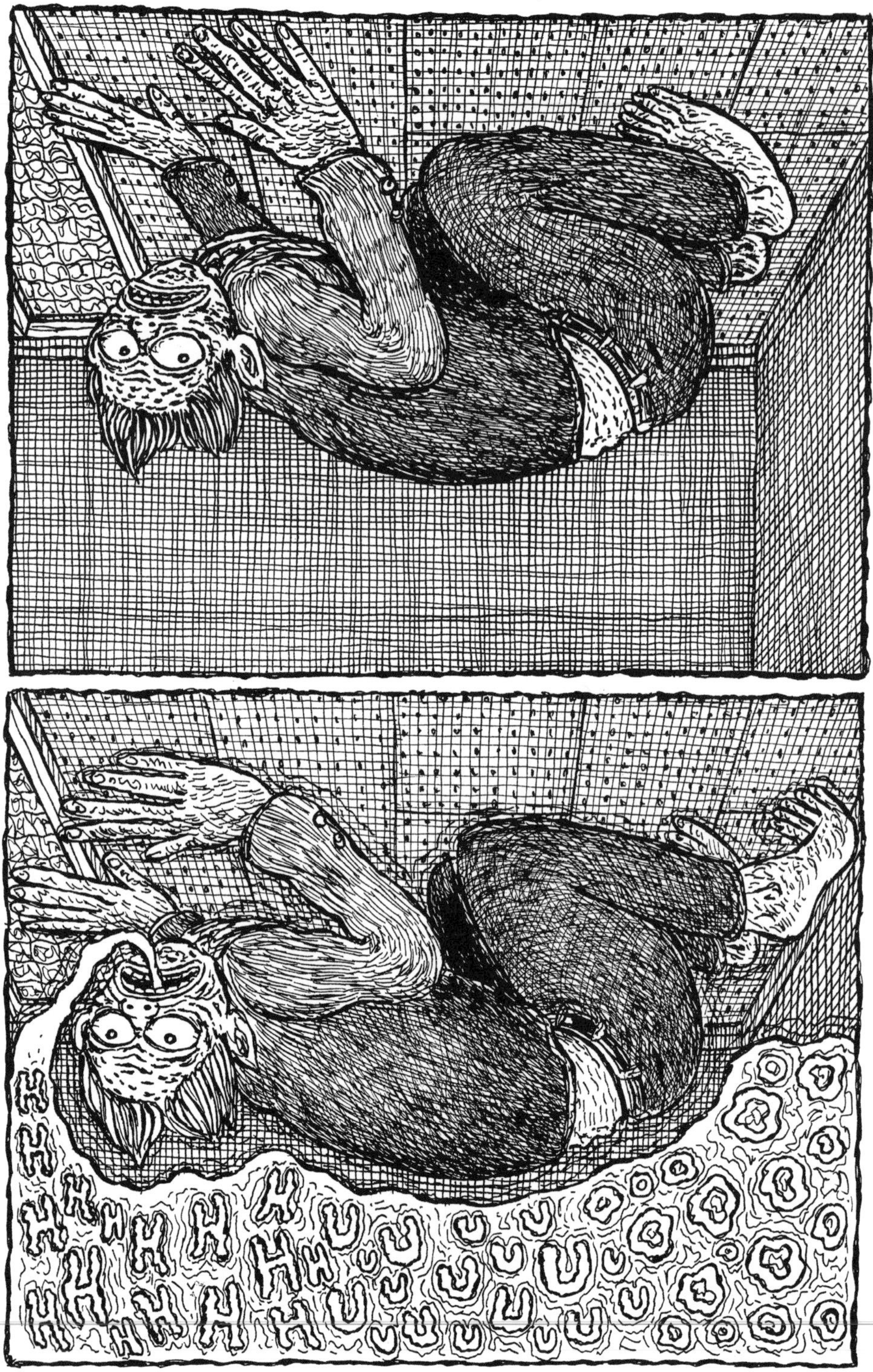
HHHHHHHHUUUUUUUUOOOOOOOO

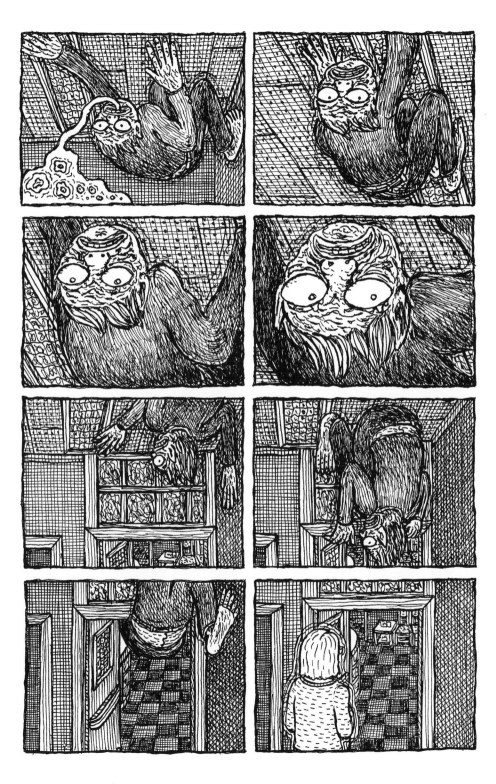

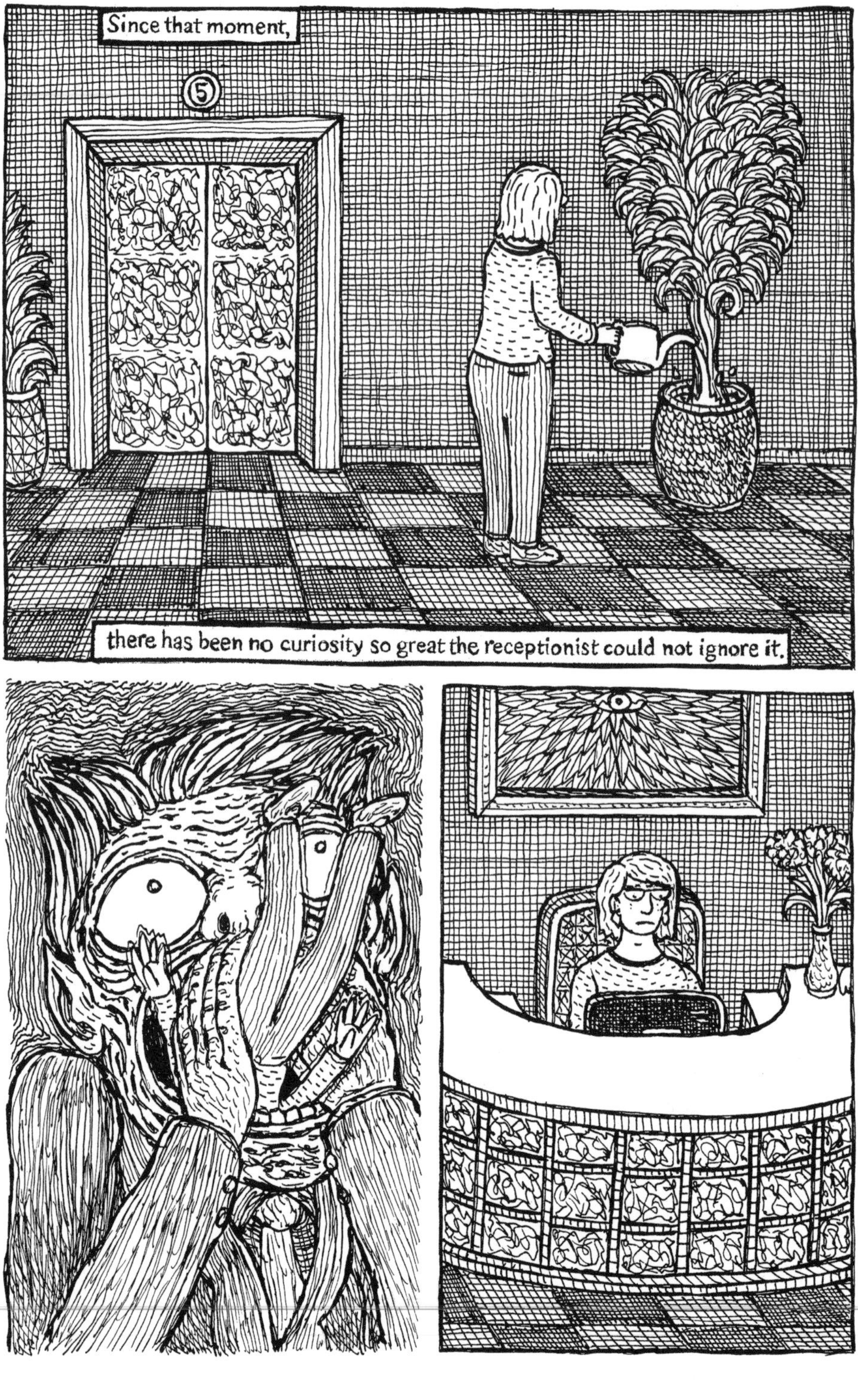
Since that moment,
there has been no curiosity so great the receptionist could not ignore it.

Unexpected...

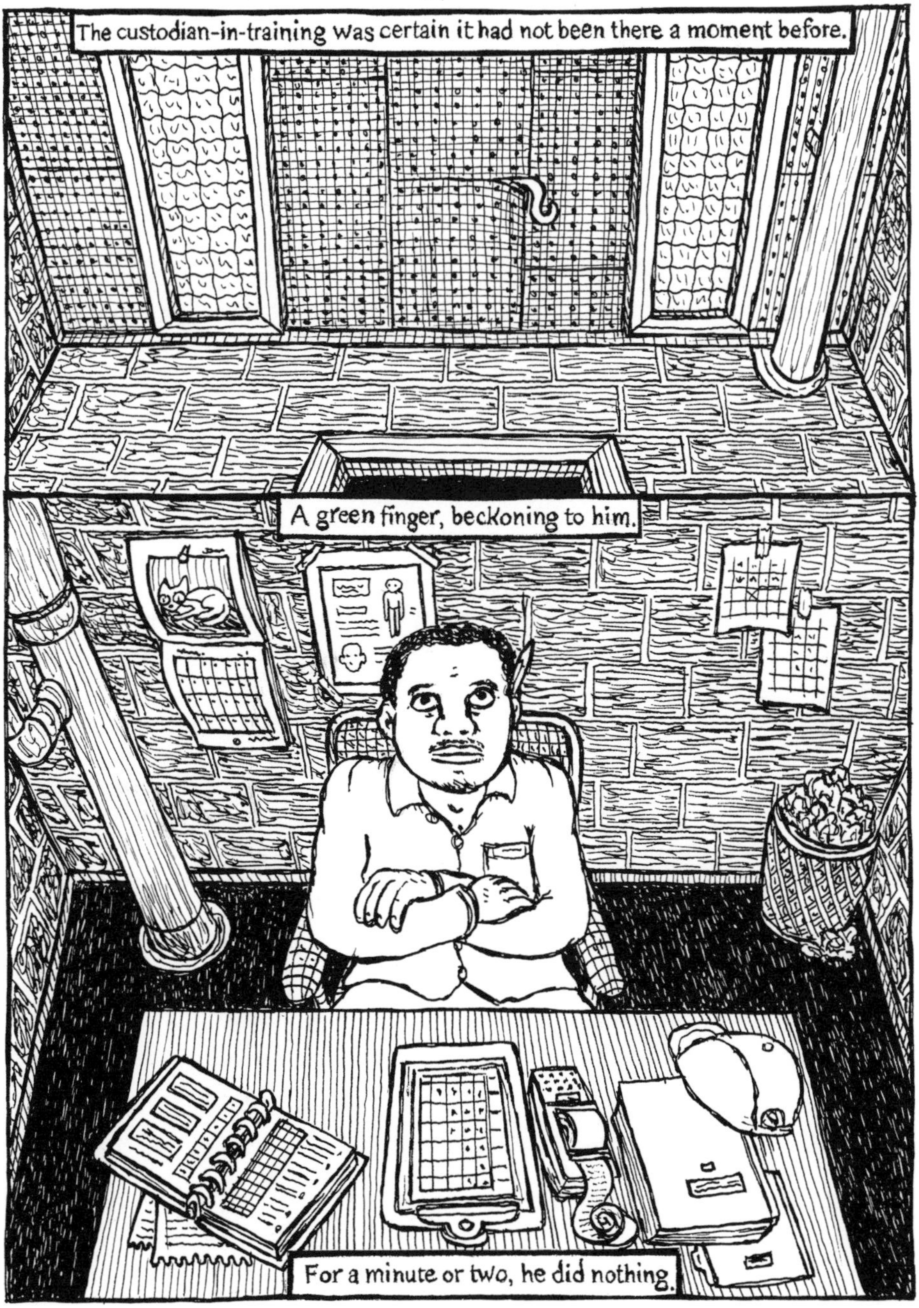
The custodian-in-training was certain it had not been there a moment before.
A green finger, beckoning to him.
For a minute or two, he did nothing.

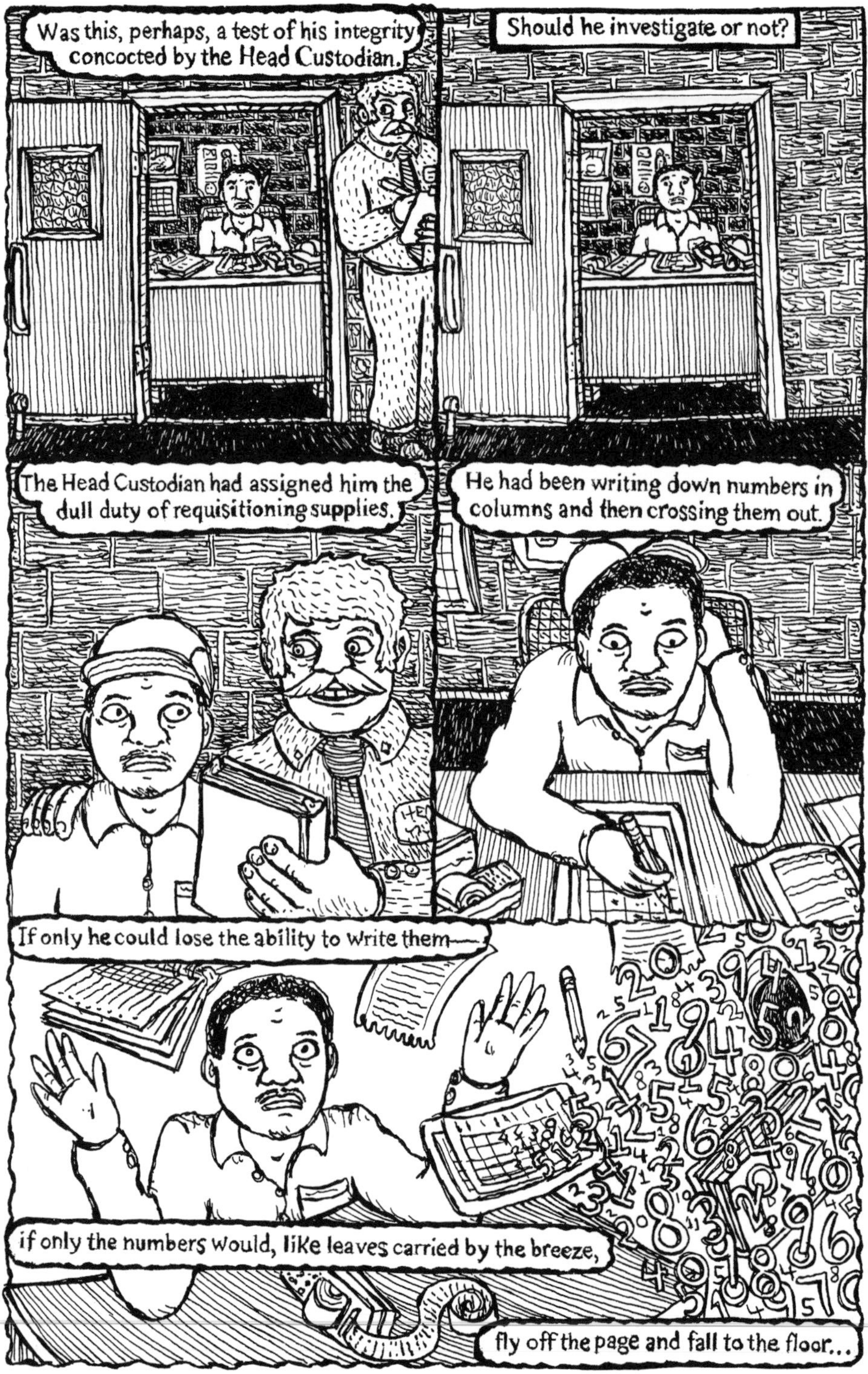
Was this, perhaps, a test of his integrity concocted by the Head Custodian.
Should he investigate or not?
The Head Custodian had assigned him the dull duty of requisitioning supplies.
He had been writing down numbers in columns and then crossing them out.
If only he could lose the ability to write them—
if only the numbers would, like leaves carried by the breeze,
fly off the page and fall to the floor...

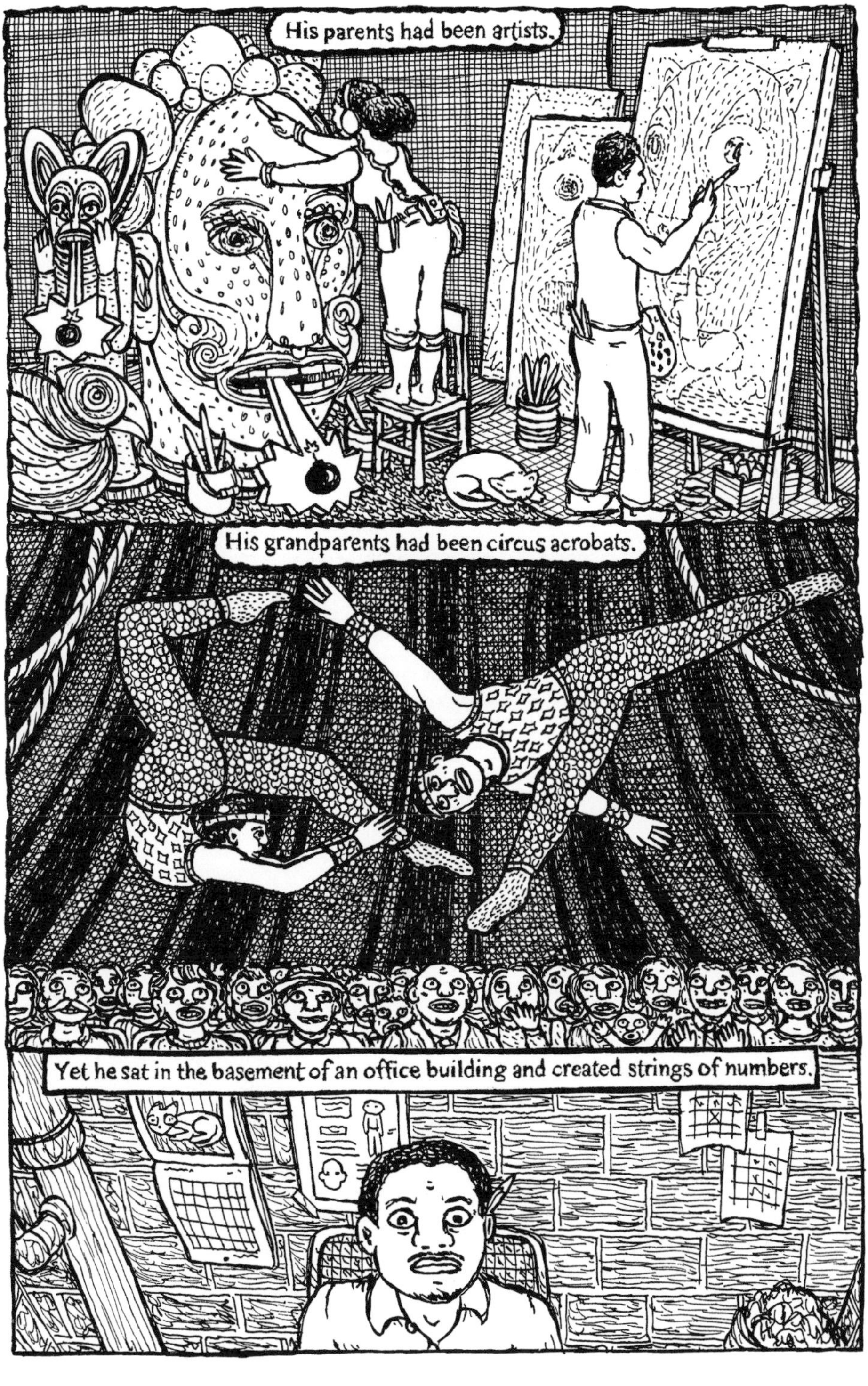
His parents had been artists.
His grandparents had been circus acrobats.
Yet he sat in the basement of an office building and created strings of numbers.

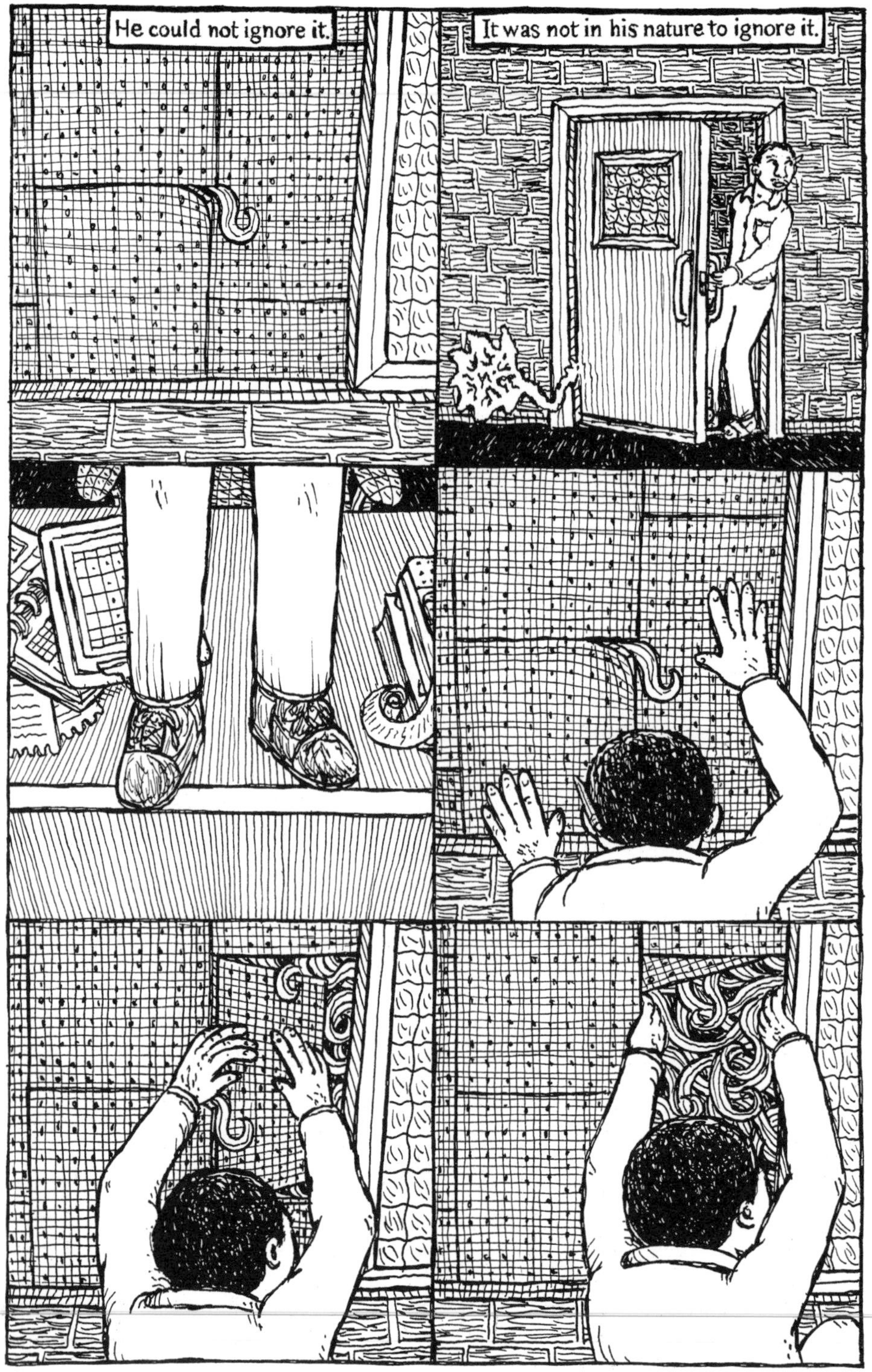
He could not ignore it.
It was not in his nature to ignore it.

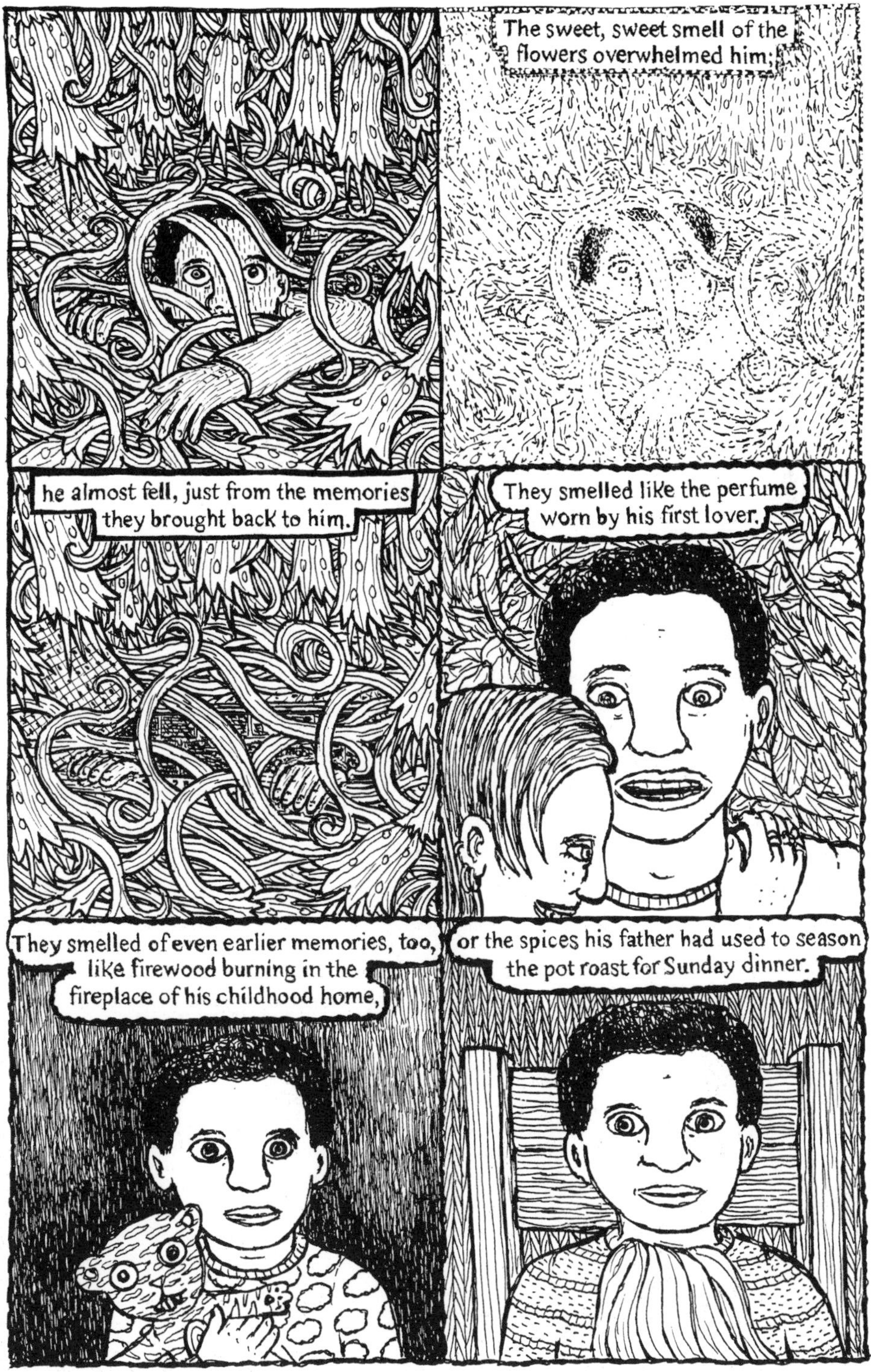
The sweet, sweet smell of the flowers overwhelmed him;
he almost fell, just from the memories they brought back to him.
They smelled like the perfume worn by his first lover.
They smelled of even earlier memories, too, like firewood burning in the fireplace of his childhood home,
or the spices his father had used to season the pot roast for Sunday dinner.

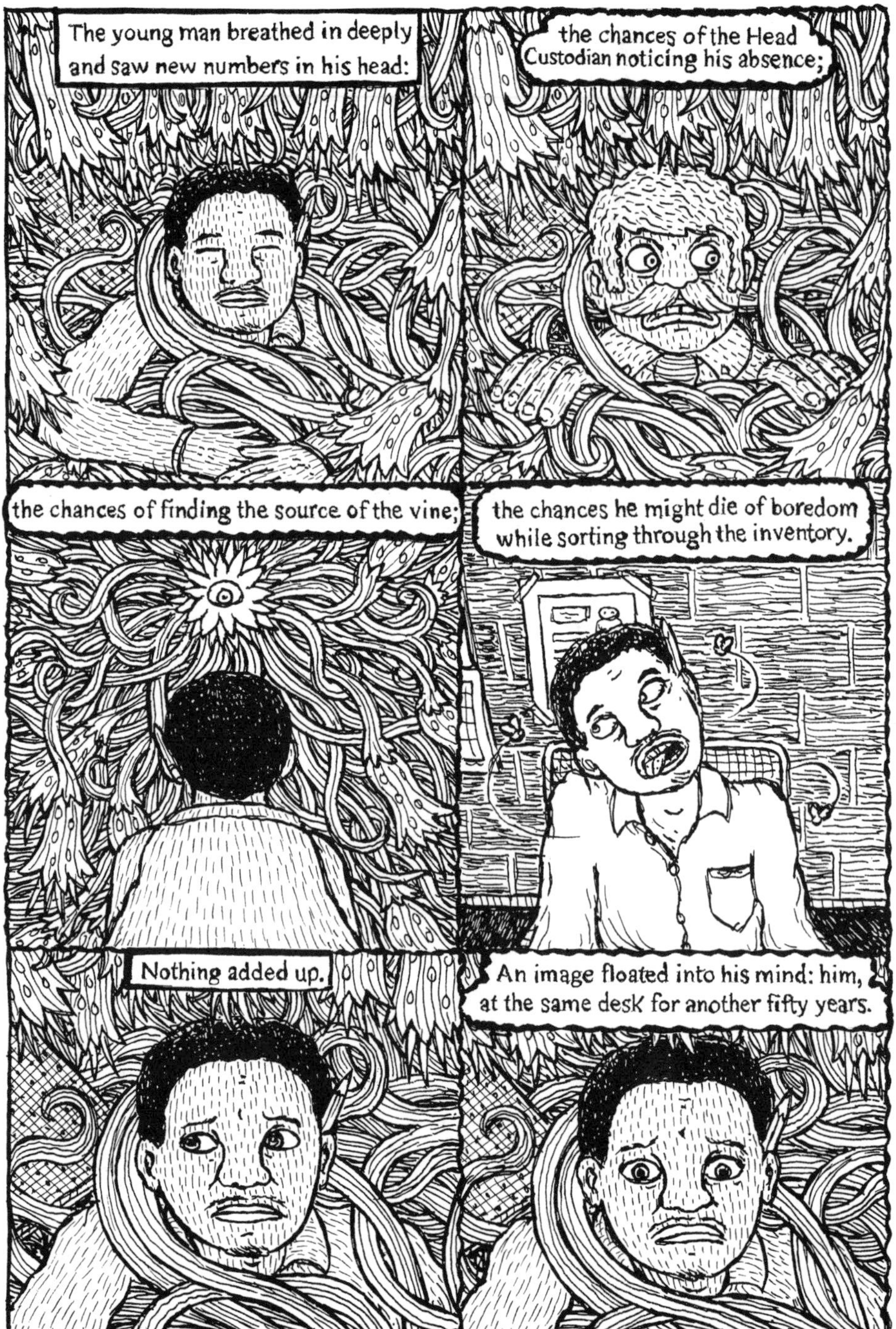
The young man breathed in deeply and saw new numbers in his head:
the chances of the Head Custodian noticing his absence;
the chances of finding the source of the vine;
the chances he might die of boredom while sorting through the inventory.
Nothing added up.
Nothing made complete sense.
An image floated into his mind: him, at the same desk for another fifty years.

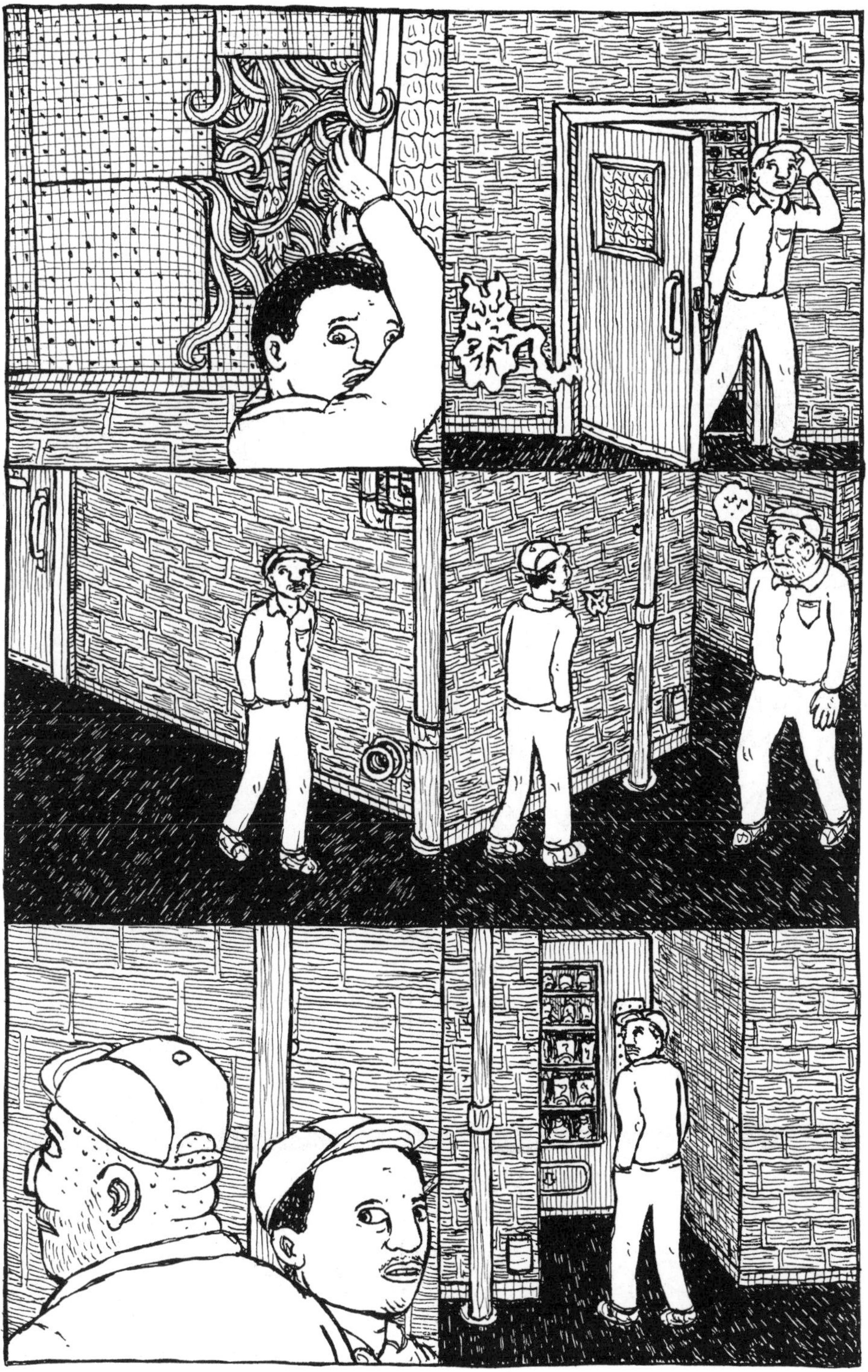

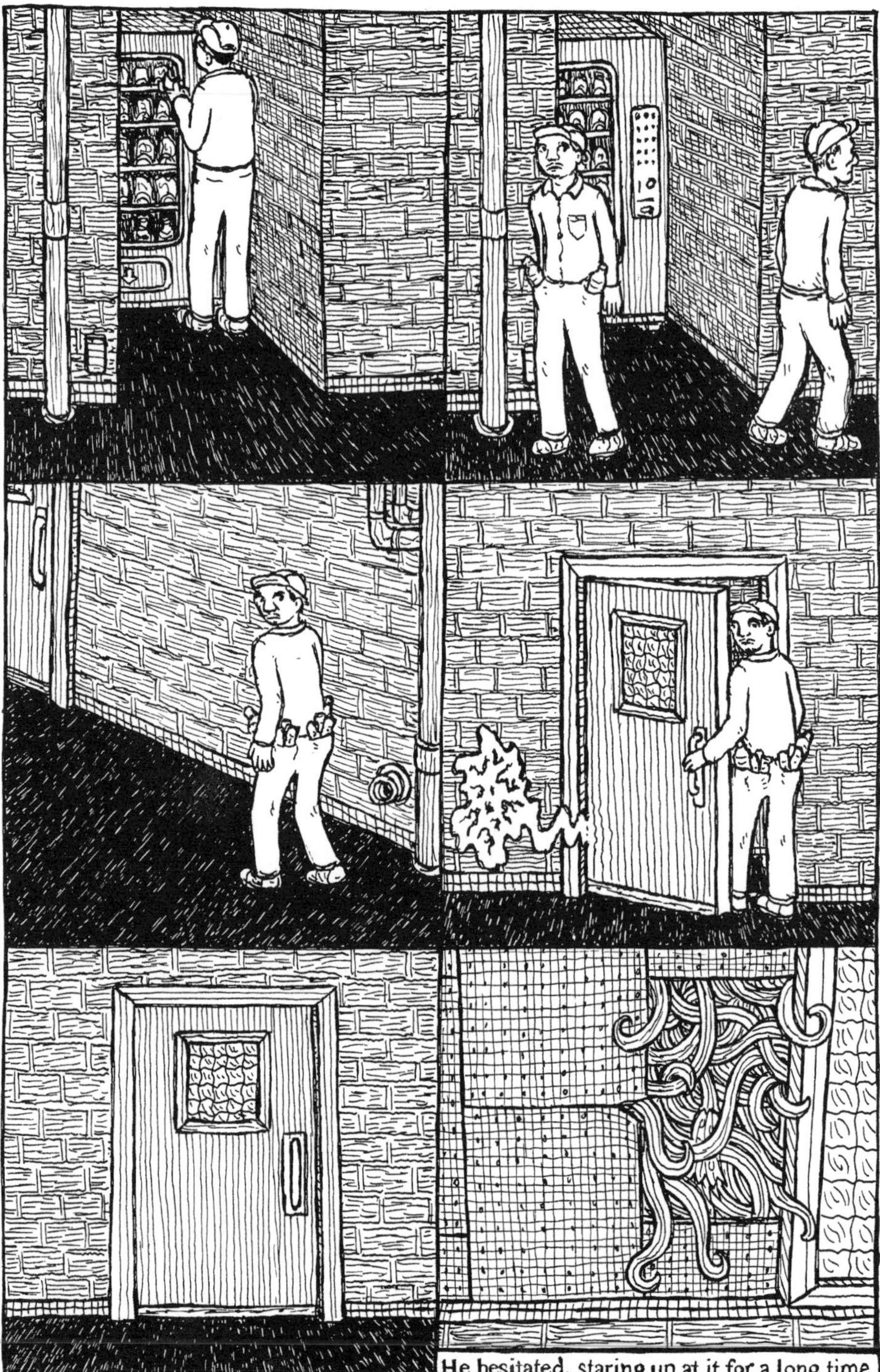
He hesitated, staring up at it for a long time.

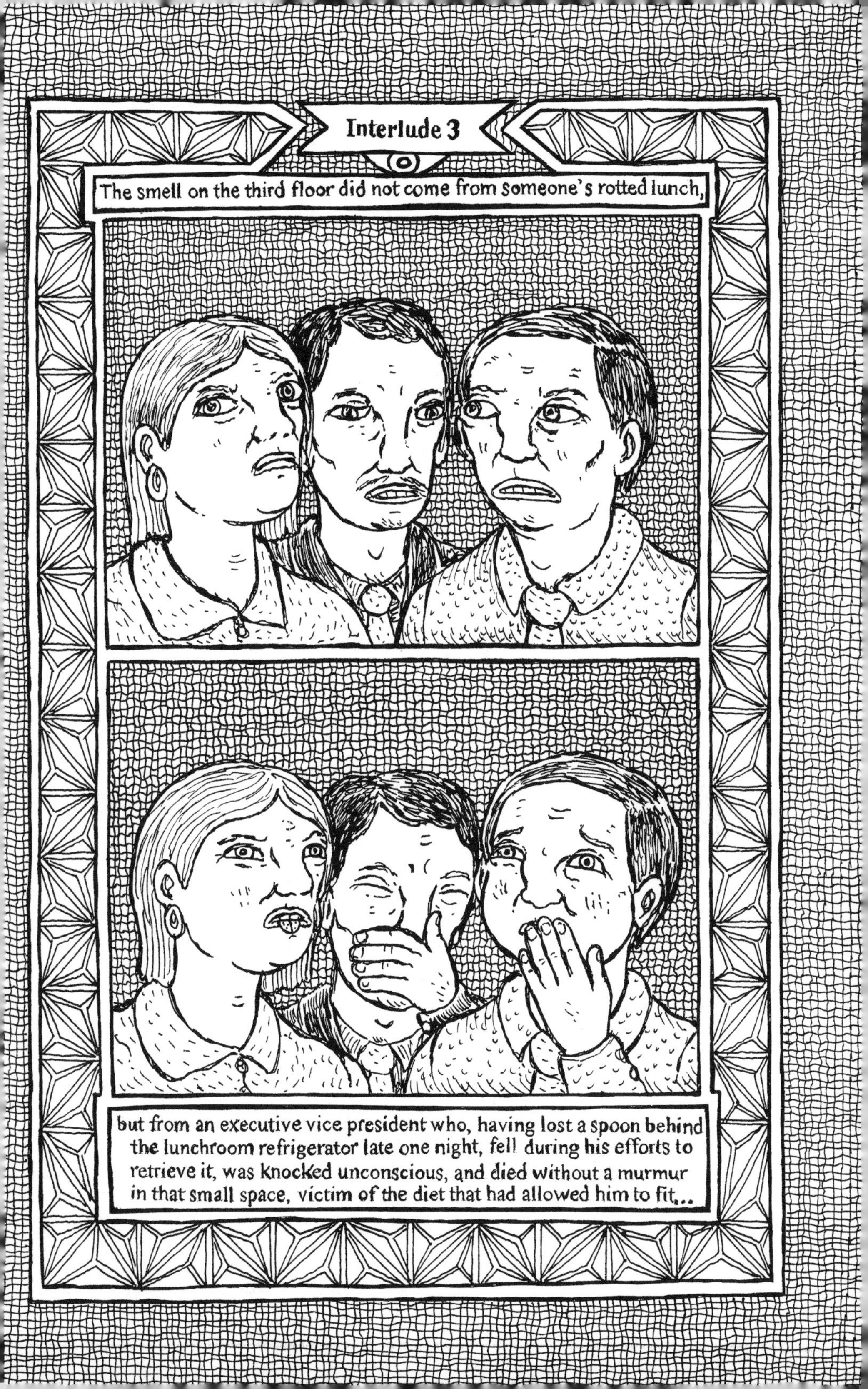
Interlude 3
The smell on the third floor did not come from someone's rotted lunch,
but from an executive vice president who, having lost a spoon behind the lunchroom refrigerator late one night, fell during his efforts to retrieve it, was knocked unconscious, and died without a murmur in that small space, victim of the diet that had allowed him to fit...

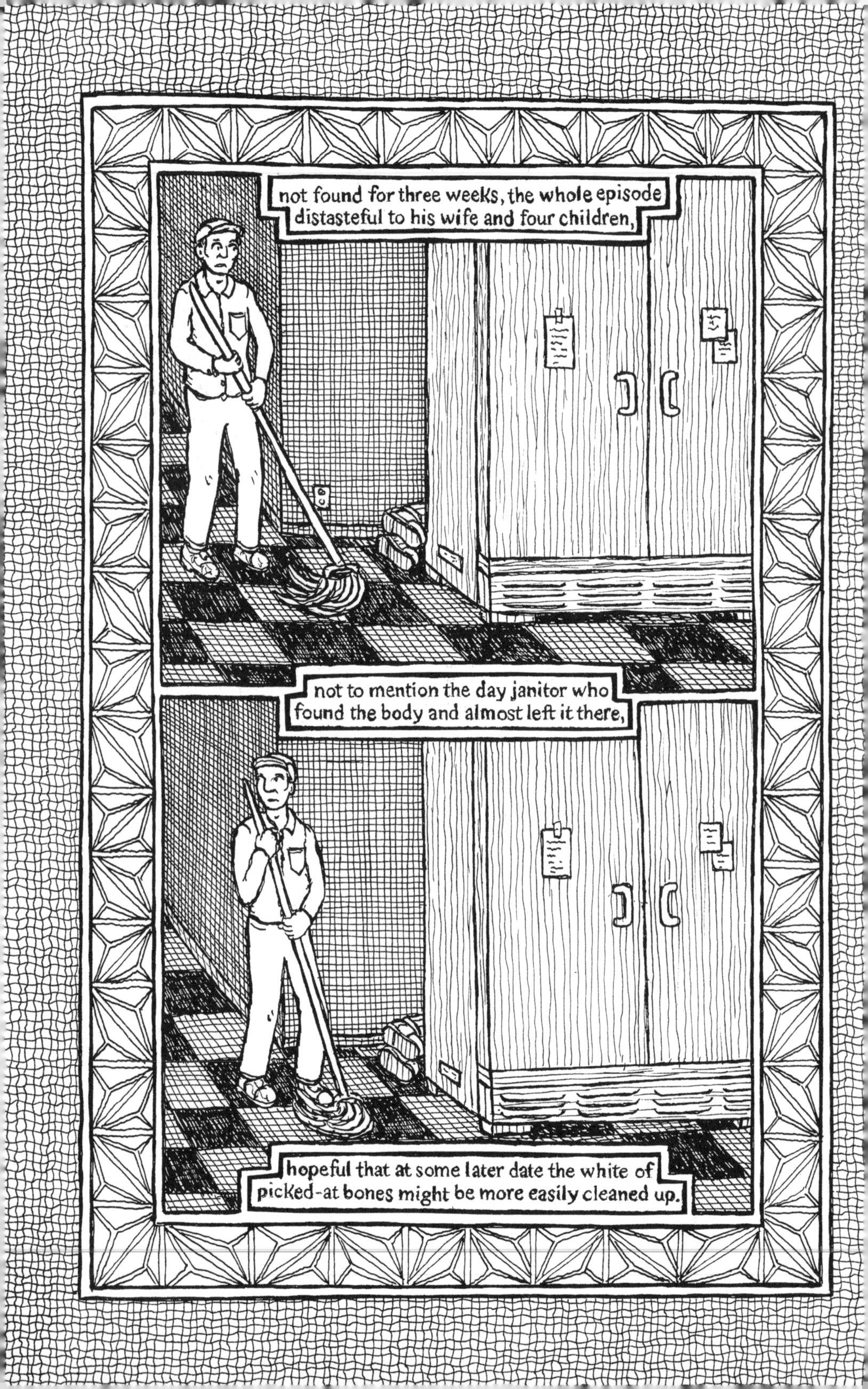
not found for three weeks, the whole episode distasteful to his wife and four children,
not to mention the day janitor who found the body and almost left it there,
hopeful that at some later date the white of picked-at bones might be more easily cleaned up.

...Beauty

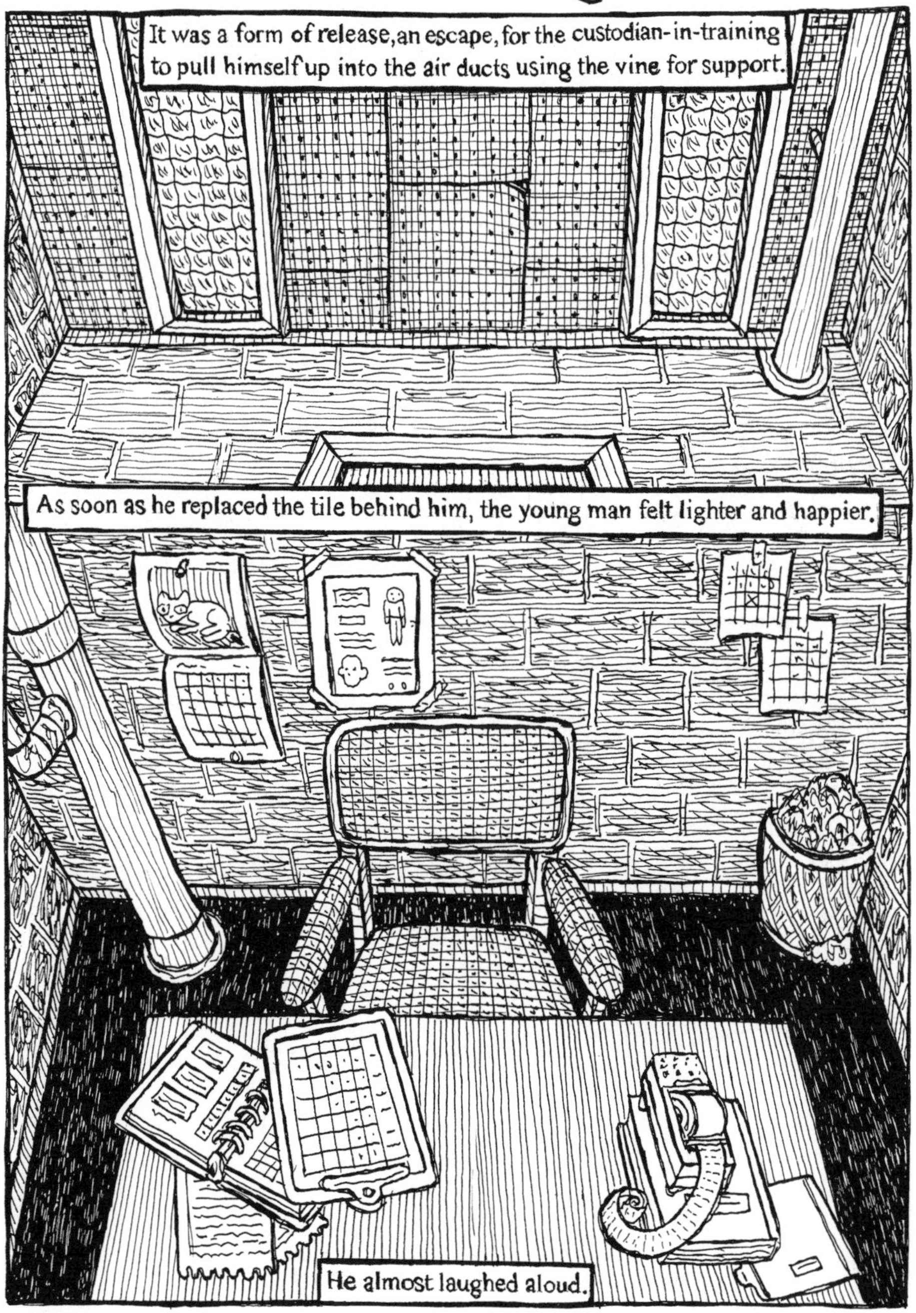
It was a form of release, an escape, for the custodian-in-training to pull himself up into the air ducts using the vine for support.
As soon as he replaced the tile behind him, the young man felt lighter and happier.
He almost laughed aloud.

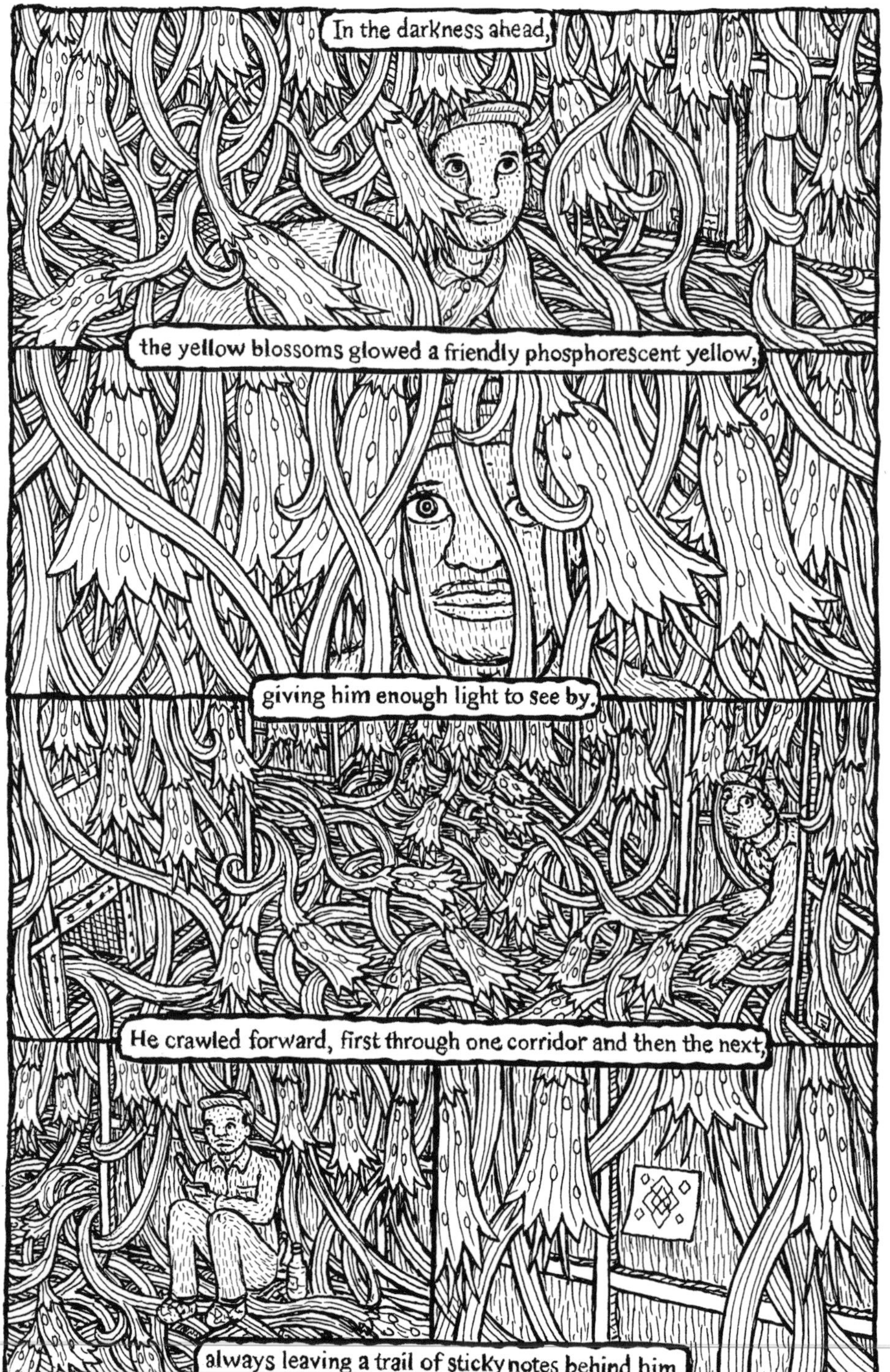
In the darkness ahead,
the yellow blossoms glowed a friendly phosphorescent yellow,
giving him enough light to see by.
He crawled forward, first through one corridor and then the next,
always leaving a trail of sticky notes behind him.

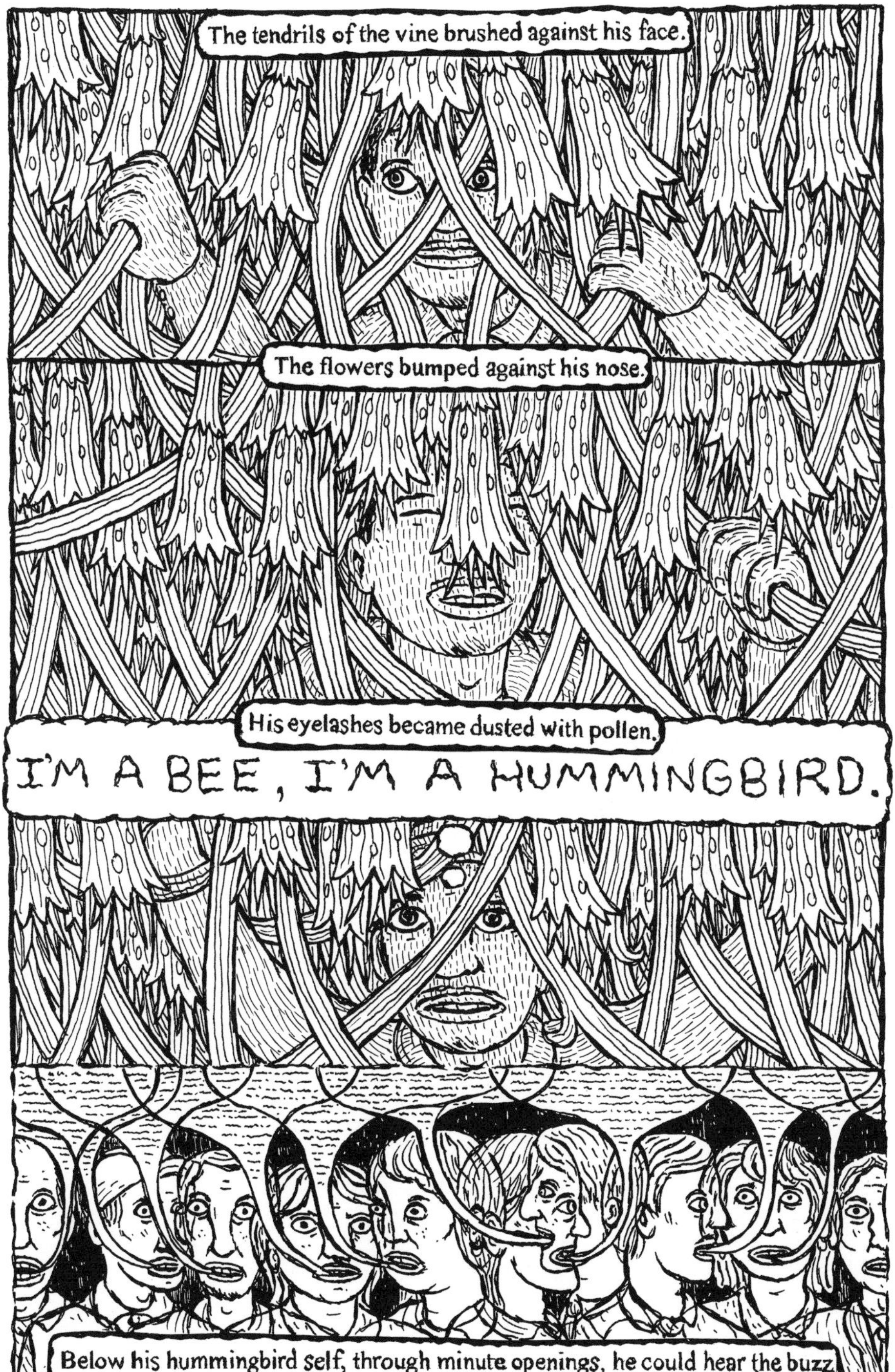

The tendrils of the vine brushed against his face.
The flowers bumped against his nose.
His eyelashes became dusted with pollen.
I'M A BEE, I'M A HUMMINGBIRD.
Below his hummingbird self, through minute openings, he could hear the buzz of conversation, the reverberation of people walking just a few feet below him.

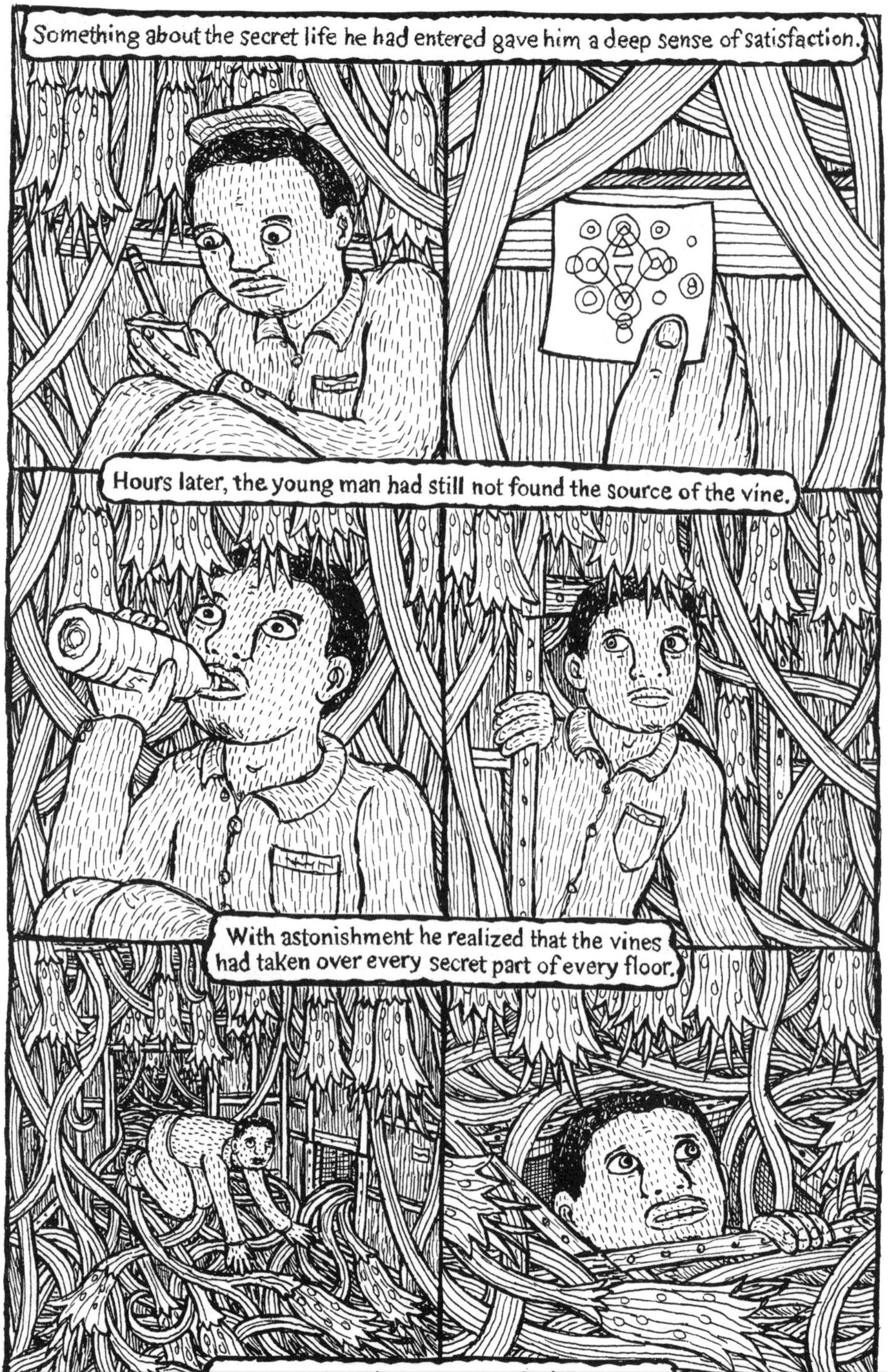

Something about the secret life he had entered gave him a deep sense of satisfaction.
Hours later, the young man had still not found the source of the vine.
With astonishment he realized that the vines had taken over every secret part of every floor.
It might take a day or more to find the source.

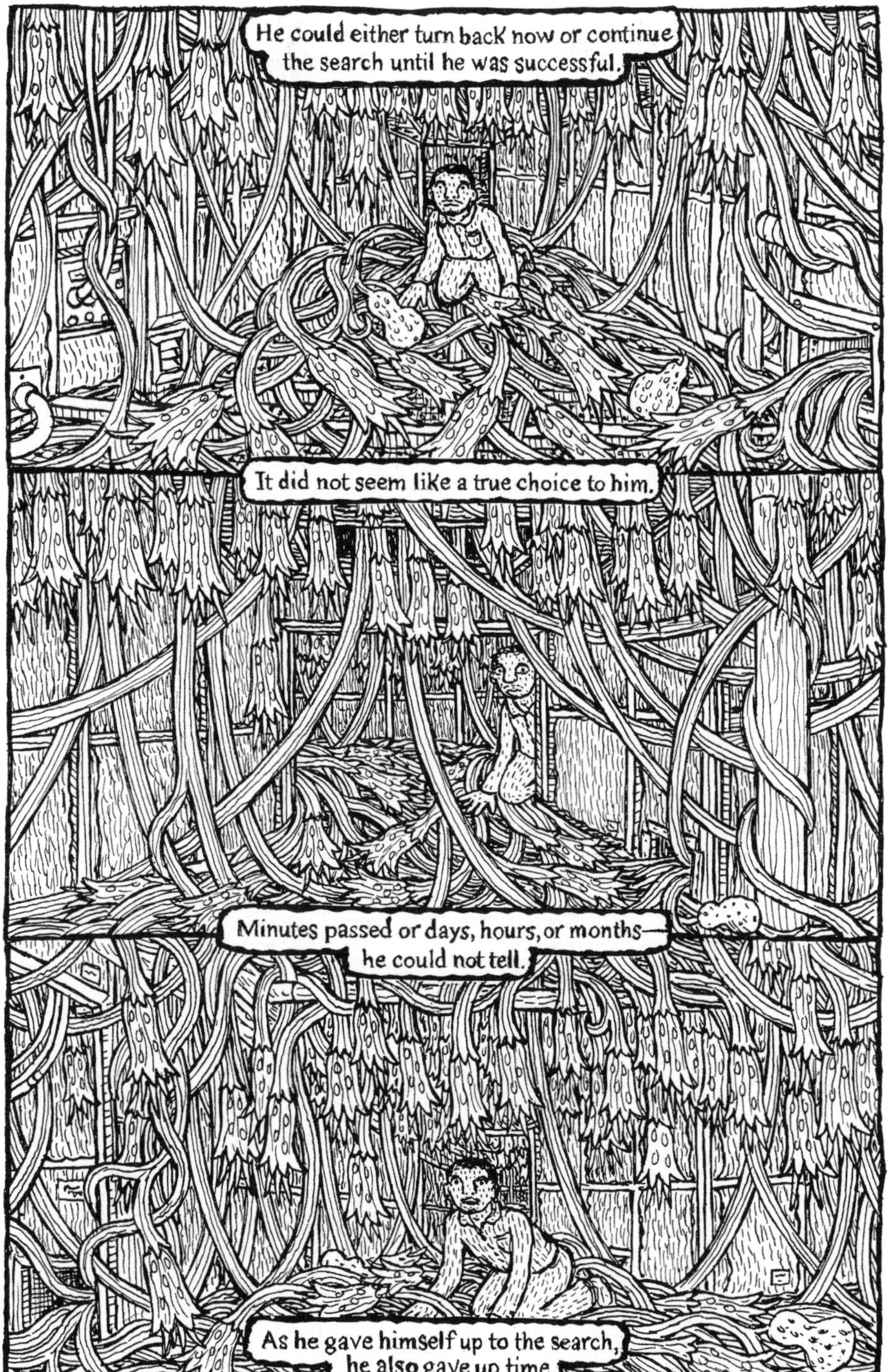
He could either turn back now or continue the search until he was successful.
It did not seem like a true choice to him.
Minutes passed or days, hours, or months—he could not tell.
As he gave himself up to the search, he also gave up time.

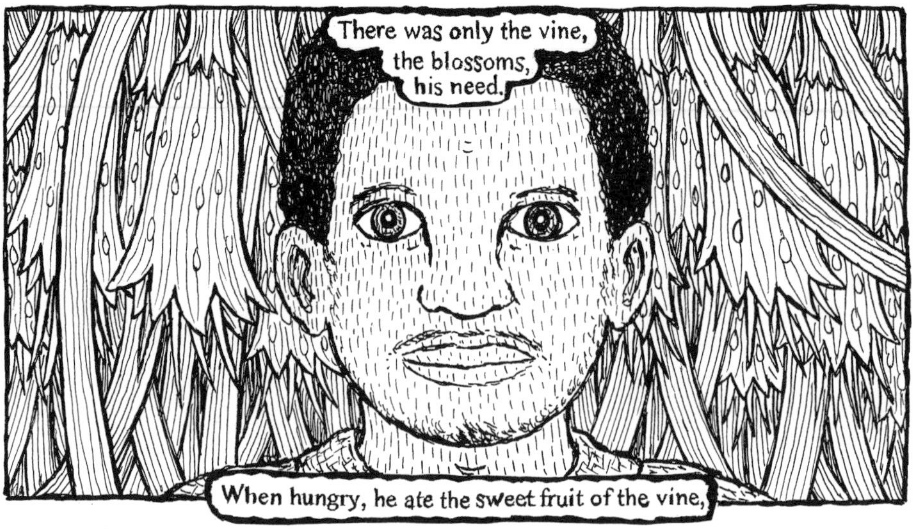
There was only the vine,
the blossoms,
his need.
When hungry, he ate the sweet fruit of the vine,

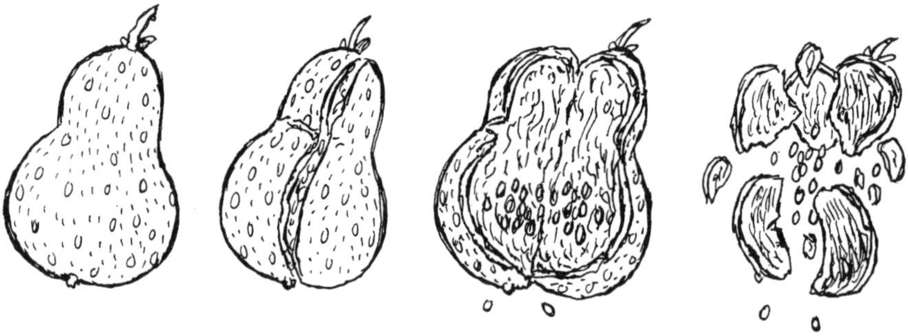

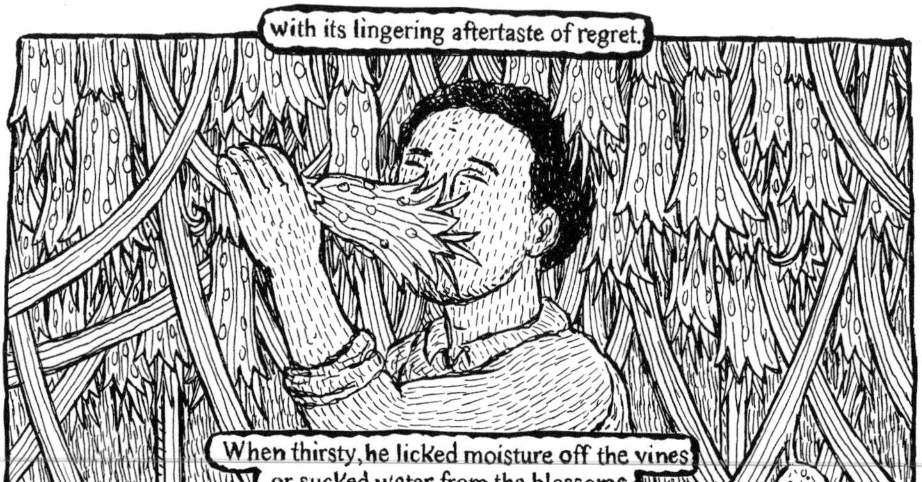
with its lingering aftertaste of regret.
When thirsty, he licked moisture off the vines
or sucked water from the blossoms.

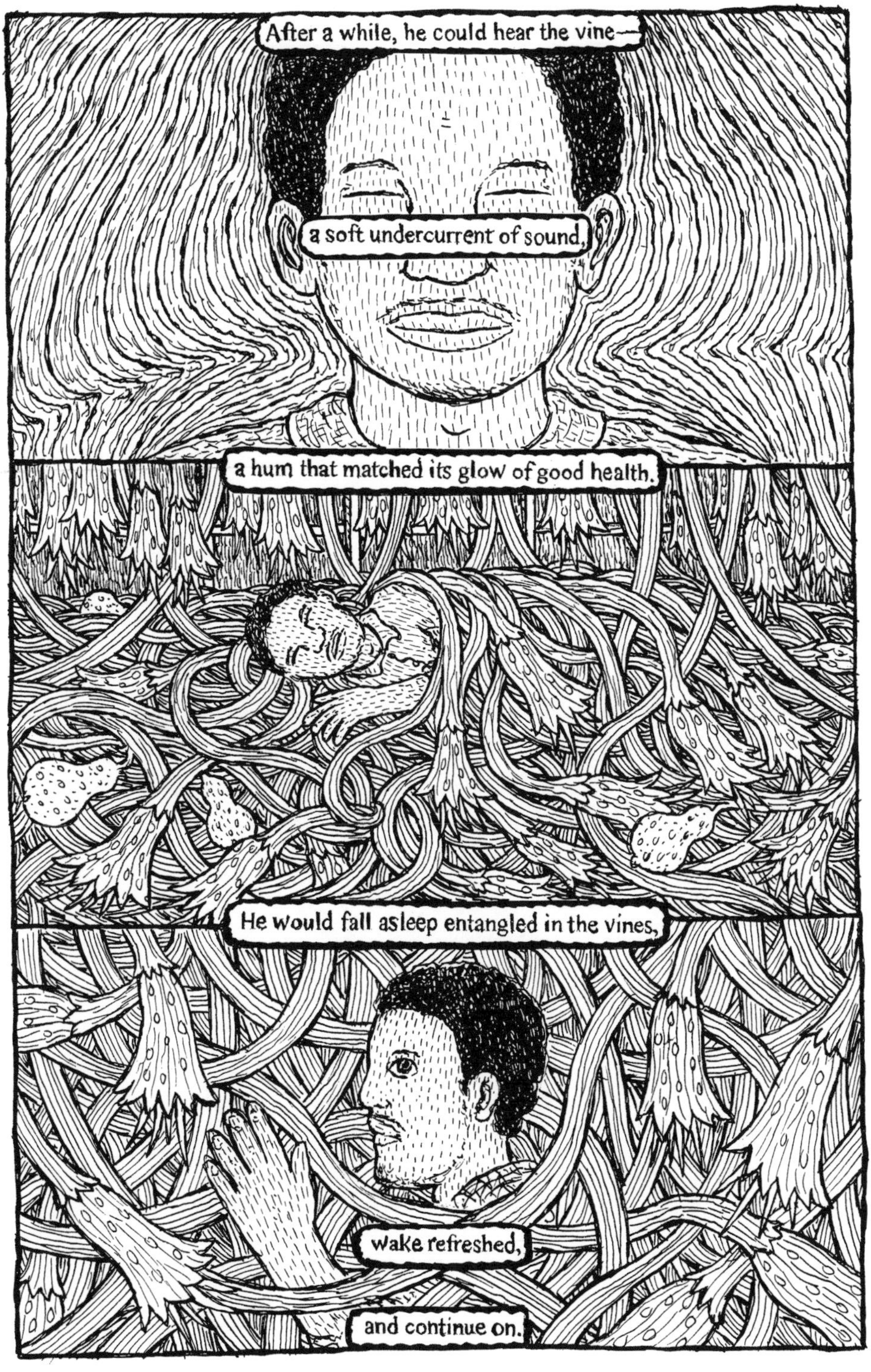
After a while, he could hear the vine—
a soft undercurrent of sound,
a hum that matched its glow of good health.
He would fall asleep entangled in the vines,
wake refreshed,
and continue on.

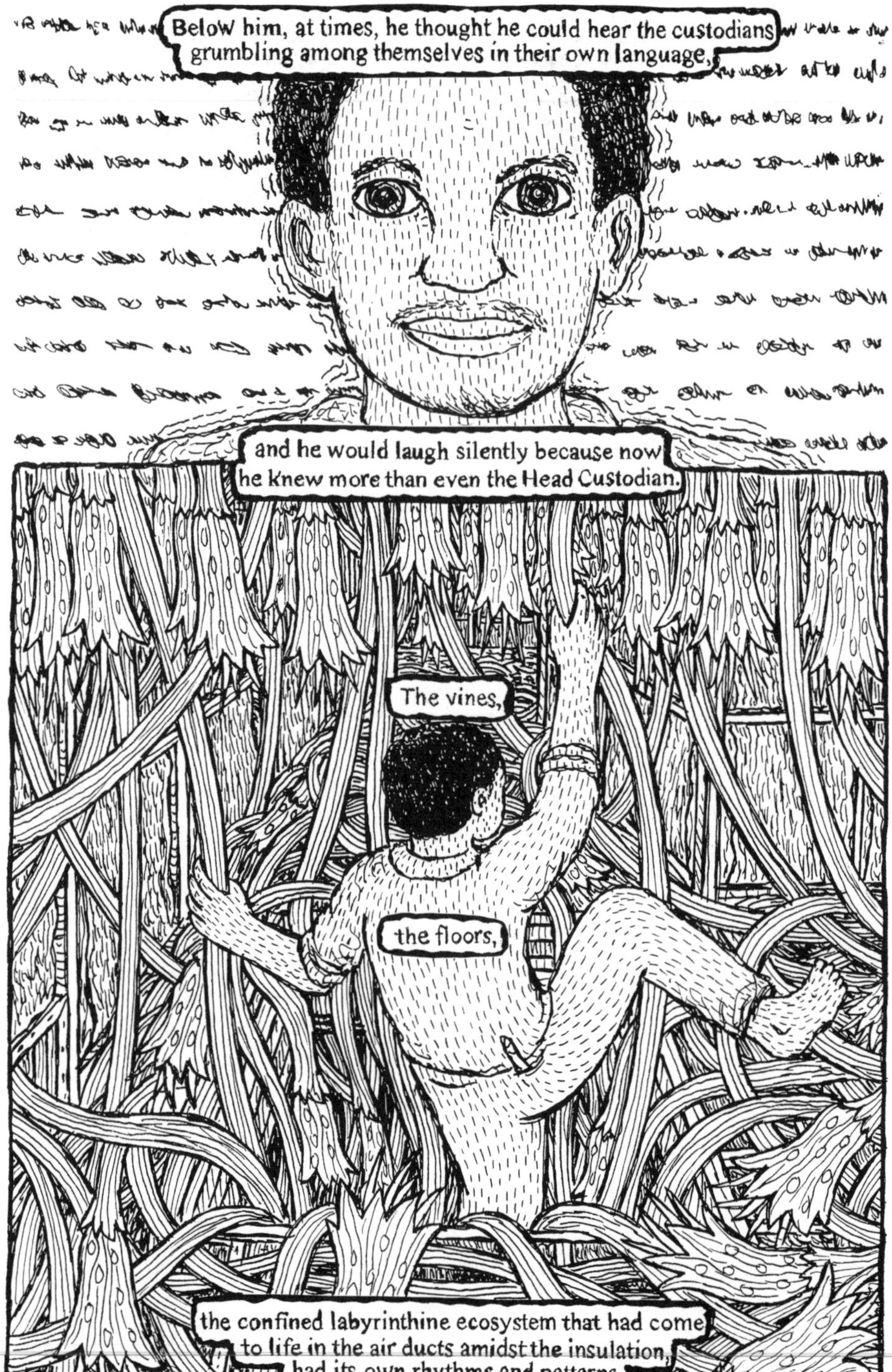
Below him, at times, he thought he could hear the custodians grumbling among themselves in their own language,
and he would laugh silently because now he knew more than even the Head Custodian.
The vines,
the floors,
the confined labyrinthine ecosystem that had come to life in the air ducts amidst the insulation, had its own rhythms and patterns.

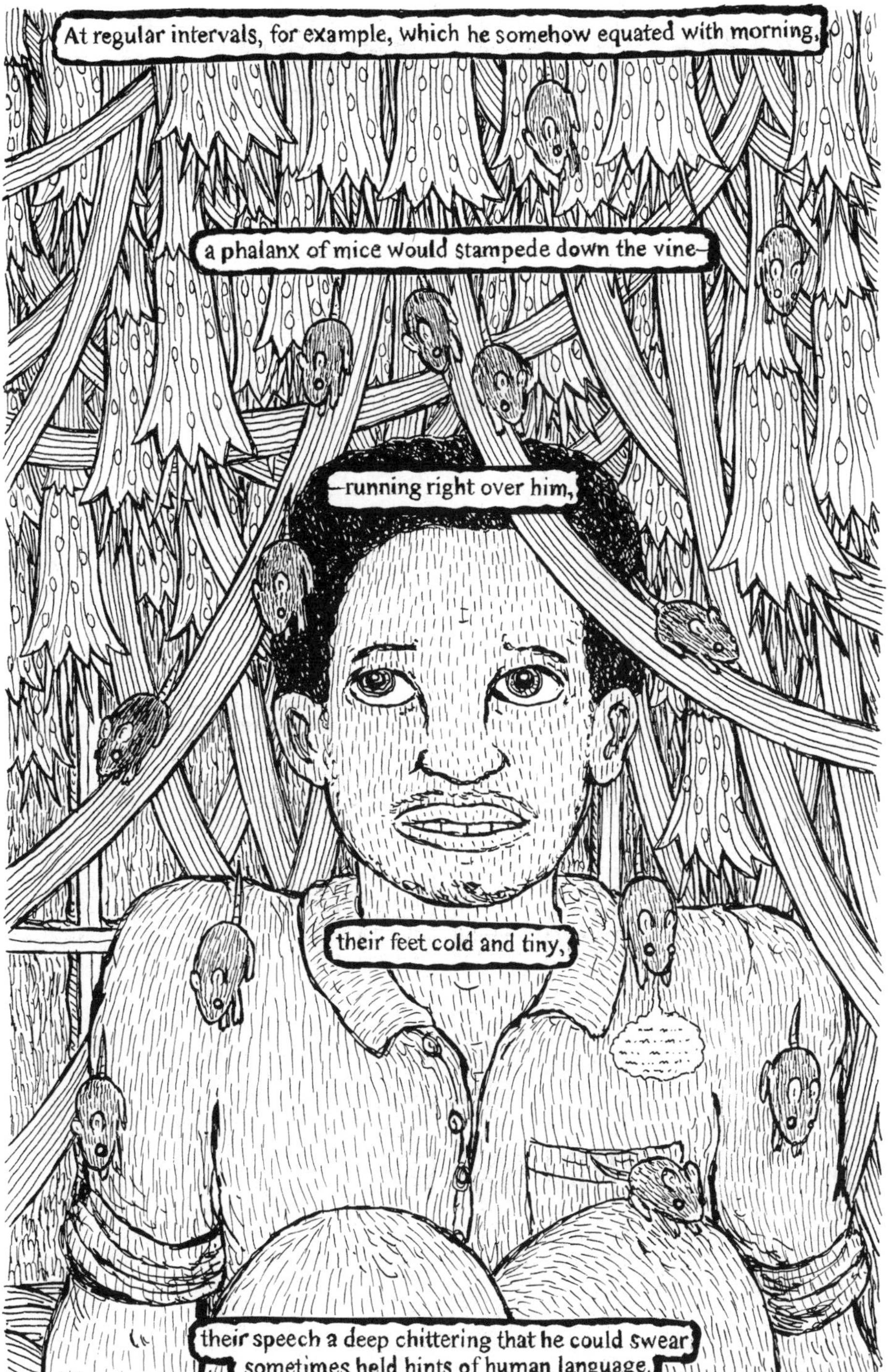
At regular intervals, for example, which he somehow equated with morning,
a phalanx of mice would stampede down the vine—
—running right over him,
their feet cold and tiny,
their speech a deep chittering that he could swear sometimes held hints of human language.

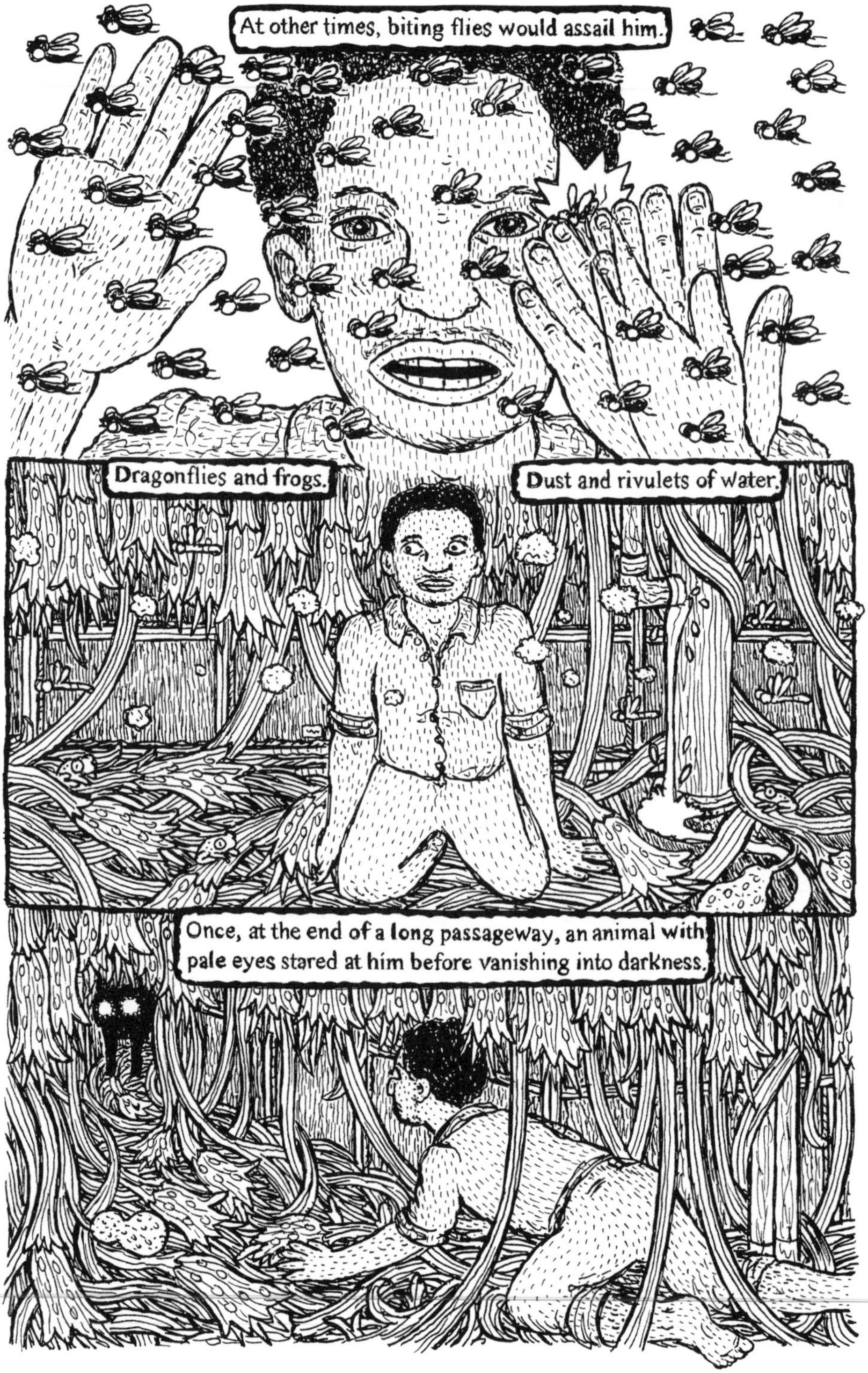
At other times, biting flies would assail him.
Dragonflies and frogs.
Dust and rivulets of water.
Once, at the end of a long passageway, an animal with pale eyes stared at him before vanishing into darkness.

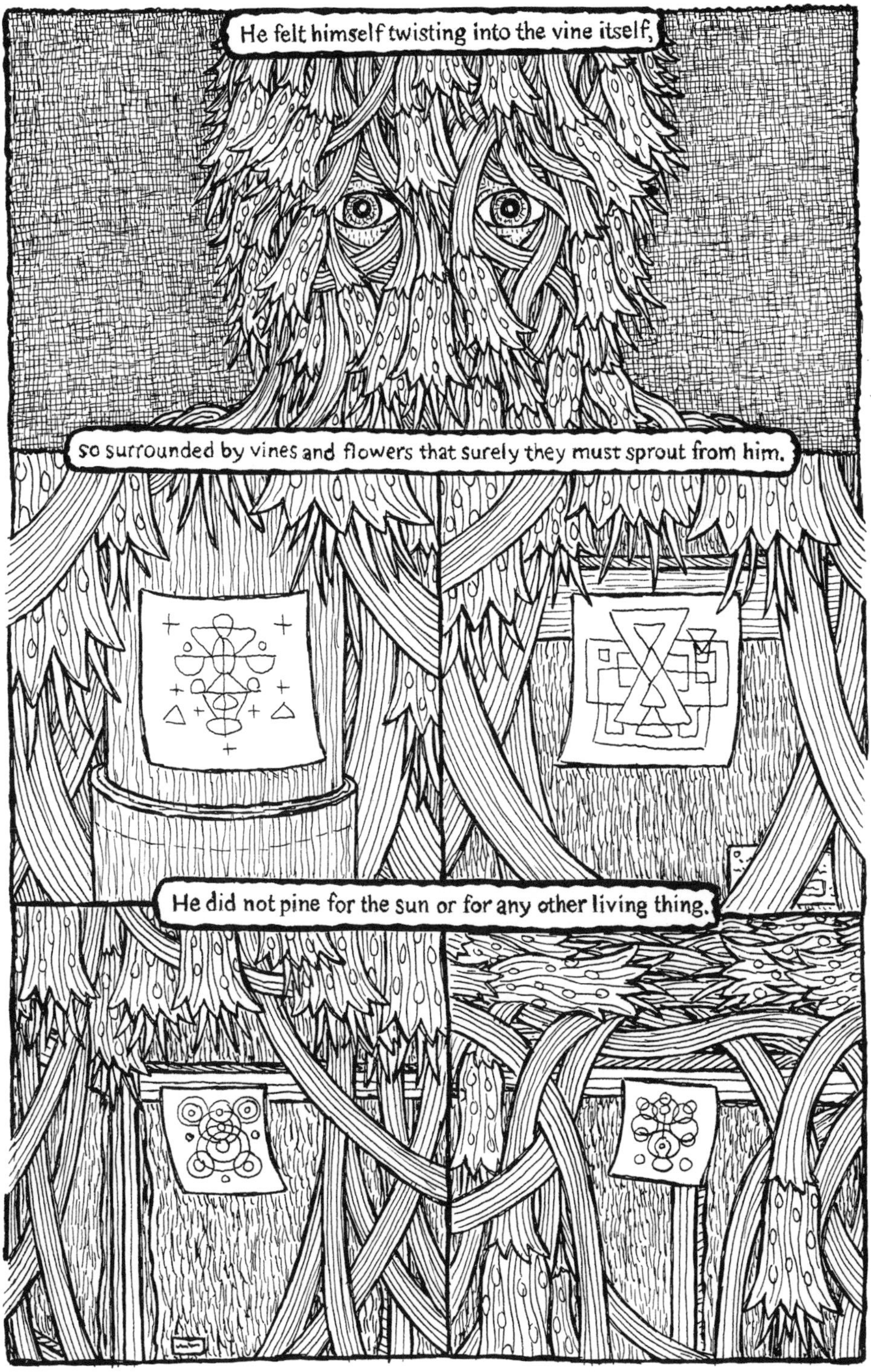
He felt himself twisting into the vine itself,
so surrounded by vines and flowers that surely they must sprout from him.
He did not pine for the sun or for any other living thing.

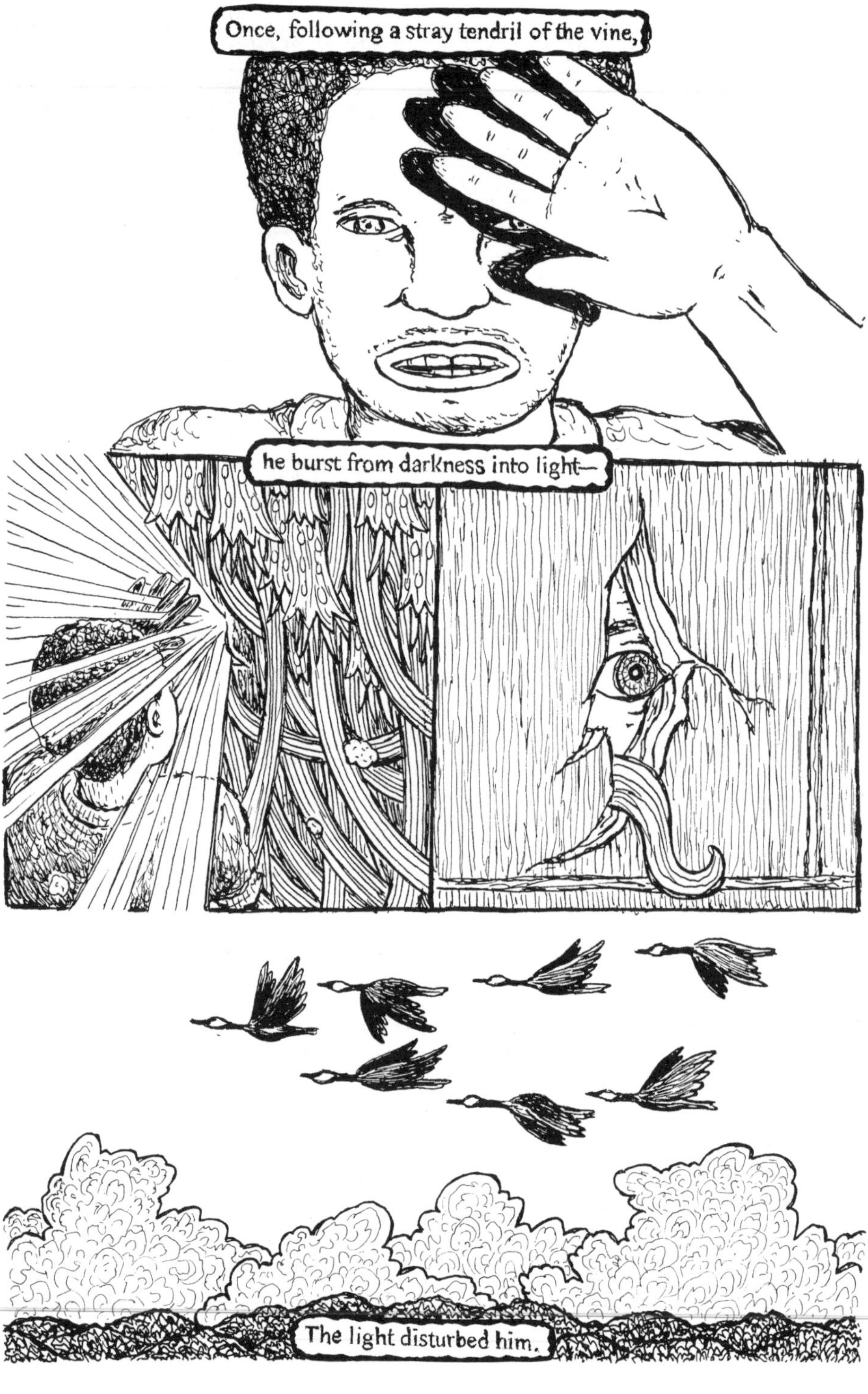
Once, following a stray tendril of the vine,
he burst from darkness into light—
The light disturbed him.

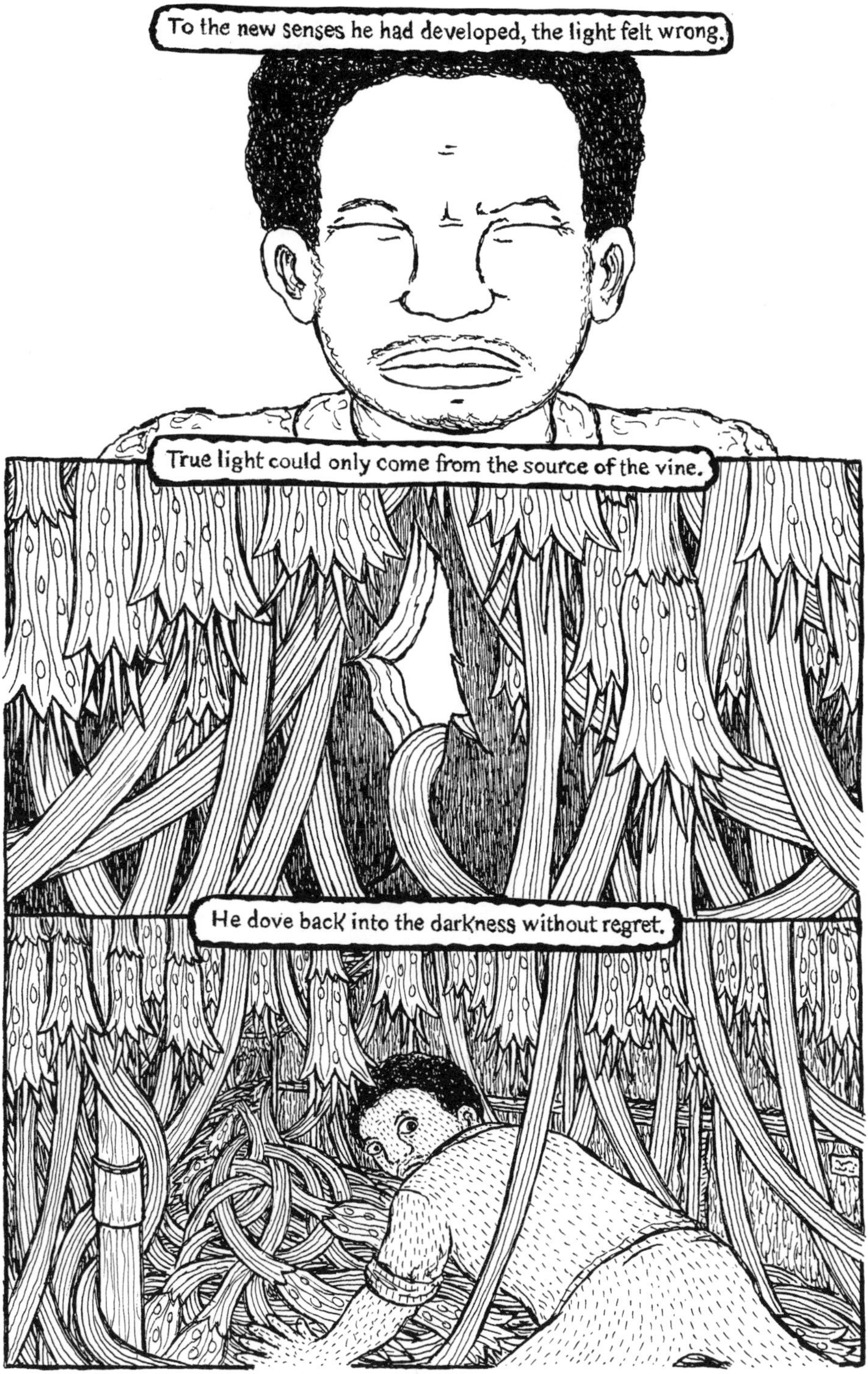
To the new senses he had developed, the light felt wrong.
True light could only come from the source of the vine.
He dove back into the darkness without regret.

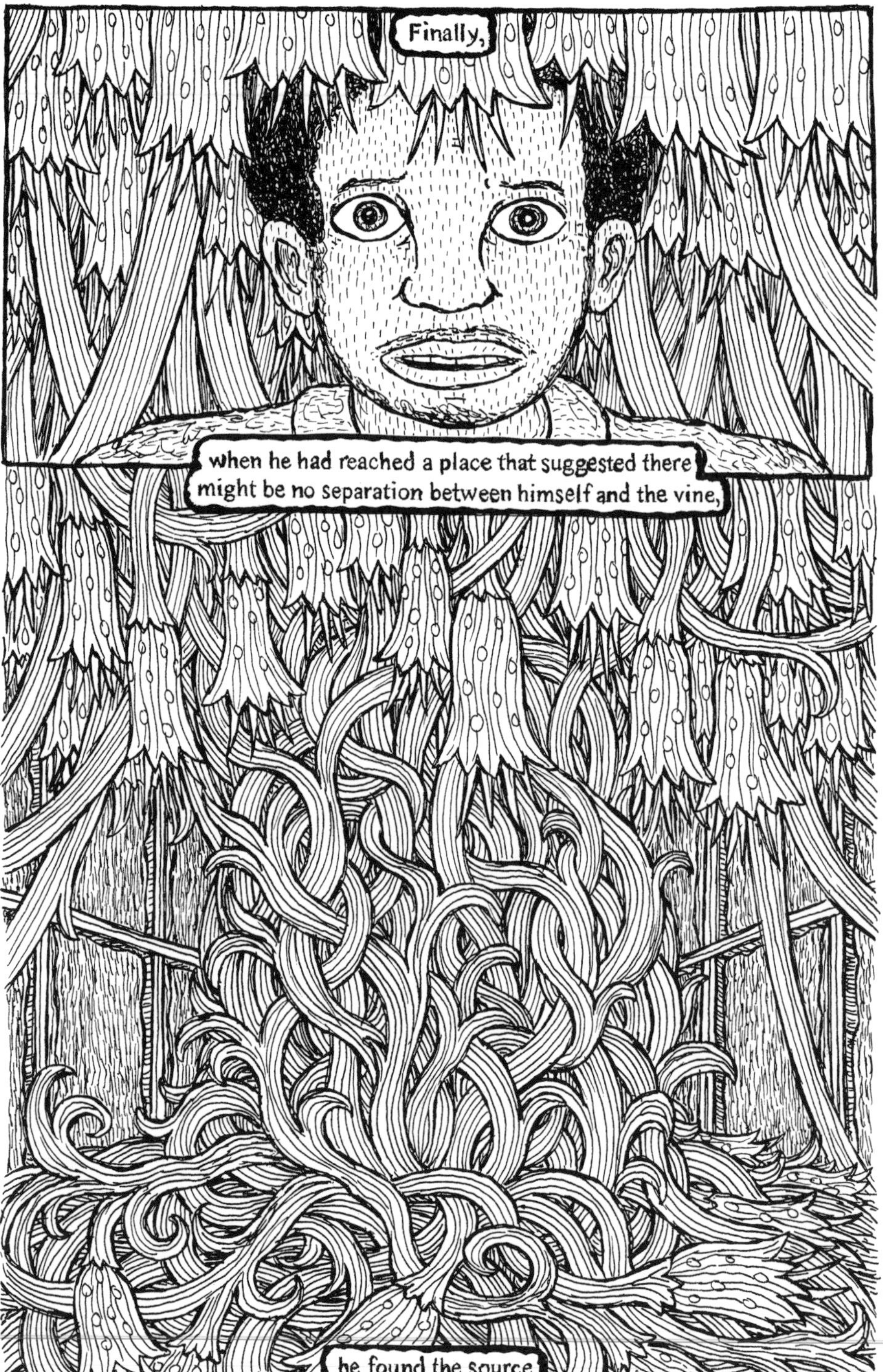
Finally,
when he had reached a place that suggested there might be no separation between himself and the vine,
he found the source.

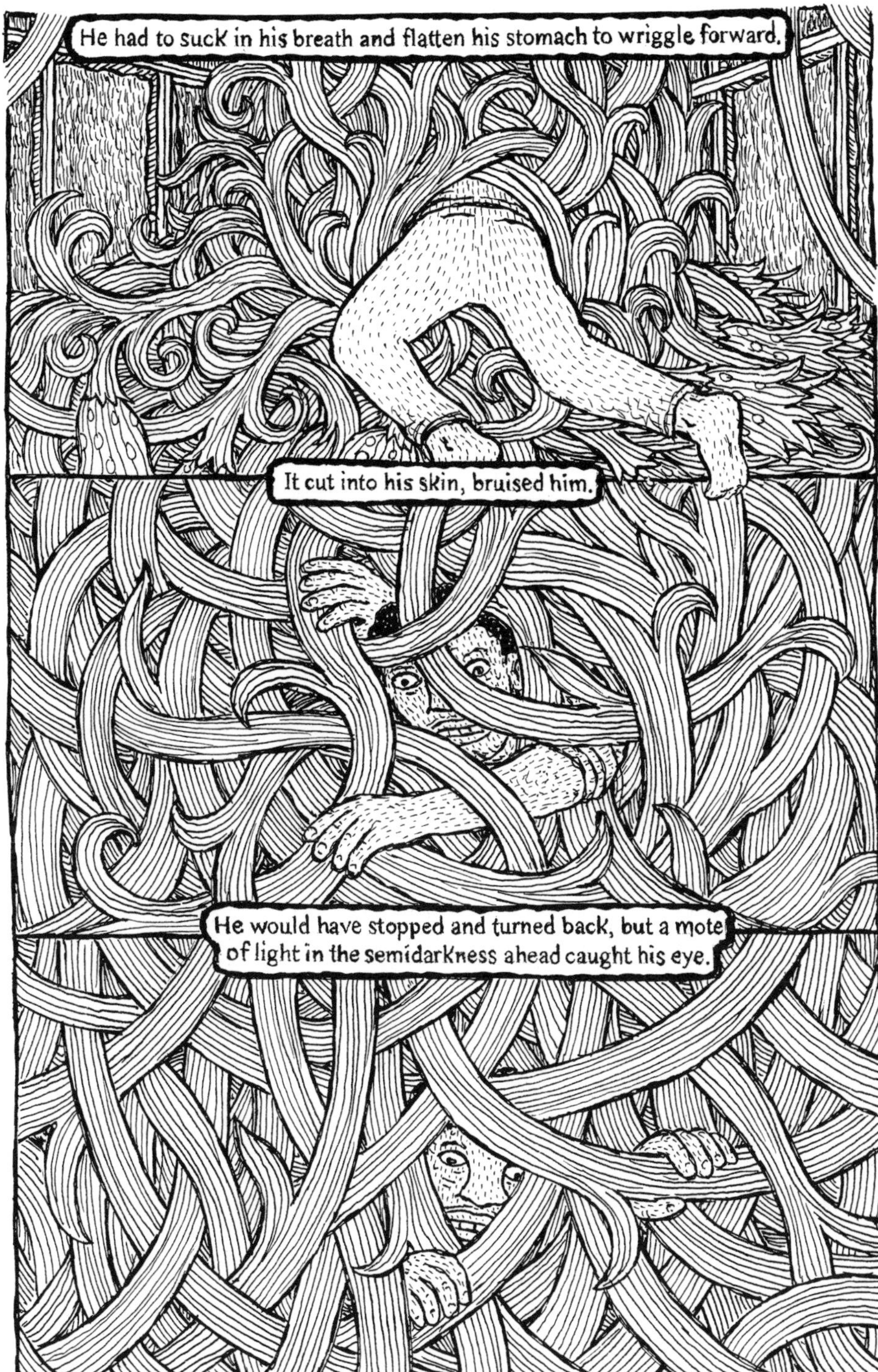
He had to suck in his breath and flatten his stomach to wriggle forward.
It cut into his skin, bruised him.
He would have stopped and turned back, but a mote of light in the semidarkness ahead caught his eye.

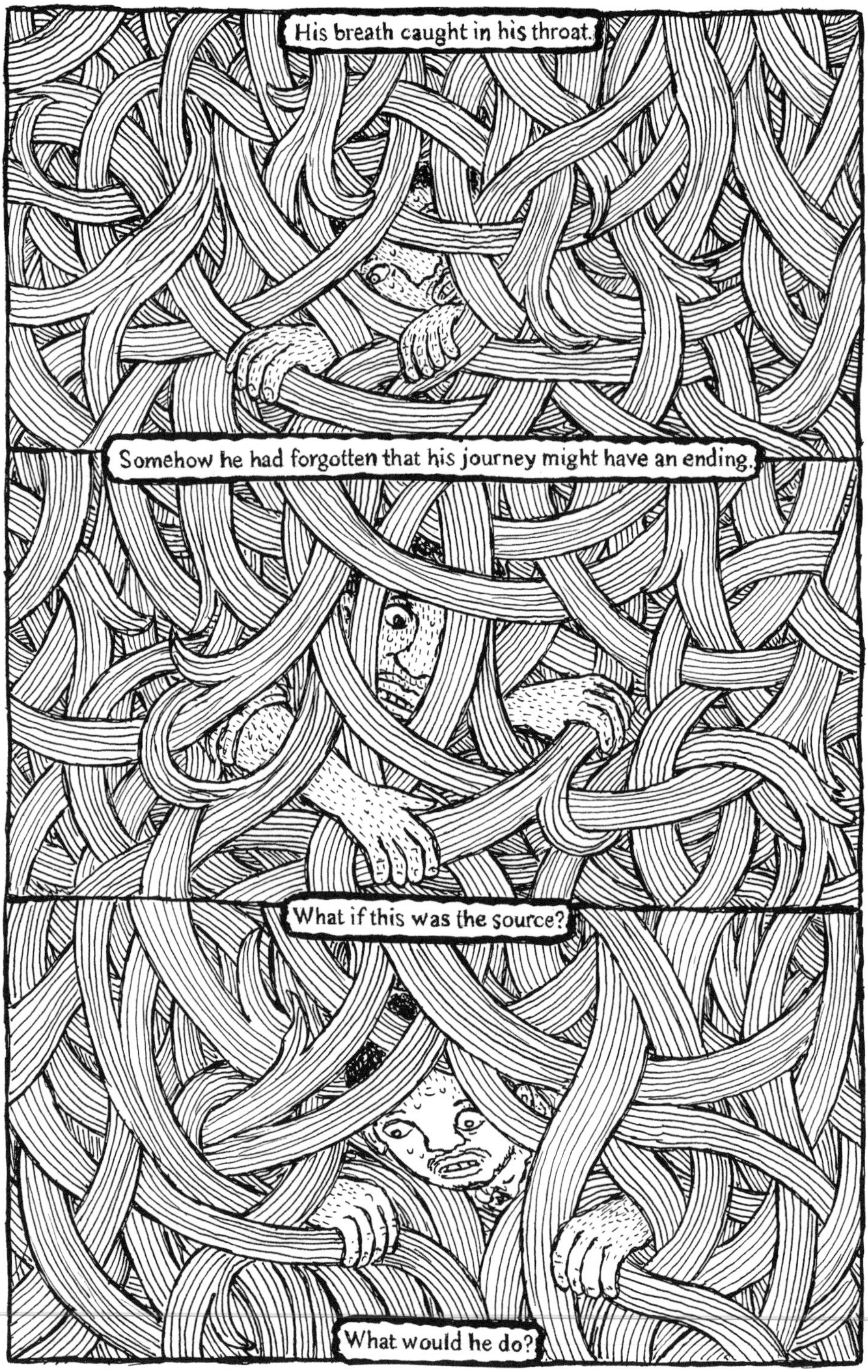
His breath caught in his throat.
Somehow he had forgotten that his journey might have an ending.
What if this was the source?
What would he do?

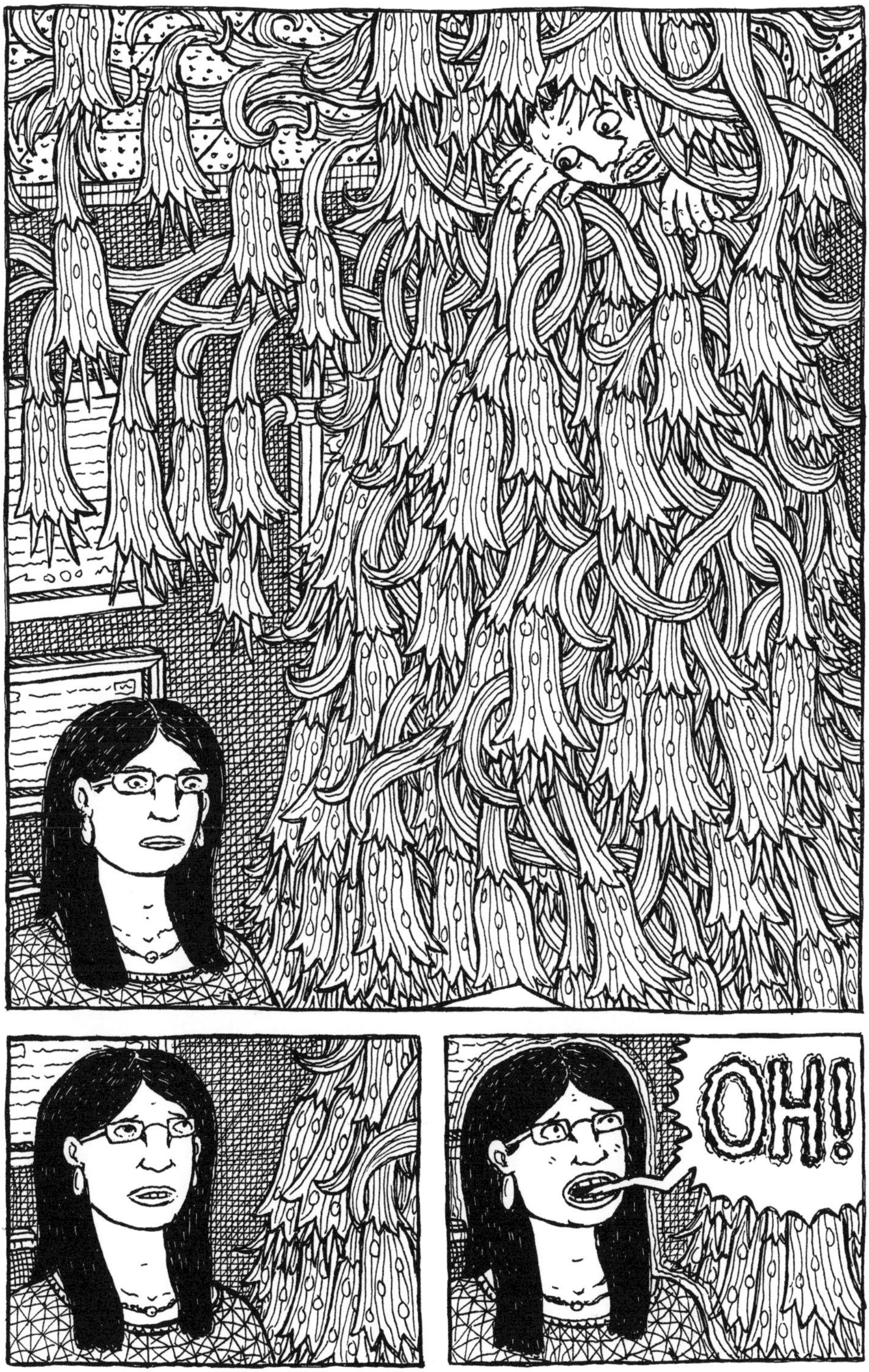
OH!

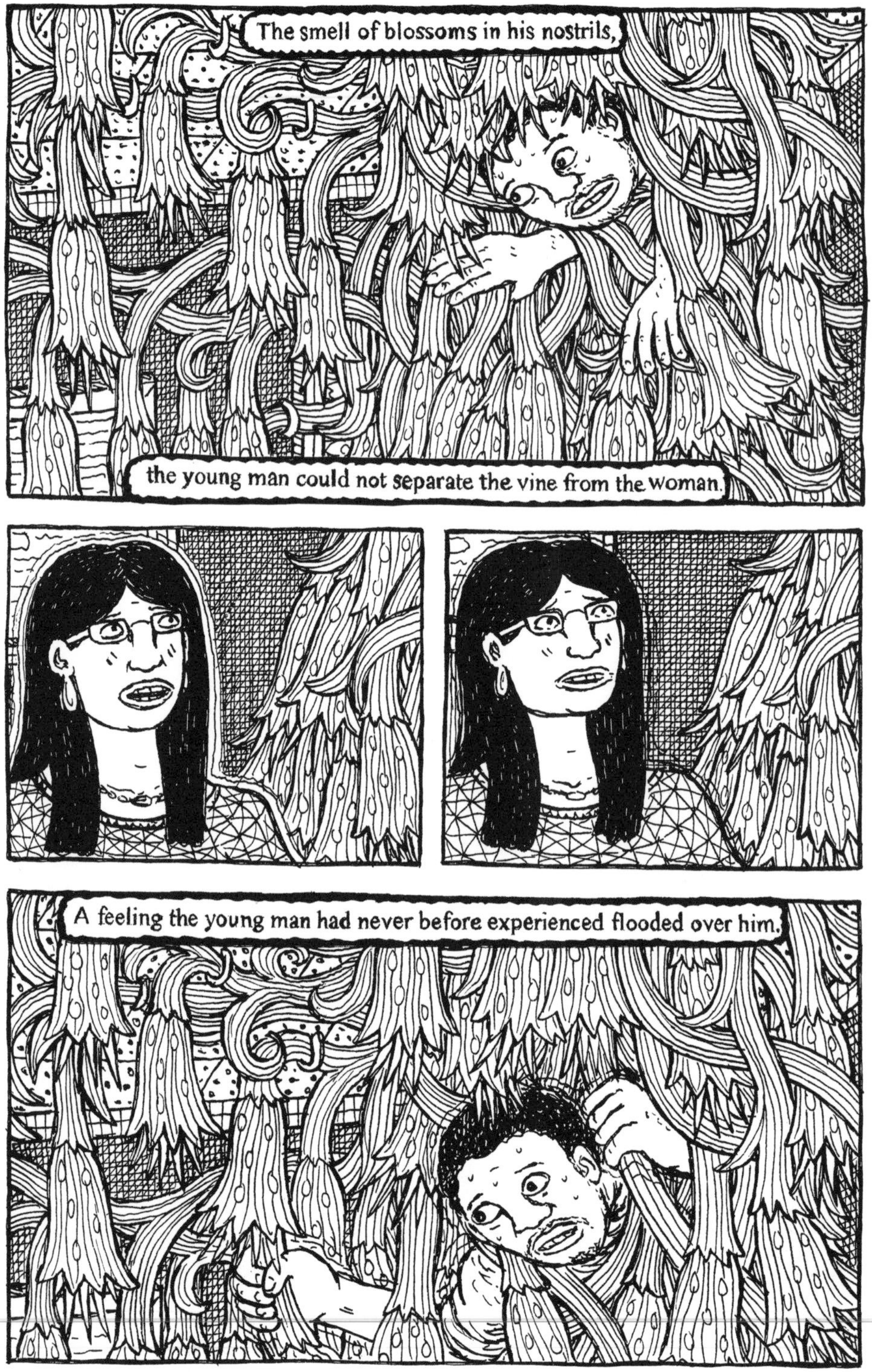
The smell of blossoms in his nostrils,
the young man could not separate the vine from the woman.
A feeling the young man had never before experienced flooded over him.

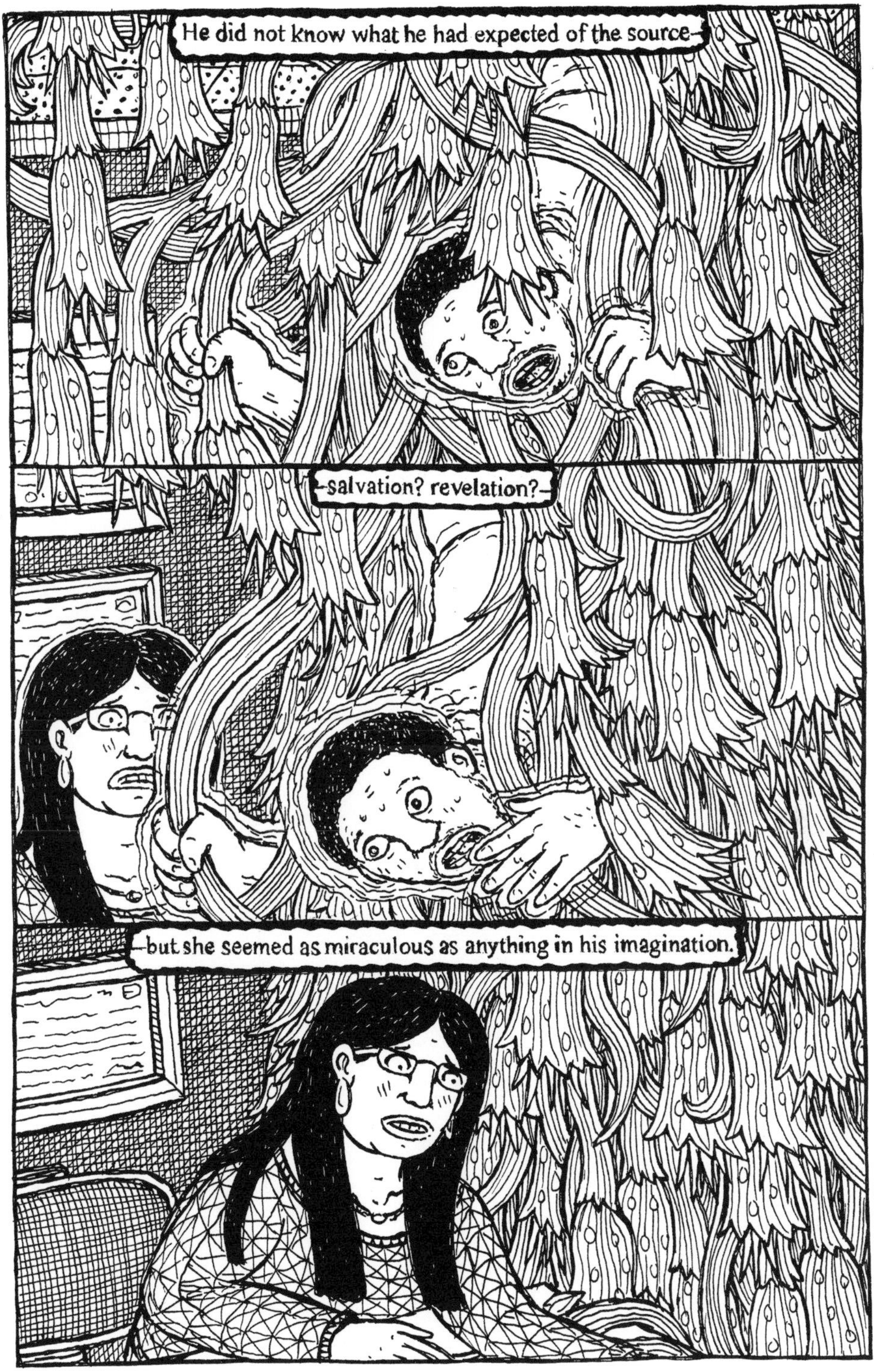
He did not know what he had expected of the source—
—salvation? revelation?—
—but she seemed as miraculous as anything in his imagination.

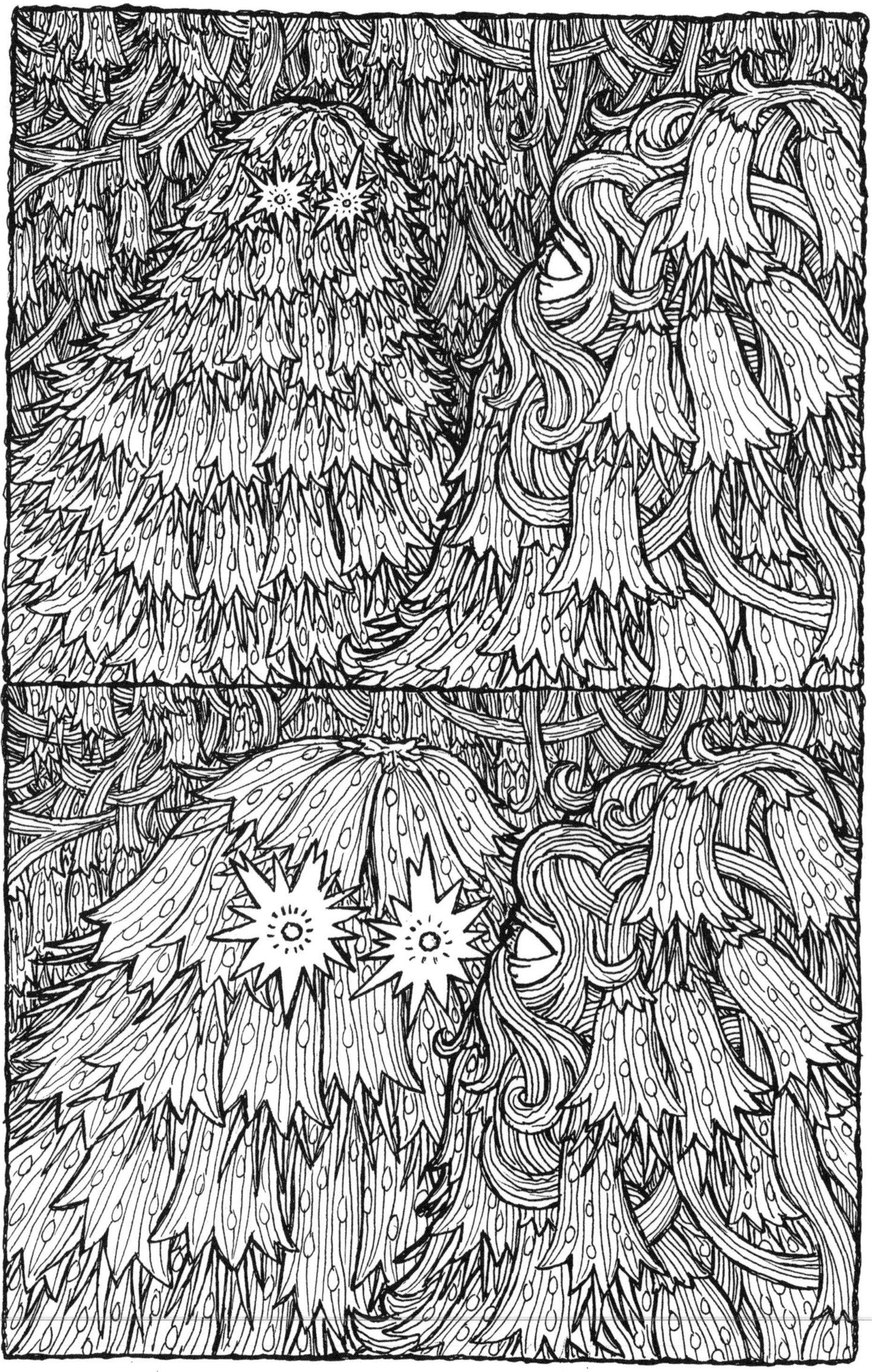

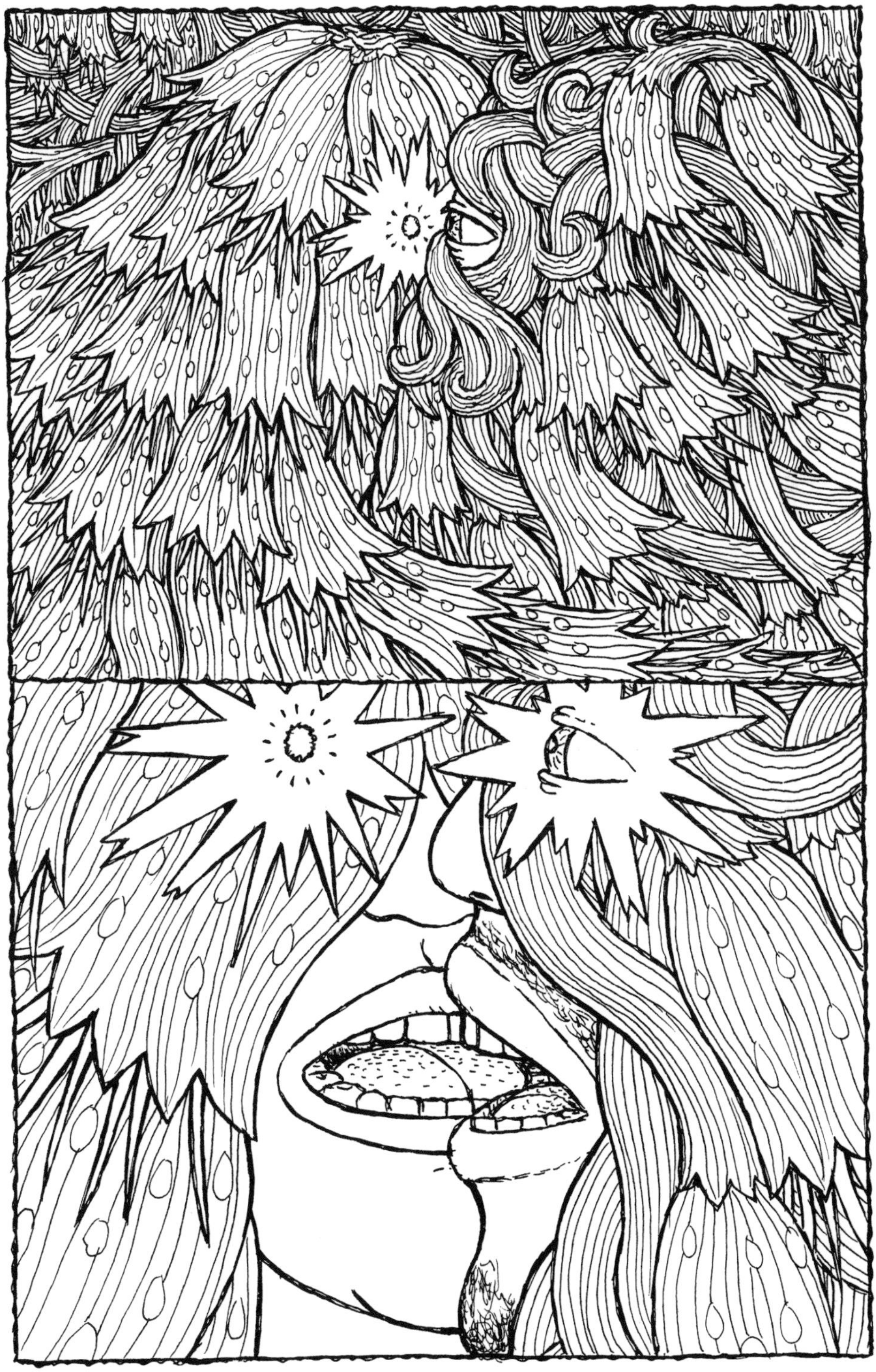

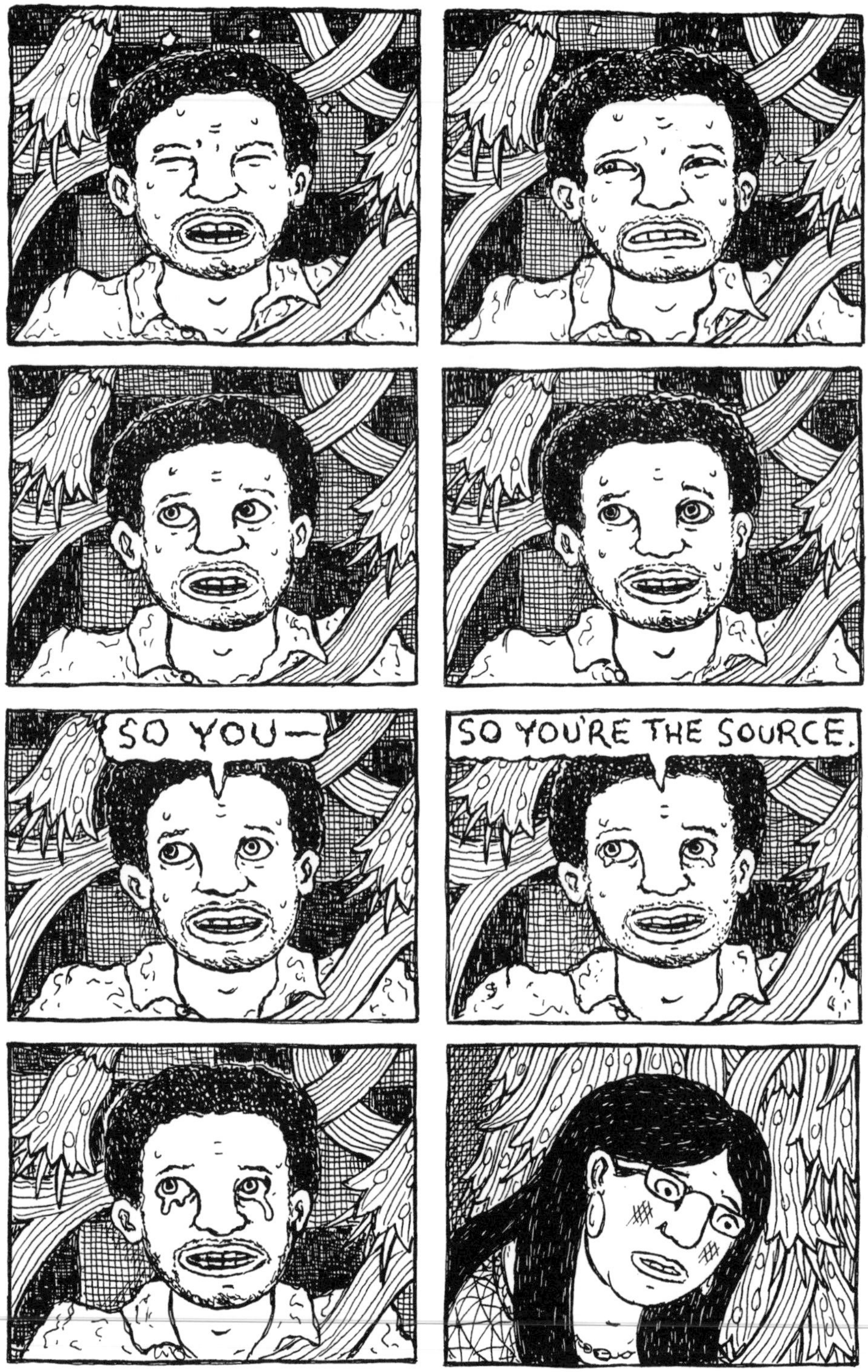
SO YOU—
SO YOU'RE THE SOURCE.

Confusion of Tongues

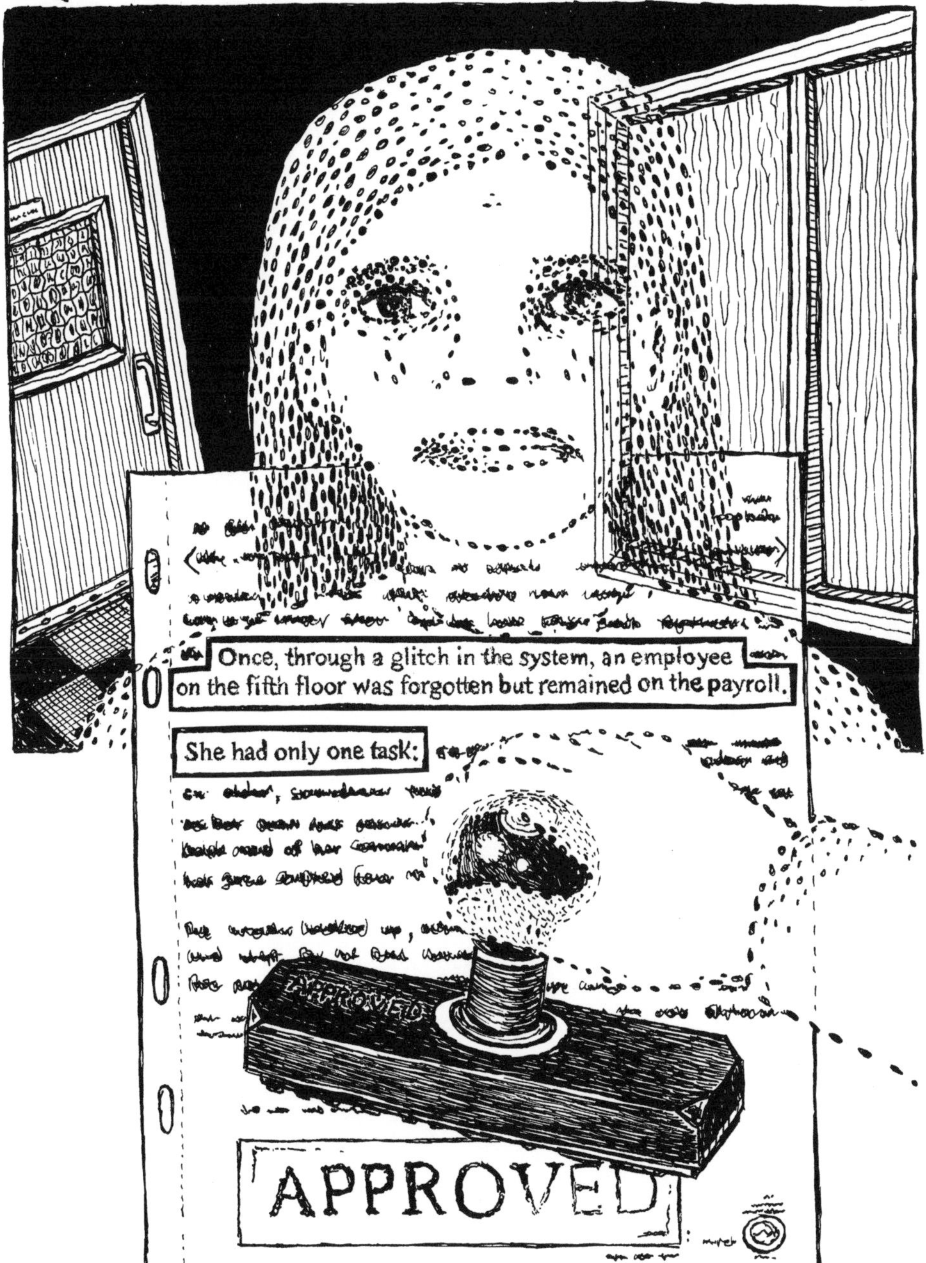
Once, through a glitch in the system, an employee on the fifth floor was forgotten but remained on the payroll.
She had only one task:
APPROVED
APPROVED

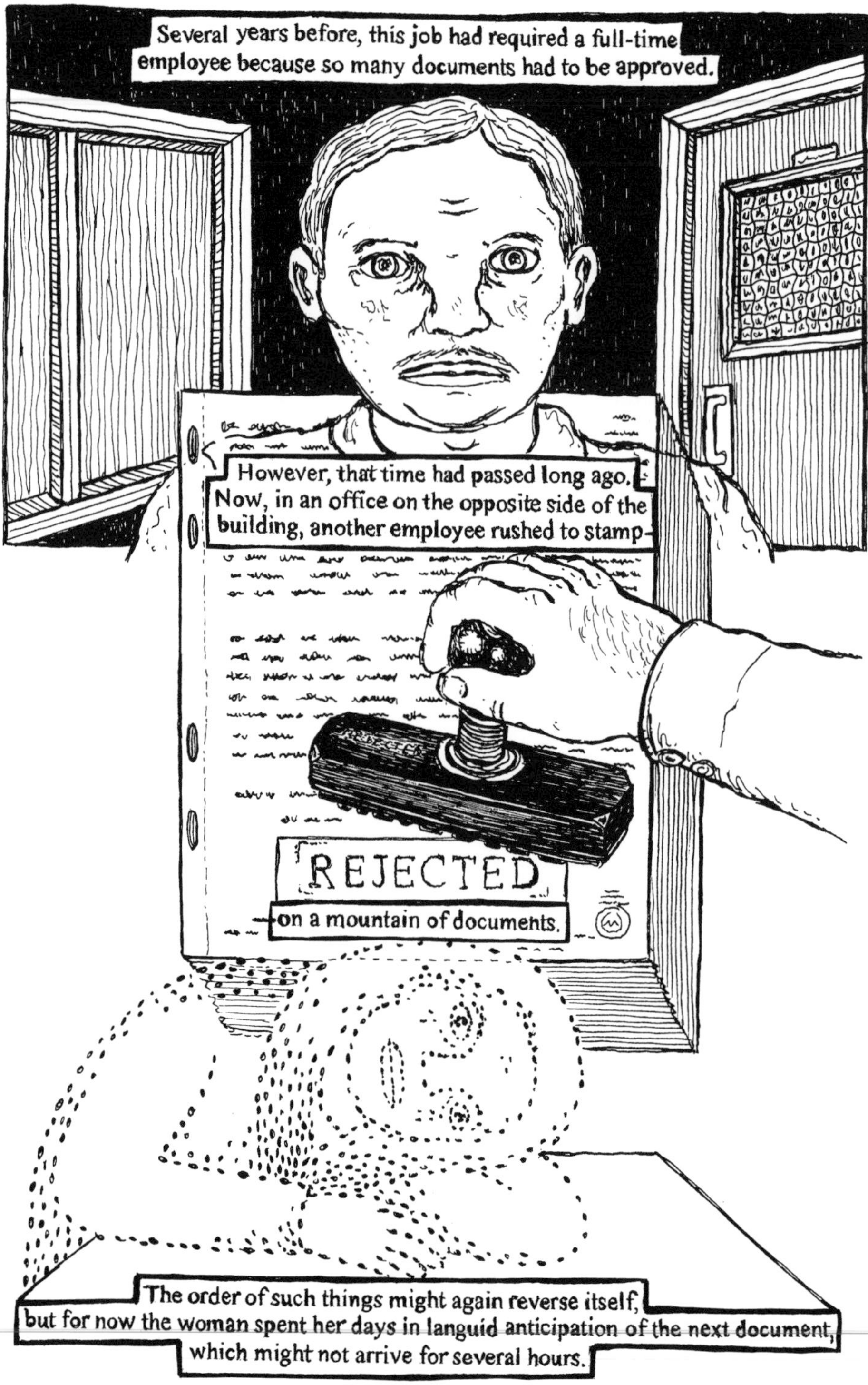
Several years before, this job had required a full-time employee because so many documents had to be approved.
However, that time had passed long ago. Now, in an office on the opposite side of the building, another employee rushed to stamp-
REJECTED
on a mountain of documents.
The order of such things might again reverse itself, but for now the woman spent her days in languid anticipation of the next document, which might not arrive for several hours.

The woman did not even have a window to distract her.

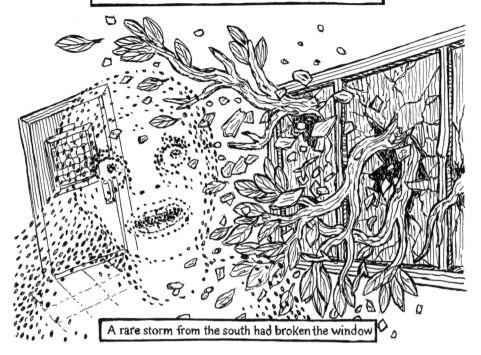

A rare storm from the south had broken the window

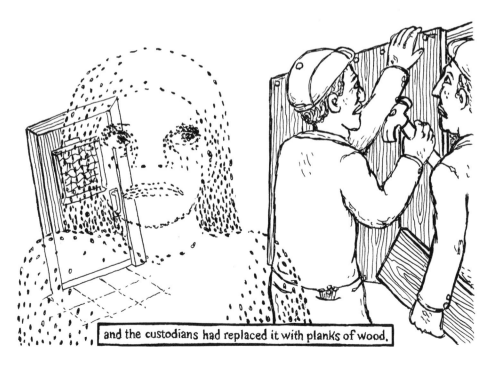

and the custodians had replaced it with planks of wood.

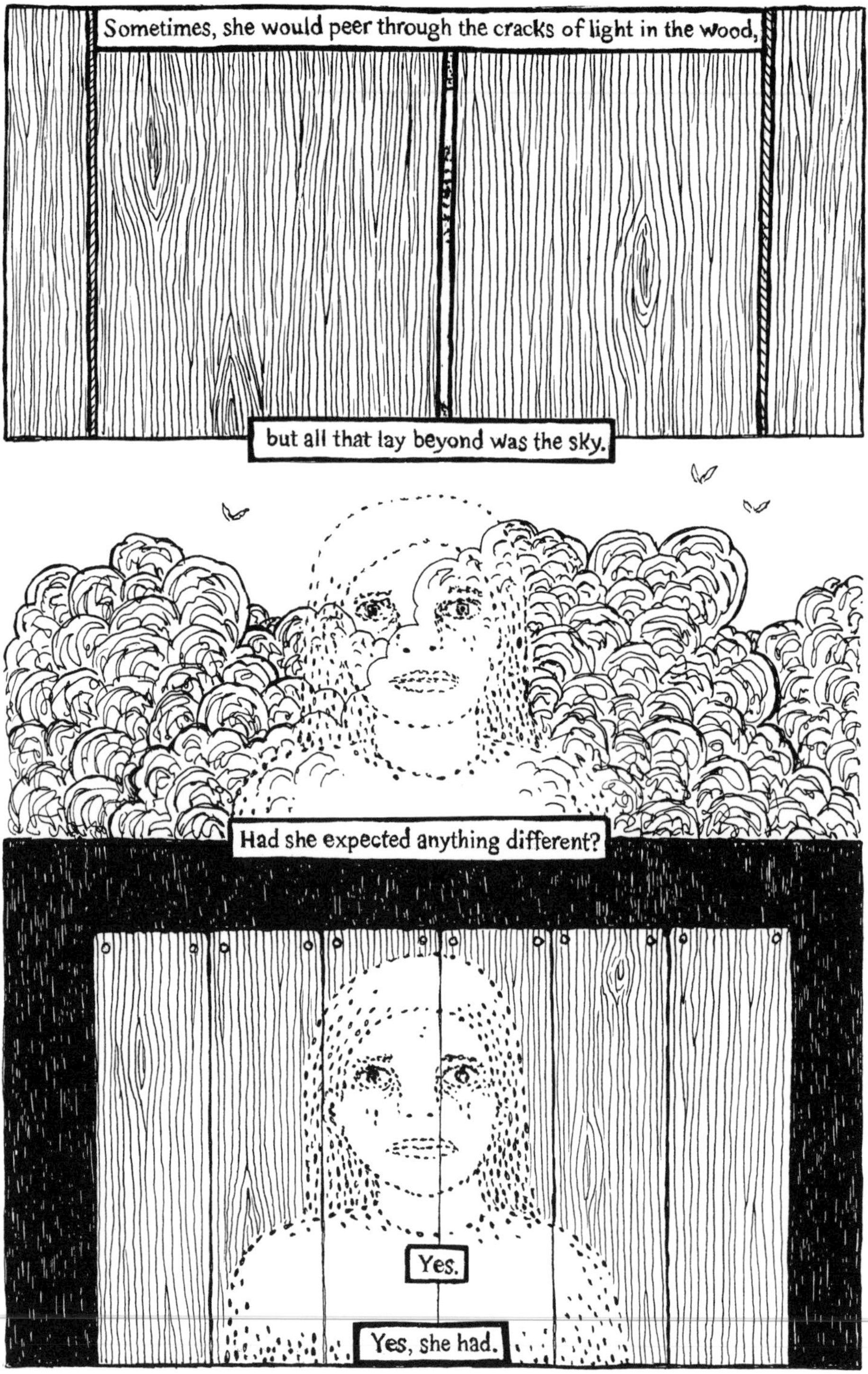
Sometimes, she would peer through the cracks of light in the wood,
but all that lay beyond was the sky.
Had she expected anything different?
Yes.
Yes, she had.

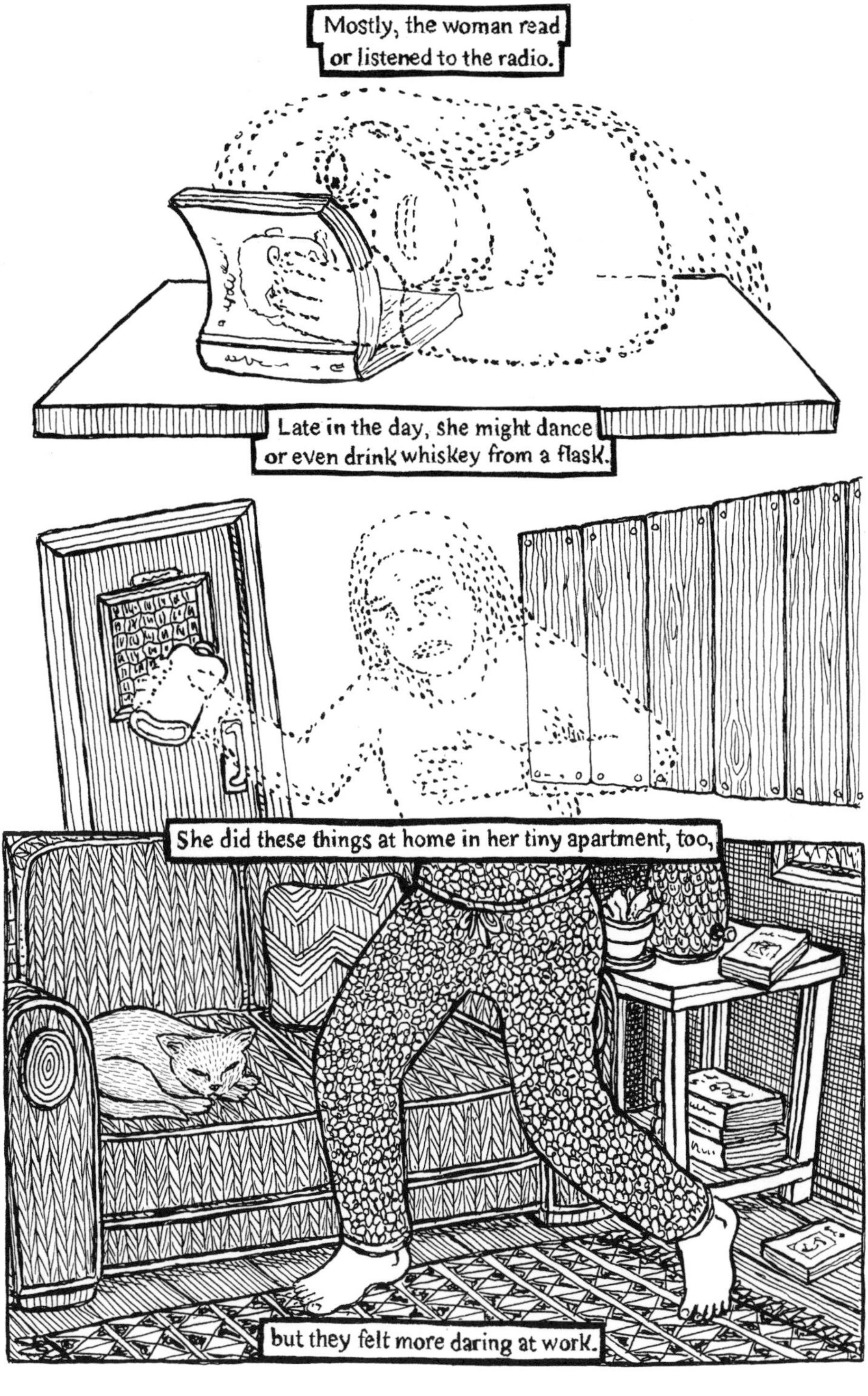

Mostly, the woman read or listened to the radio.
Late in the day, she might dance or even drink whiskey from a flask.
She did these things at home in her tiny apartment, too,
but they felt more daring at work.

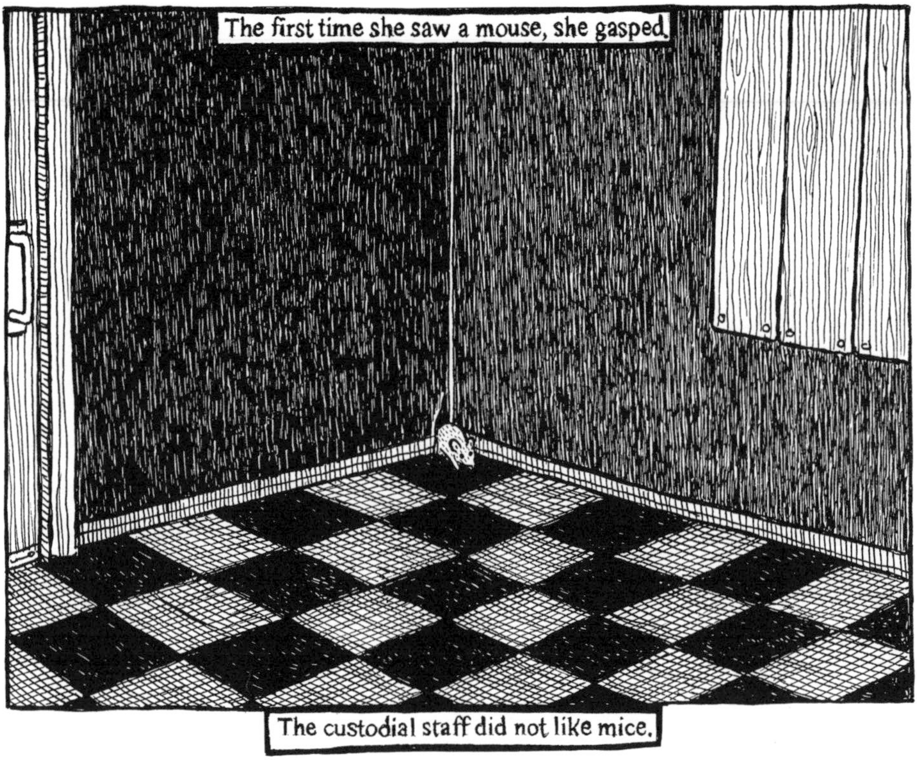
The first time she saw a mouse, she gasped.
The custodial staff did not like mice.

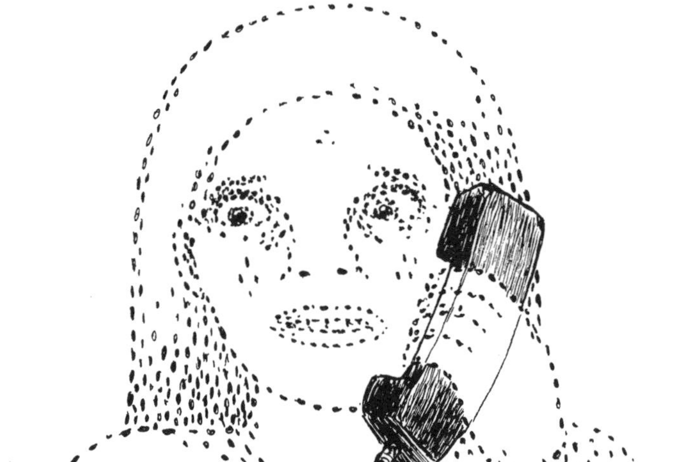

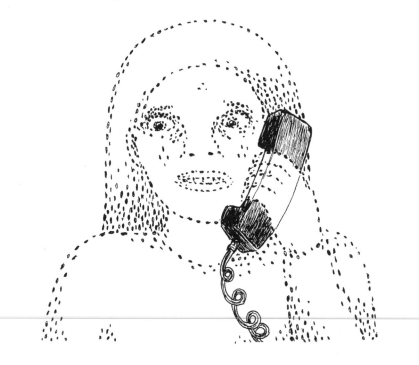

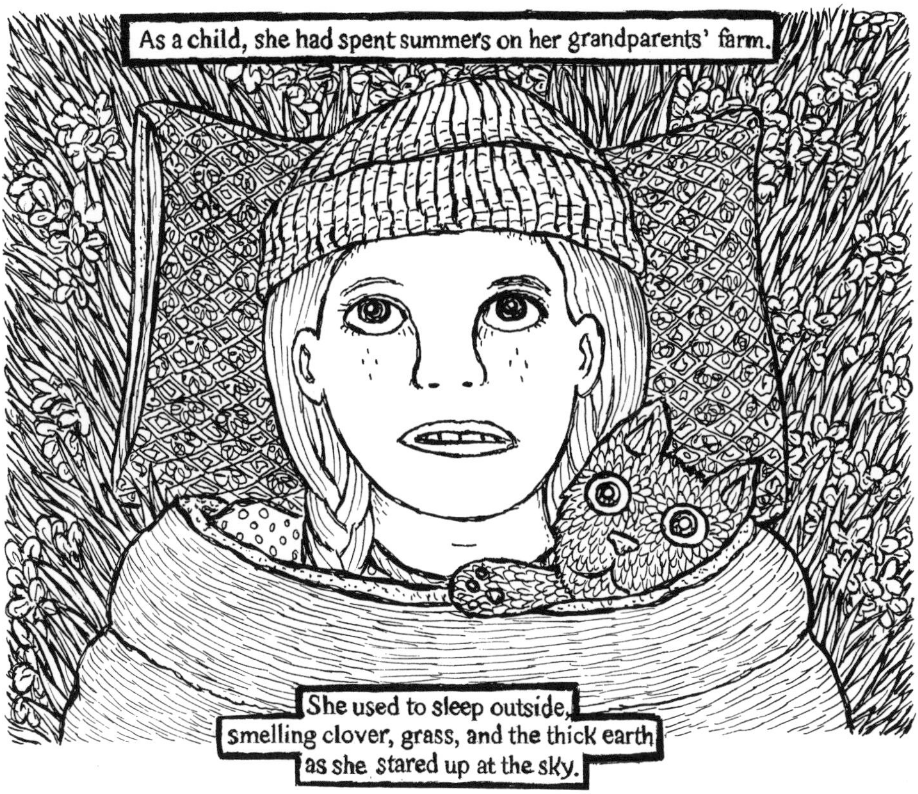
As a child, she had spent summers on her grandparents' farm.
She used to sleep outside, smelling clover, grass, and the thick earth as she stared up at the sky.

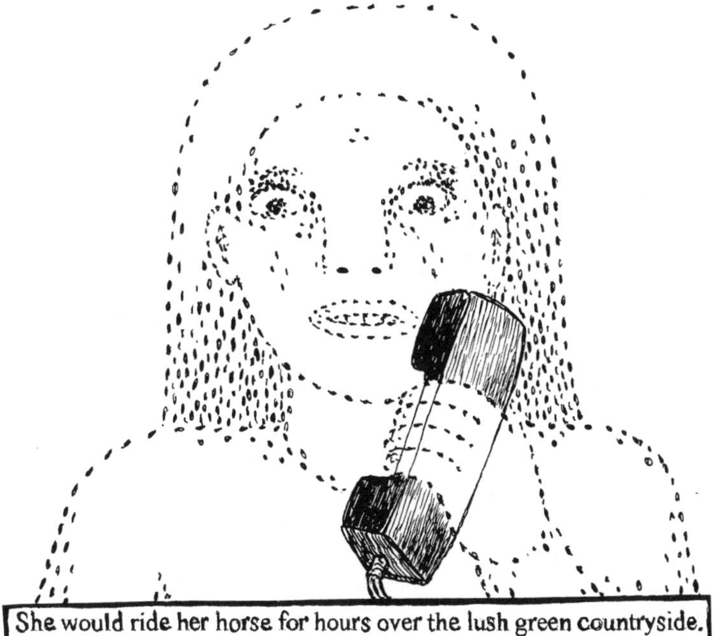
She would ride her horse for hours over the lush green countryside.

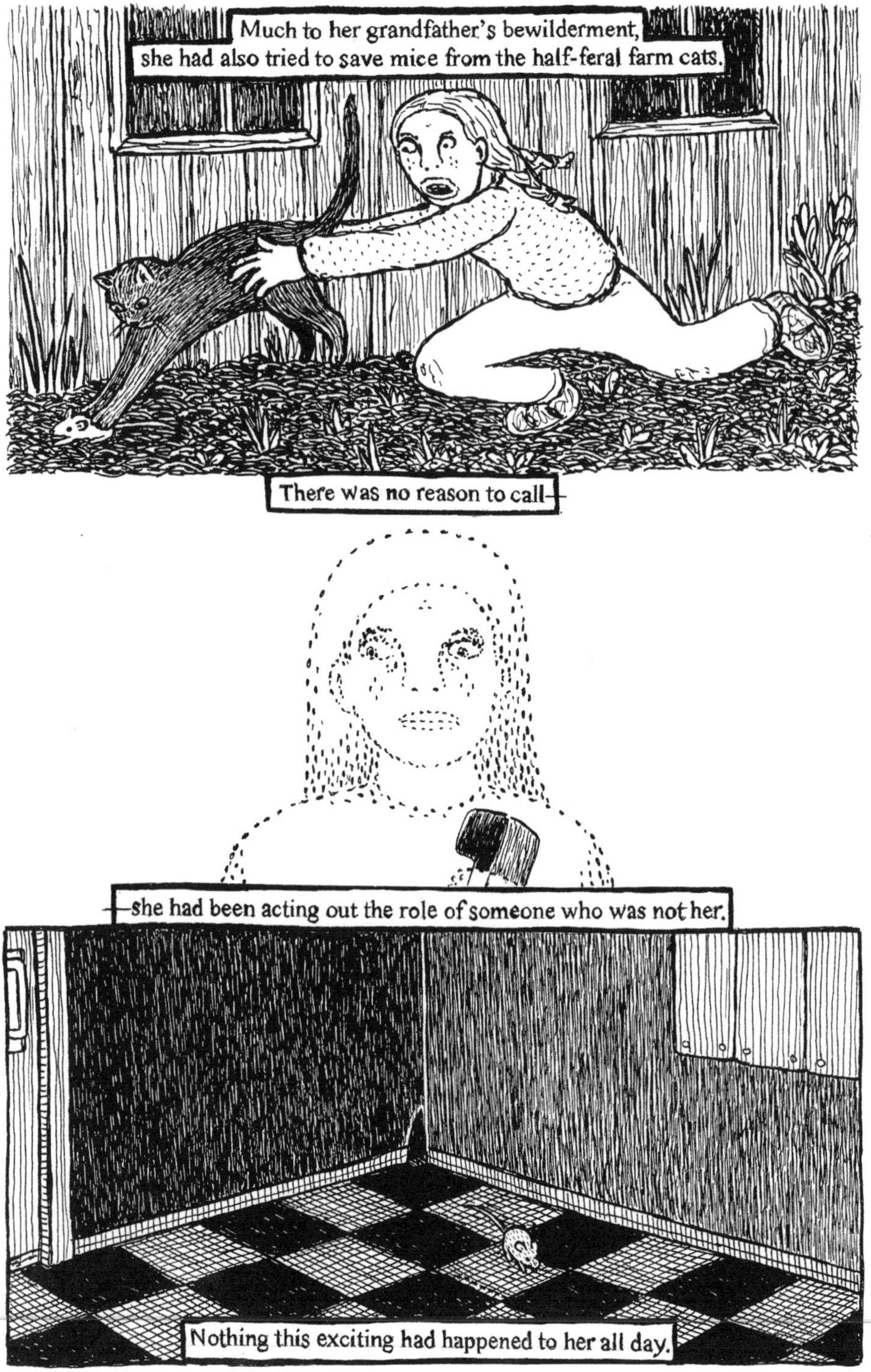
Much to her grandfather's bewilderment, she had also tried to save mice from the half-feral farm cats.
There was no reason to call—
—she had been acting out the role of someone who was not her.
Nothing this exciting had happened to her all day.

The next day, the woman began to bring breadcrumbs, seeds, and other scraps from her apartment.

She even went to the store to buy cheese.

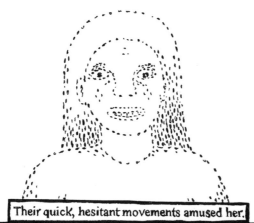

Their quick, hesitant movements amused her.

Their psychic abilities impressed her as well;

they always disappeared at least fifteen minutes before the courier arrived with the latest document to enjoy the stamp of approval.

She found herself trying out names for the mice:

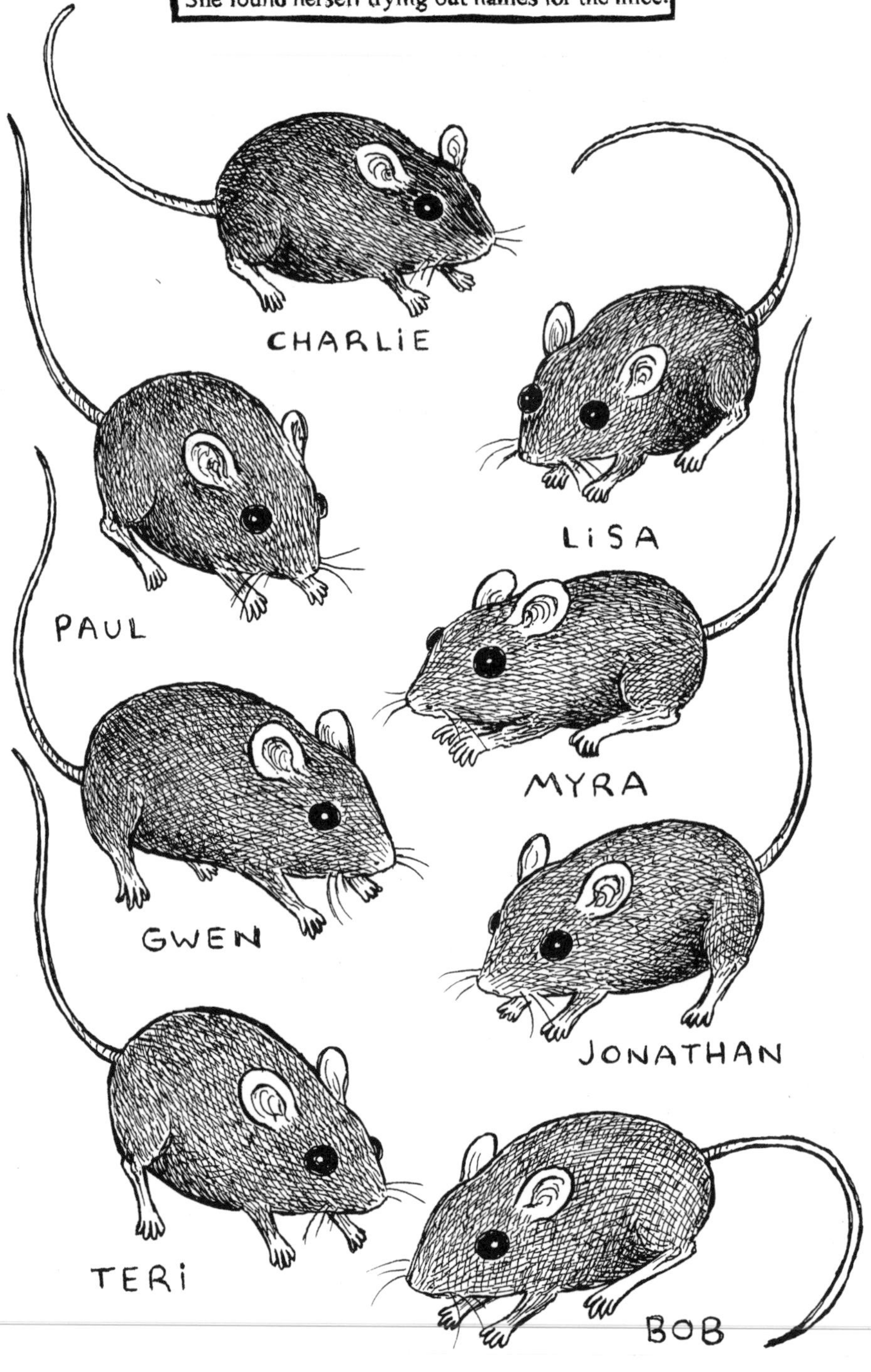
CHARLIE
LISA
PAUL
MYRA
GWEN
JONATHAN
TERI
BOB

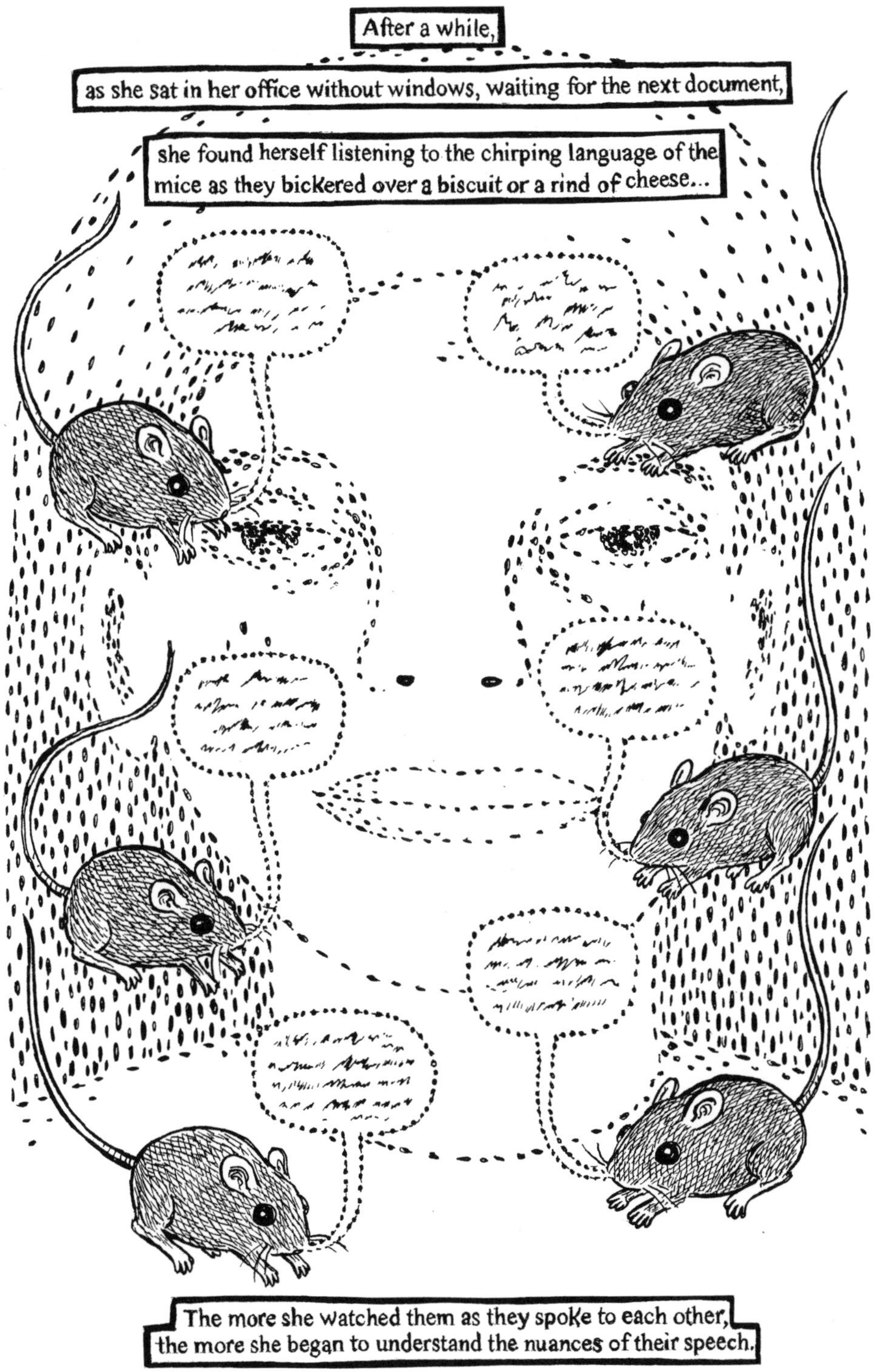
After a while,
as she sat in her office without windows, waiting for the next document,
she found herself listening to the chirping language of the mice as they bickered over a biscuit or a rind of cheese...
The more she watched them as they spoke to each other, the more she began to understand the nuances of their speech.

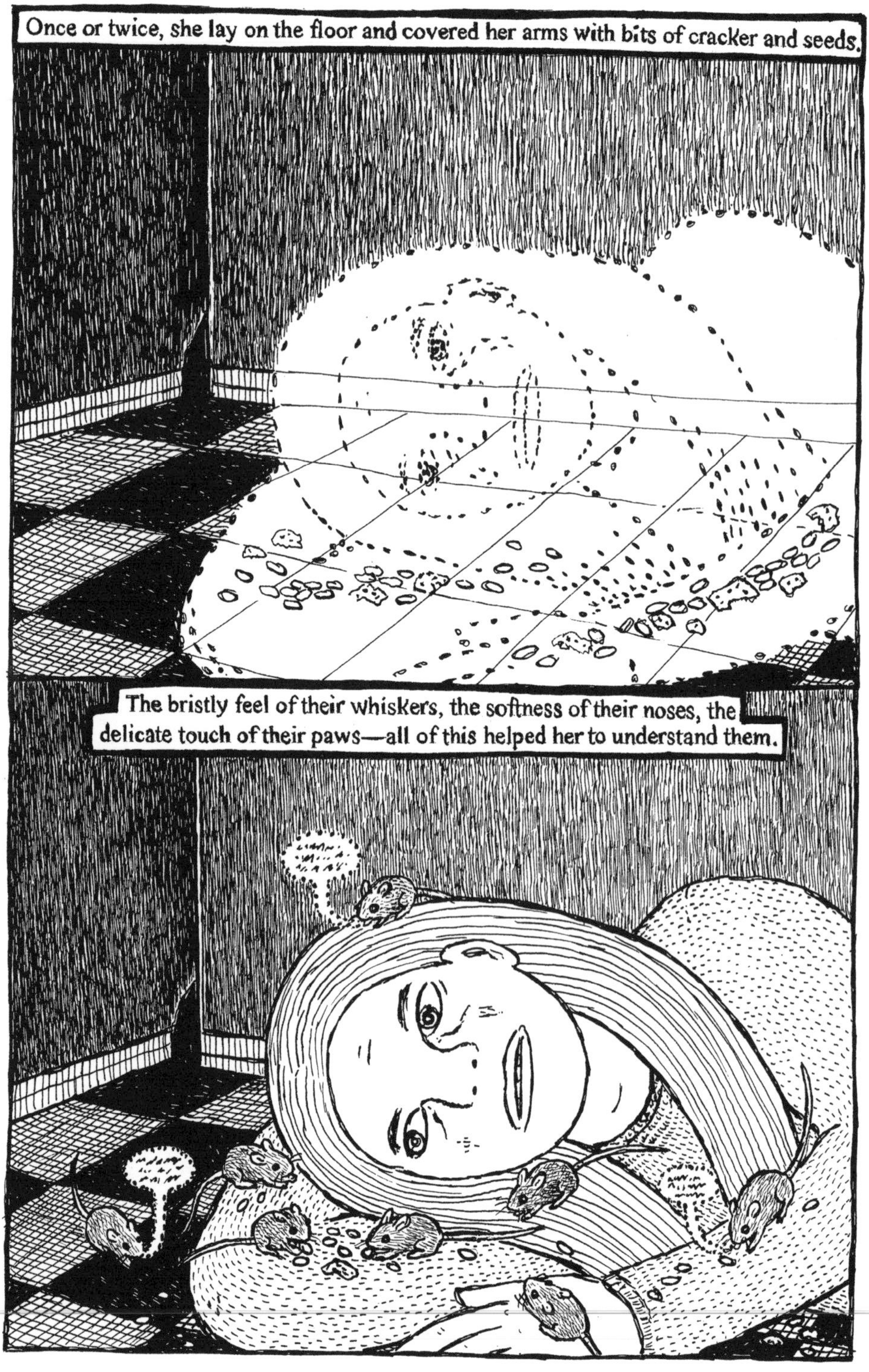
Once or twice, she lay on the floor and covered her arms with bits of cracker and seeds.
The bristly feel of their whiskers, the softness of their noses, the delicate touch of their paws—all of this helped her to understand them.

Several years passed.

The woman's hair became flecked with gray.

Her father and mother both died within a year of each other.

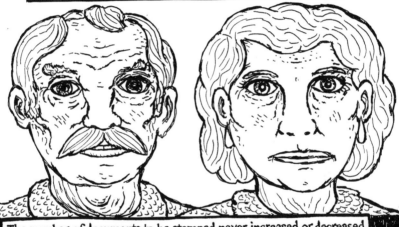

The number of documents to be stamped never increased or decreased.

Her entwined states of being friendless and alone were broken by all-too-infrequent periods of happiness that only made her feel worse when they ended, abruptly.

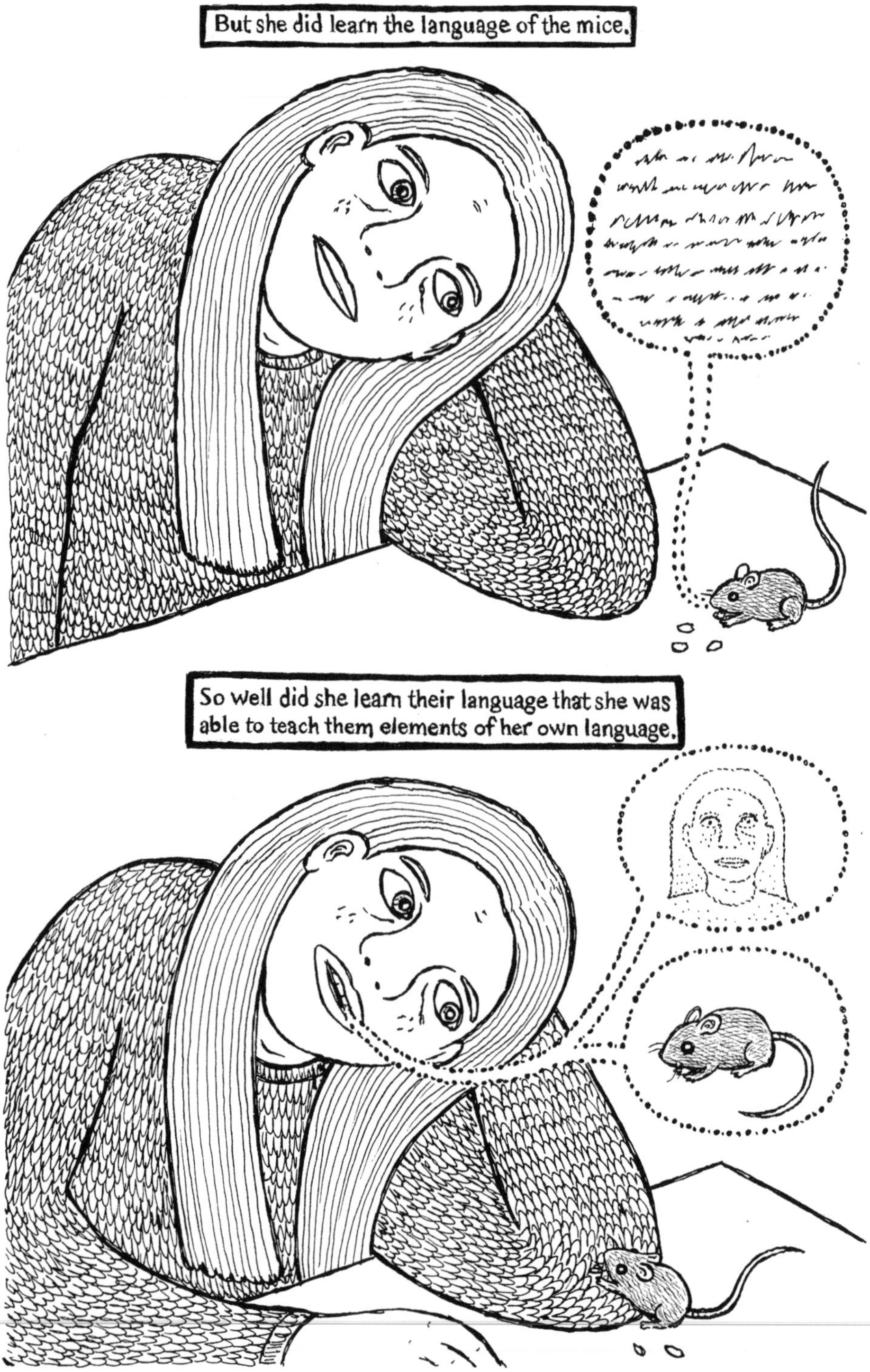
But she did learn the language of the mice.
So well did she learn their language that she was able to teach them elements of her own language.

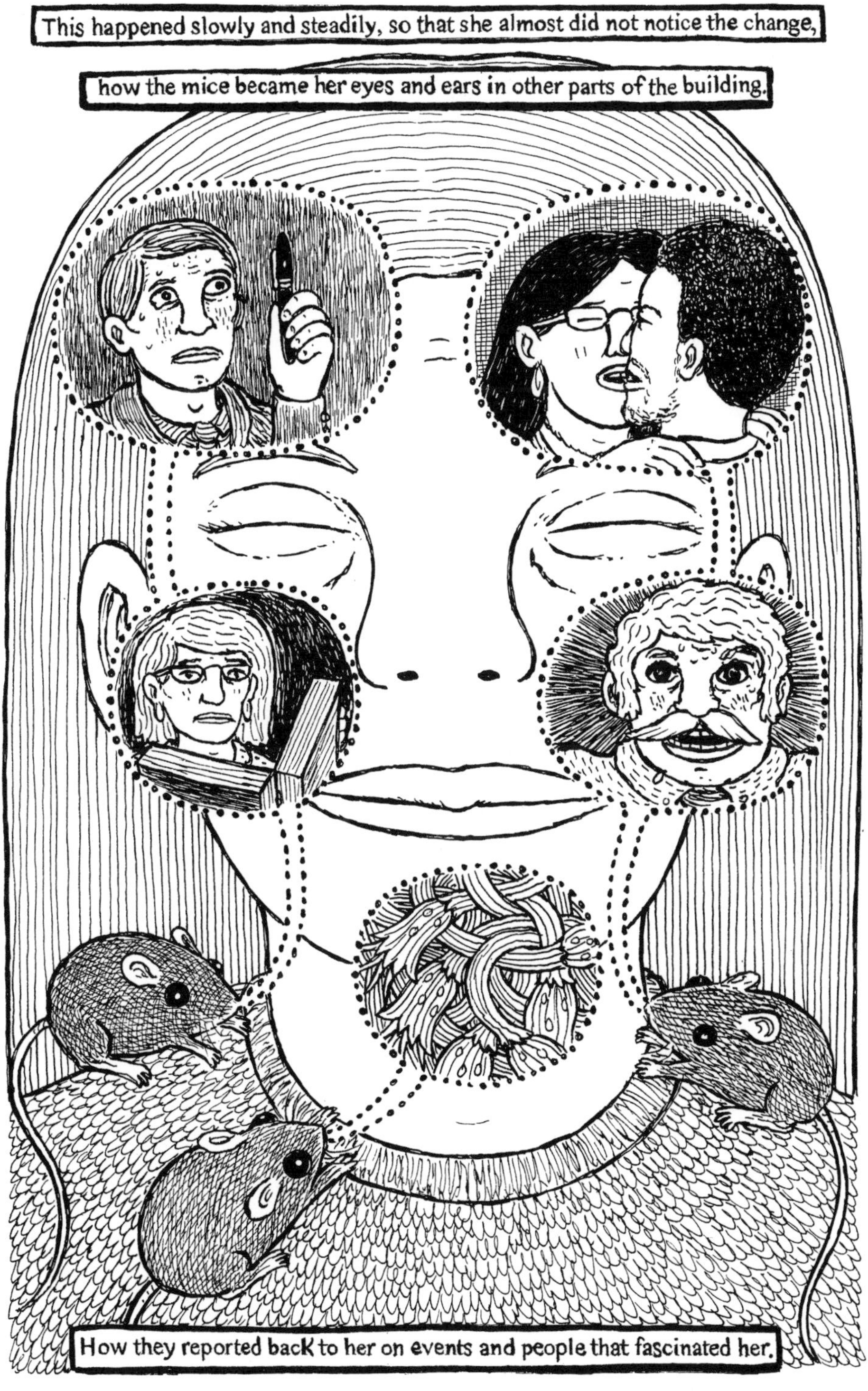
This happened slowly and steadily, so that she almost did not notice the change,
how the mice became her eyes and ears in other parts of the building.
How they reported back to her on events and people that fascinated her.

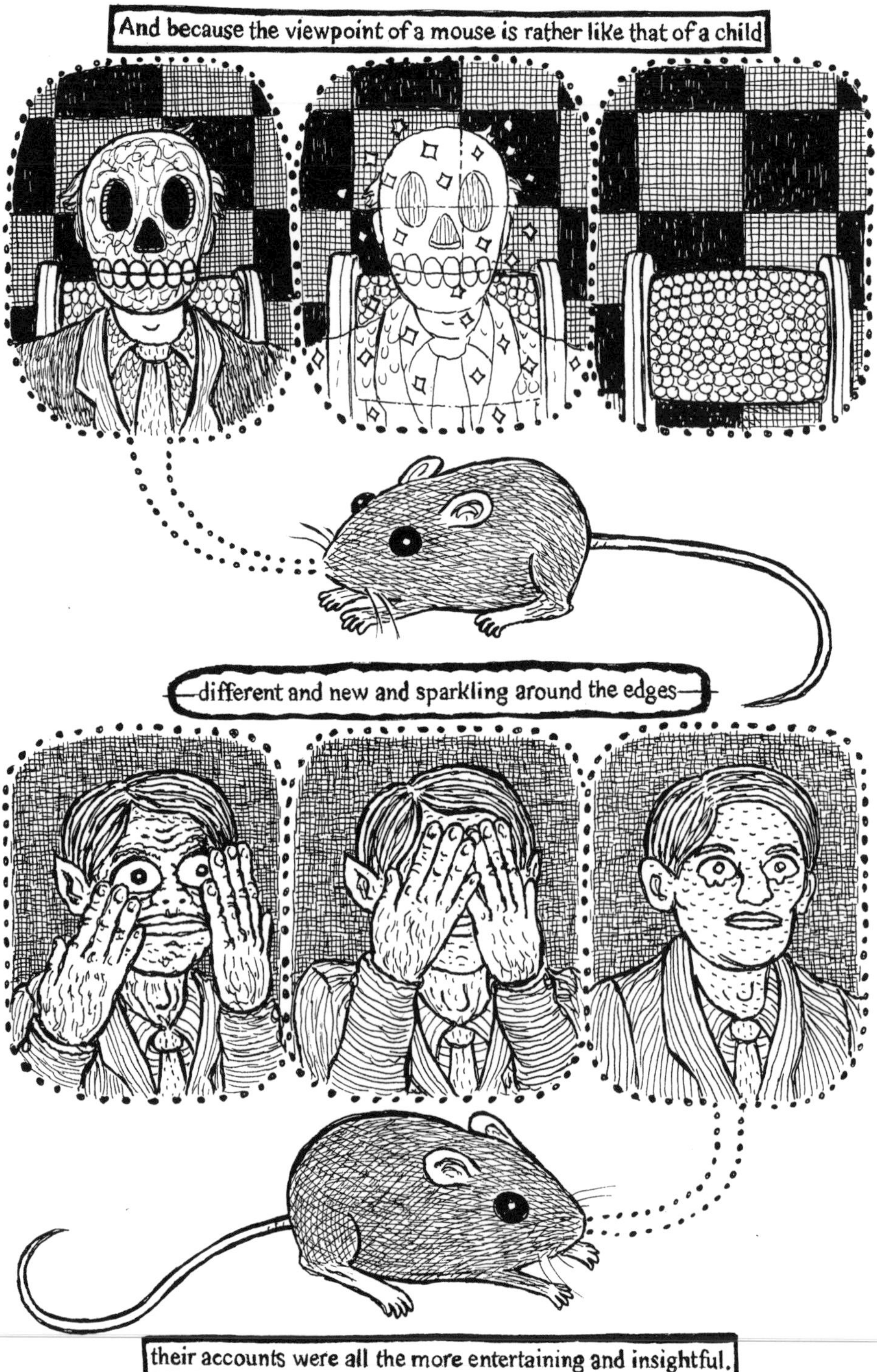
And because the viewpoint of a mouse is rather like that of a child
different and new and sparkling around the edges
their accounts were all the more entertaining and insightful.

The woman let her hair grow long and did not bother to dye the gray out of it.

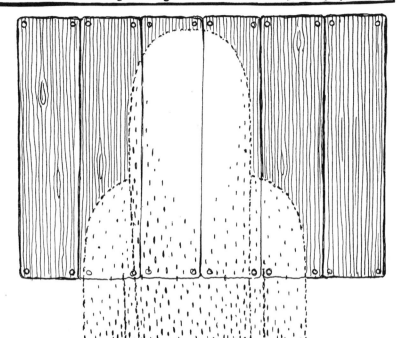

She wore long patchwork skirts and slippers.

She stopped drinking whiskey.

She no longer even bothered to say hello to the infrequent courier.

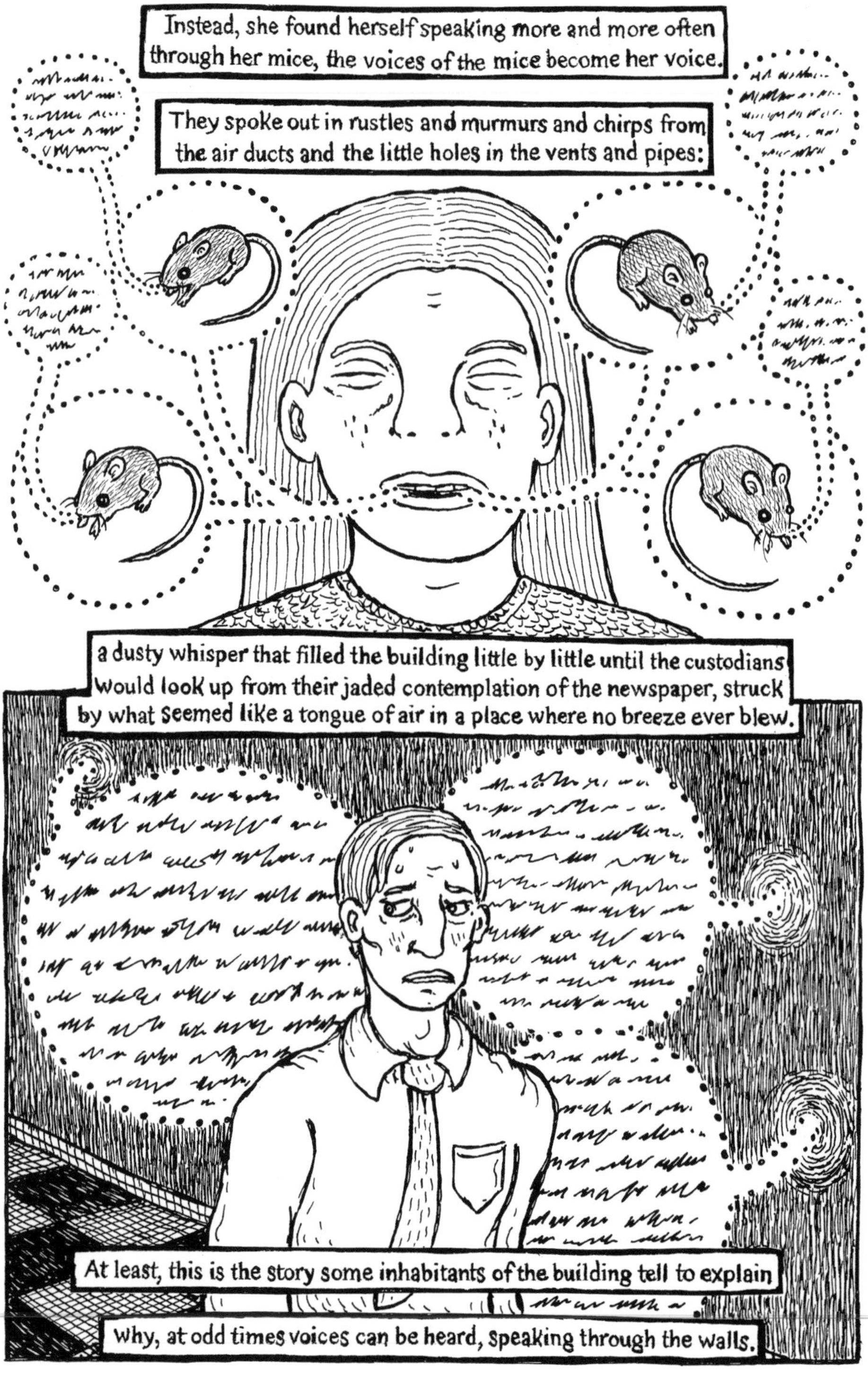
Instead, she found herself speaking more and more often through her mice, the voices of the mice become her voice.
They spoke out in rustles and murmurs and chirps from the air ducts and the little holes in the vents and pipes:
a dusty whisper that filled the building little by little until the custodians would look up from their jaded contemplation of the newspaper, struck by what seemed like a tongue of air in a place where no breeze ever blew.
At least, this is the story some inhabitants of the building tell to explain
why, at odd times voices can be heard, speaking through the walls.

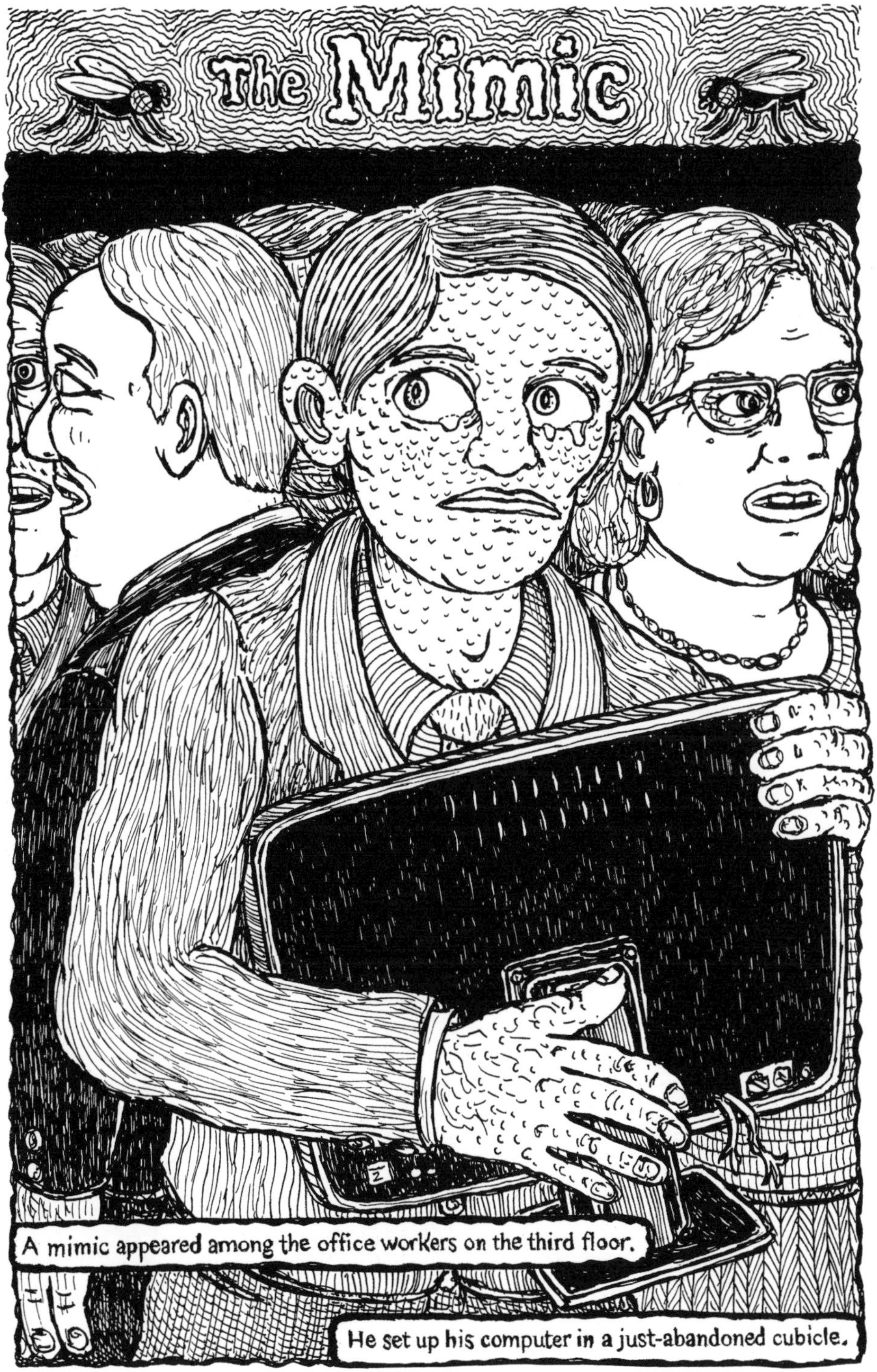
The Mimic
A mimic appeared among the office workers on the third floor.
He set up his computer in a just-abandoned cubicle.

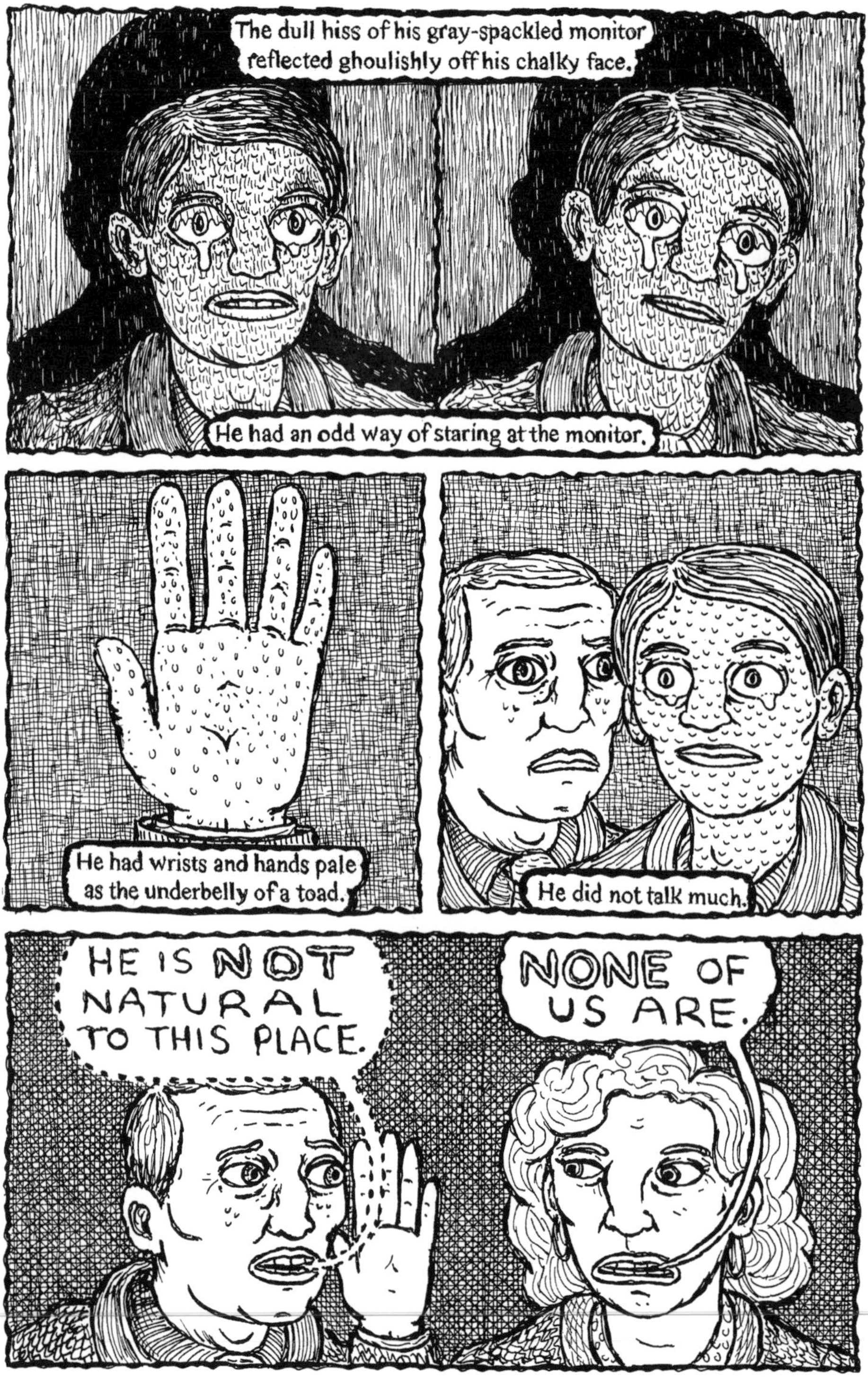
The dull hiss of his gray-spackled monitor reflected ghoulishly off his chalky face.
He had an odd way of staring at the monitor.
He had wrists and hands pale as the underbelly of a toad.
He did not talk much.
HE IS NOT NATURAL TO THIS PLACE.
NONE OF US ARE.

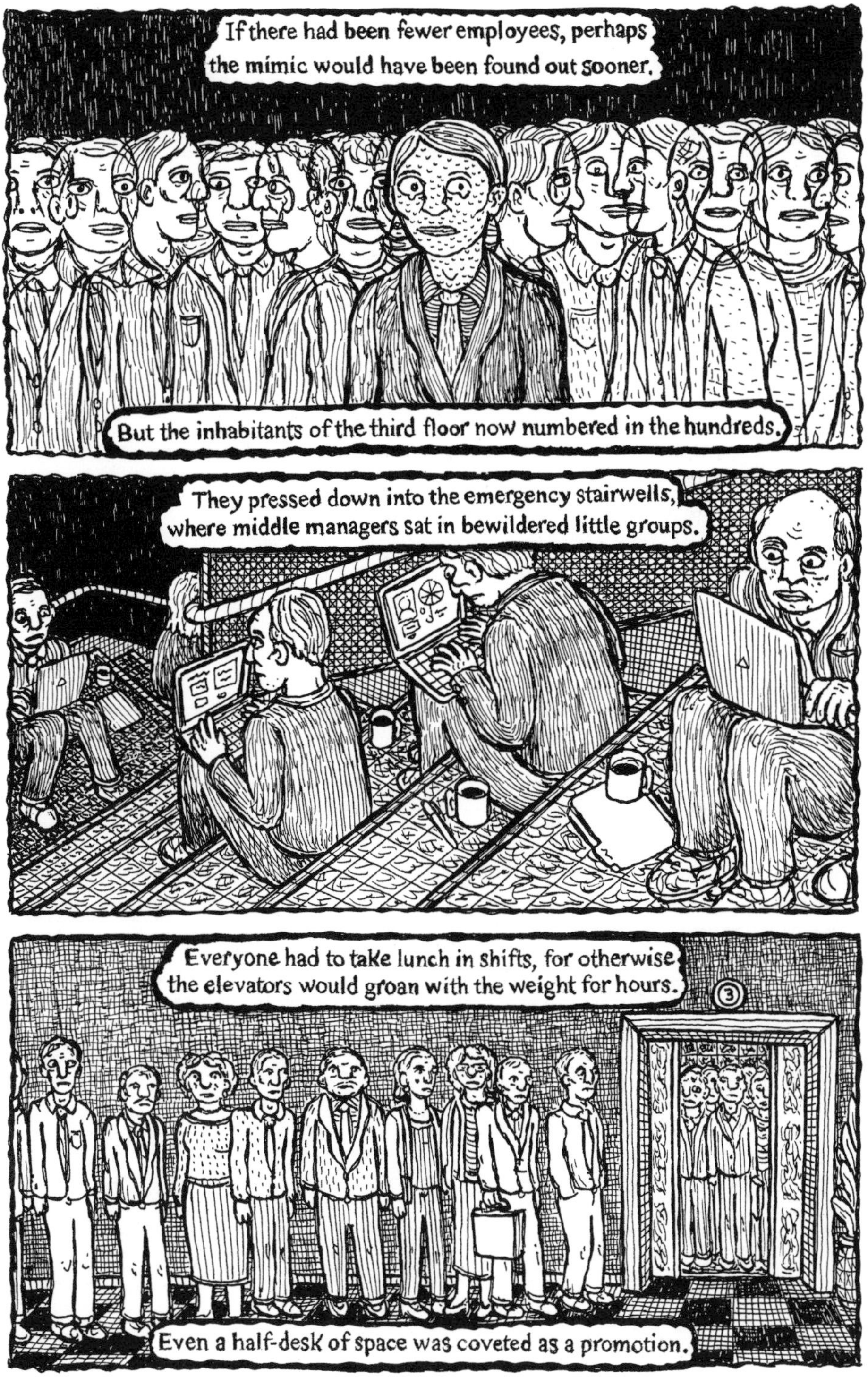
If there had been fewer employees, perhaps the mimic would have been found out sooner.
But the inhabitants of the third floor now numbered in the hundreds.
They pressed down into the emergency stairwells, where middle managers sat in bewildered little groups.
Everyone had to take lunch in shifts, for otherwise the elevators would groan with the weight for hours.
3
Even a half-desk of space was coveted as a promotion.

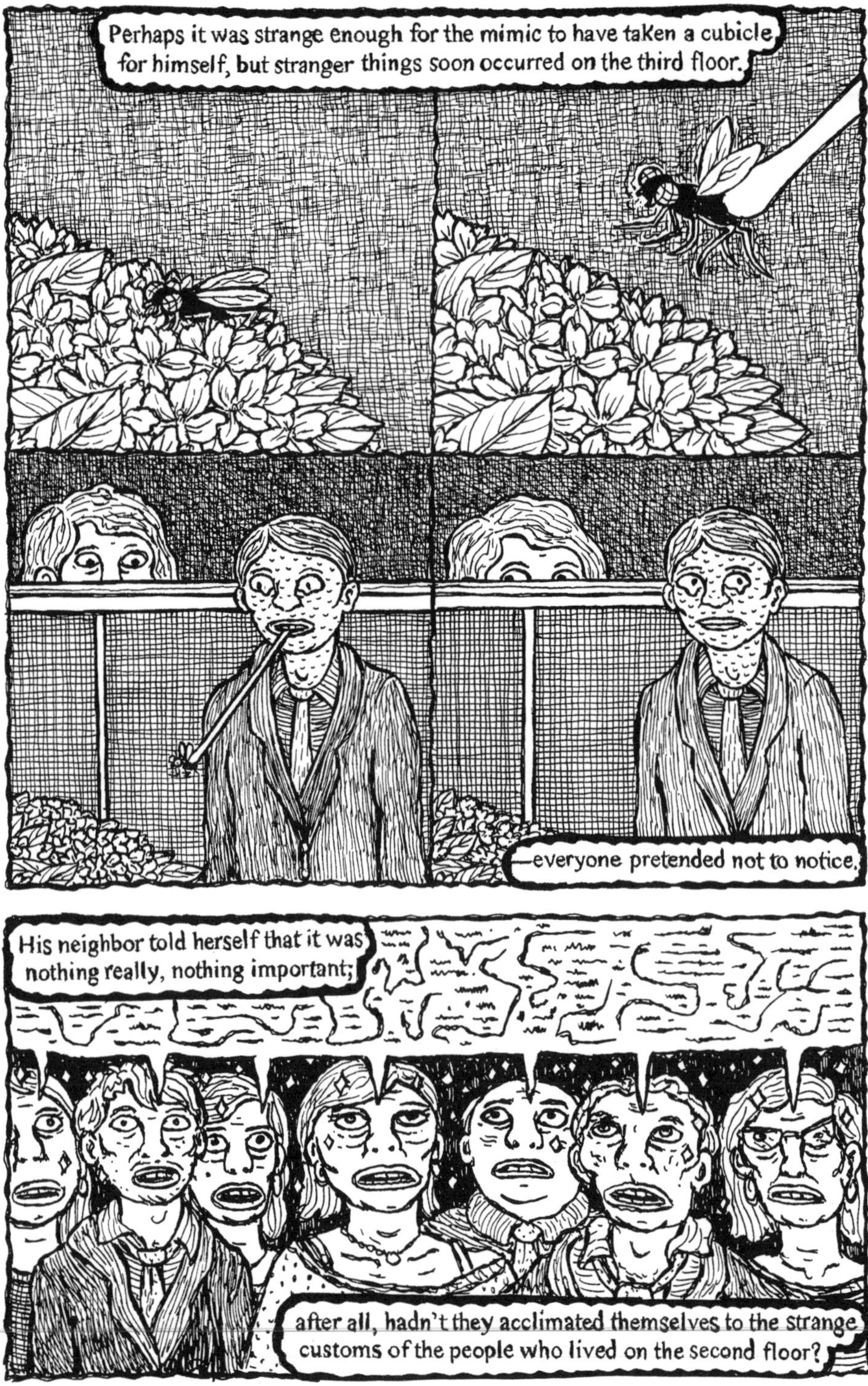

Perhaps it was strange enough for the mimic to have taken a cubicle for himself, but stranger things soon occurred on the third floor.
—everyone pretended not to notice.
His neighbor told herself that it was nothing really, nothing important;
after all, hadn't they acclimated themselves to the strange customs of the people who lived on the second floor?

Gradually, they noticed several other strange things about their new coworker.

For example, despite the dress code, he did not actually wear shoes;

his feet just resembled shoes.

And when he ate his open-faced sandwiches of thick green paste,

he swallowed as if pushing his food down like a frog.

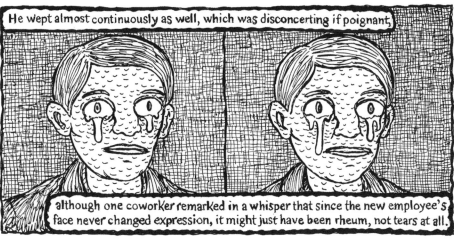

He wept almost continuously as well, which was disconcerting if poignant,

although one coworker remarked in a whisper that since the new employee's face never changed expression, it might just have been rheum, not tears at all.

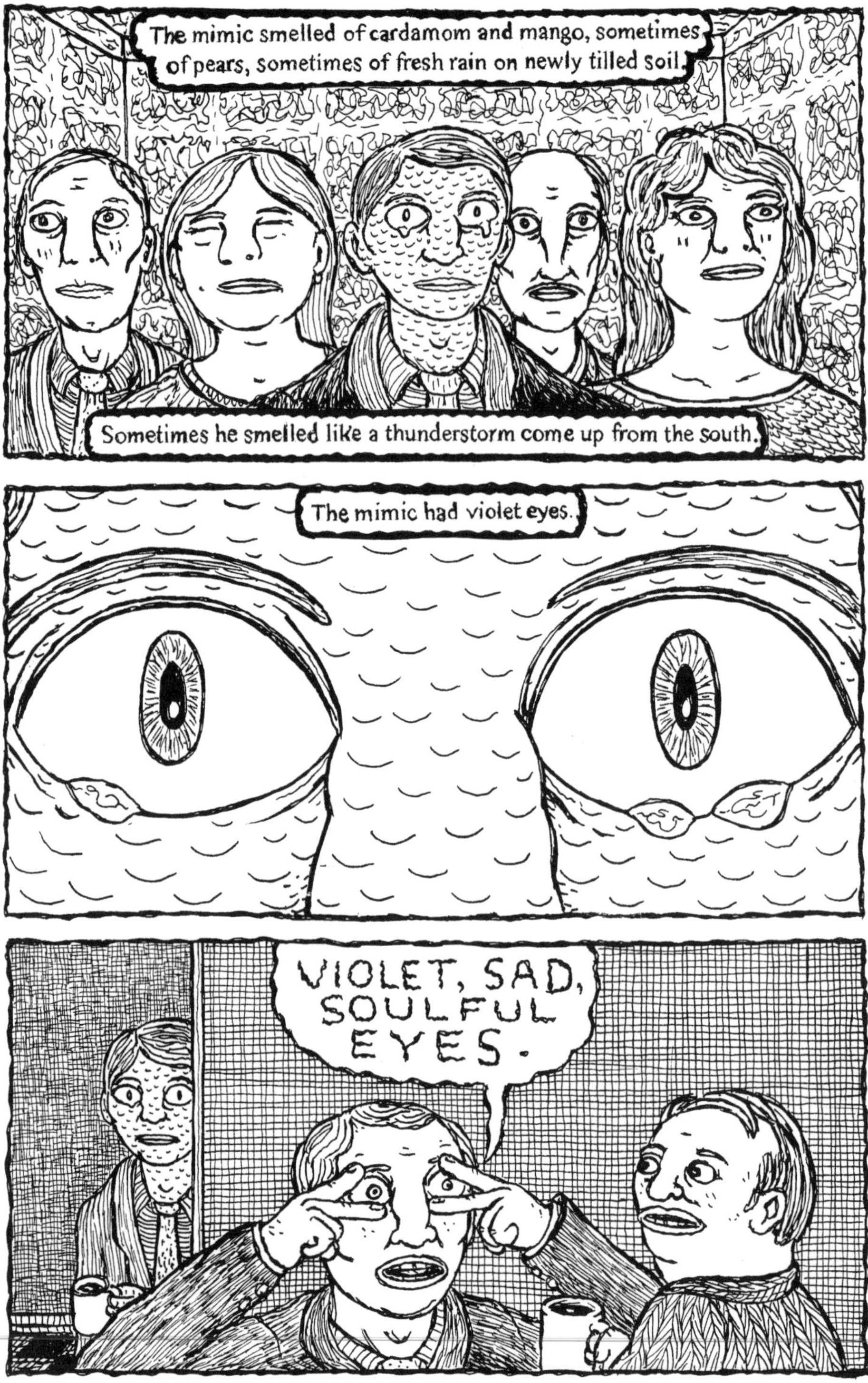
The mimic smelled of cardamom and mango, sometimes of pears, sometimes of fresh rain on newly tilled soil.
Sometimes he smelled like a thunderstorm come up from the south.
The mimic had violet eyes.
VIOLET, SAD, SOULFUL EYES.

Anyone who looked into those eyes found themselves falling.

They would remember events or people they had not thought of in years.

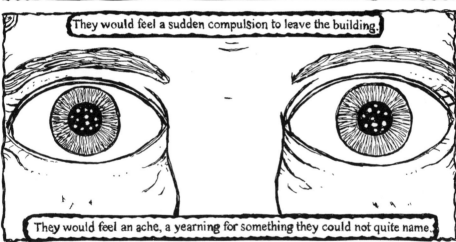

They would feel a sudden compulsion to leave the building.

They would feel an ache, a yearning for something they could not quite name.

For this reason, most people avoided looking at the mimic directly.

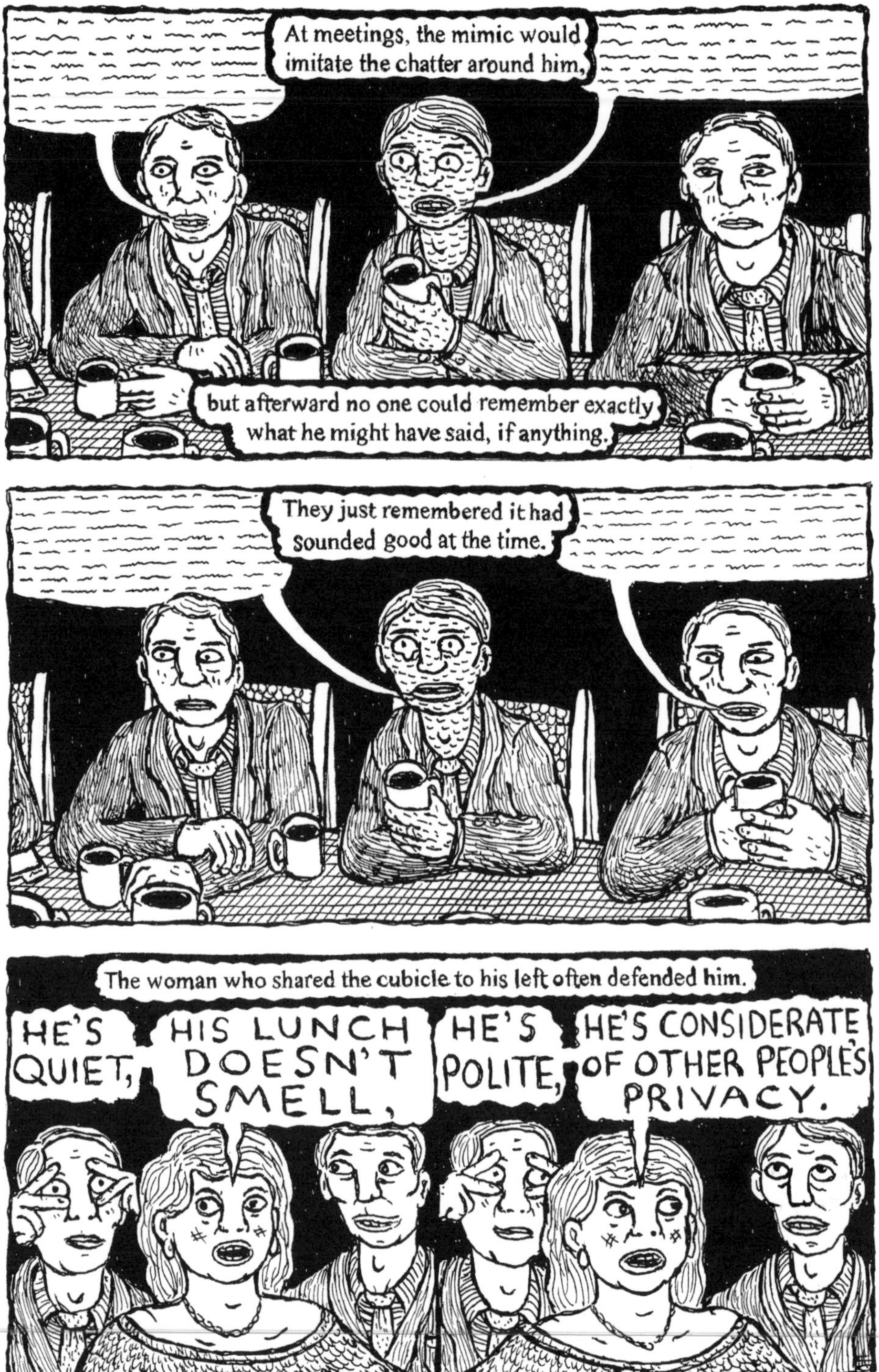
At meetings, the mimic would imitate the chatter around him,
but afterward no one could remember exactly what he might have said, if anything.
They just remembered it had sounded good at the time.
The woman who shared the cubicle to his left often defended him.
HE'S QUIET,
HIS LUNCH DOESN'T SMELL,
HE'S POLITE,
HE'S CONSIDERATE OF OTHER PEOPLE'S PRIVACY.

For long hours, the mimic stared out the window toward the south,

and wept the tears that might not be tears at all.

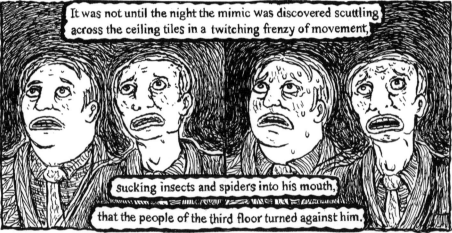

It was not until the night the mimic was discovered scuttling across the ceiling tiles in a twitching frenzy of movement,

sucking insects and spiders into his mouth,

that the people of the third floor turned against him.

The sight was too strange for them.

It did not mimic them at all.

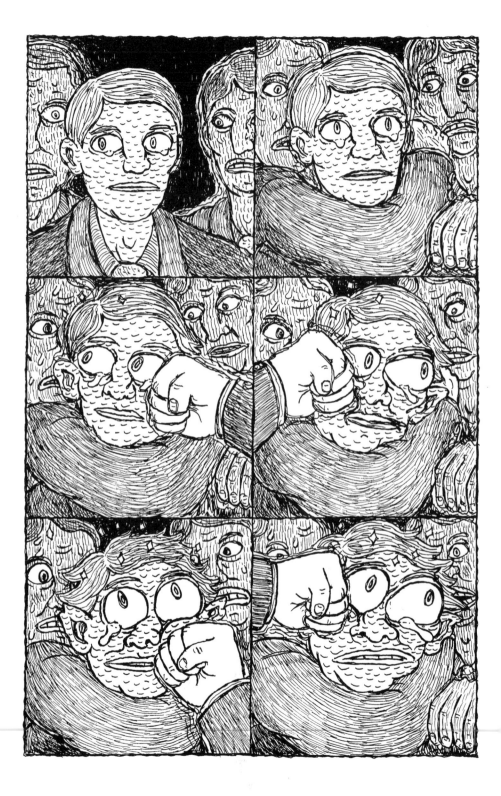

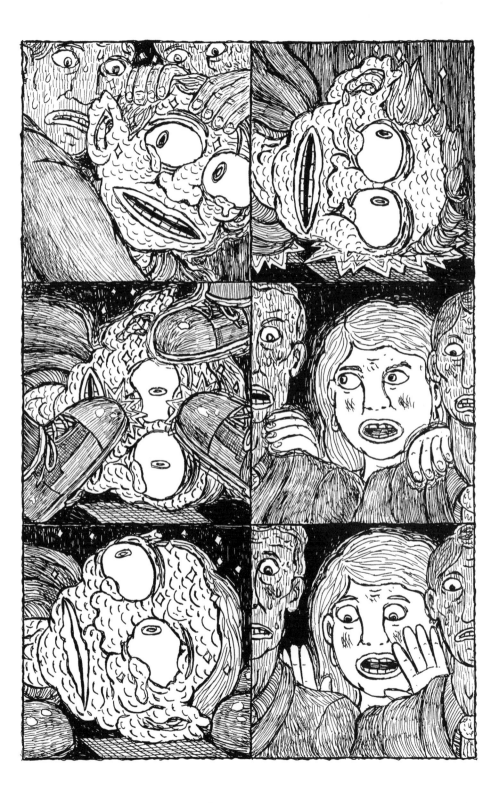

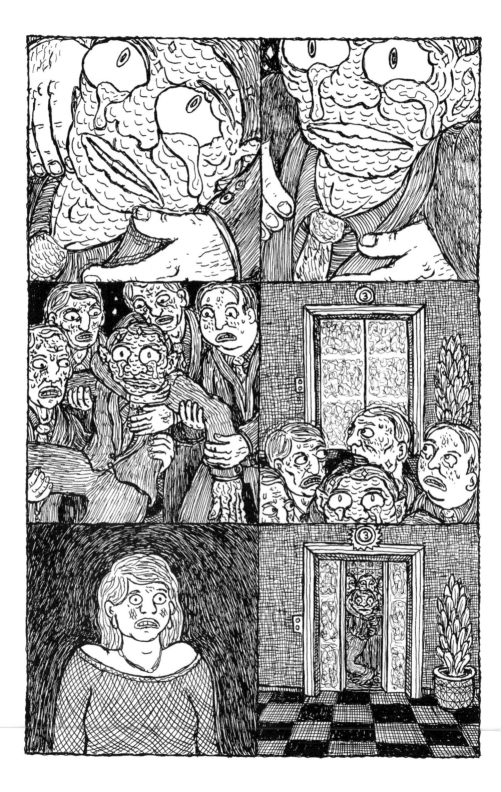

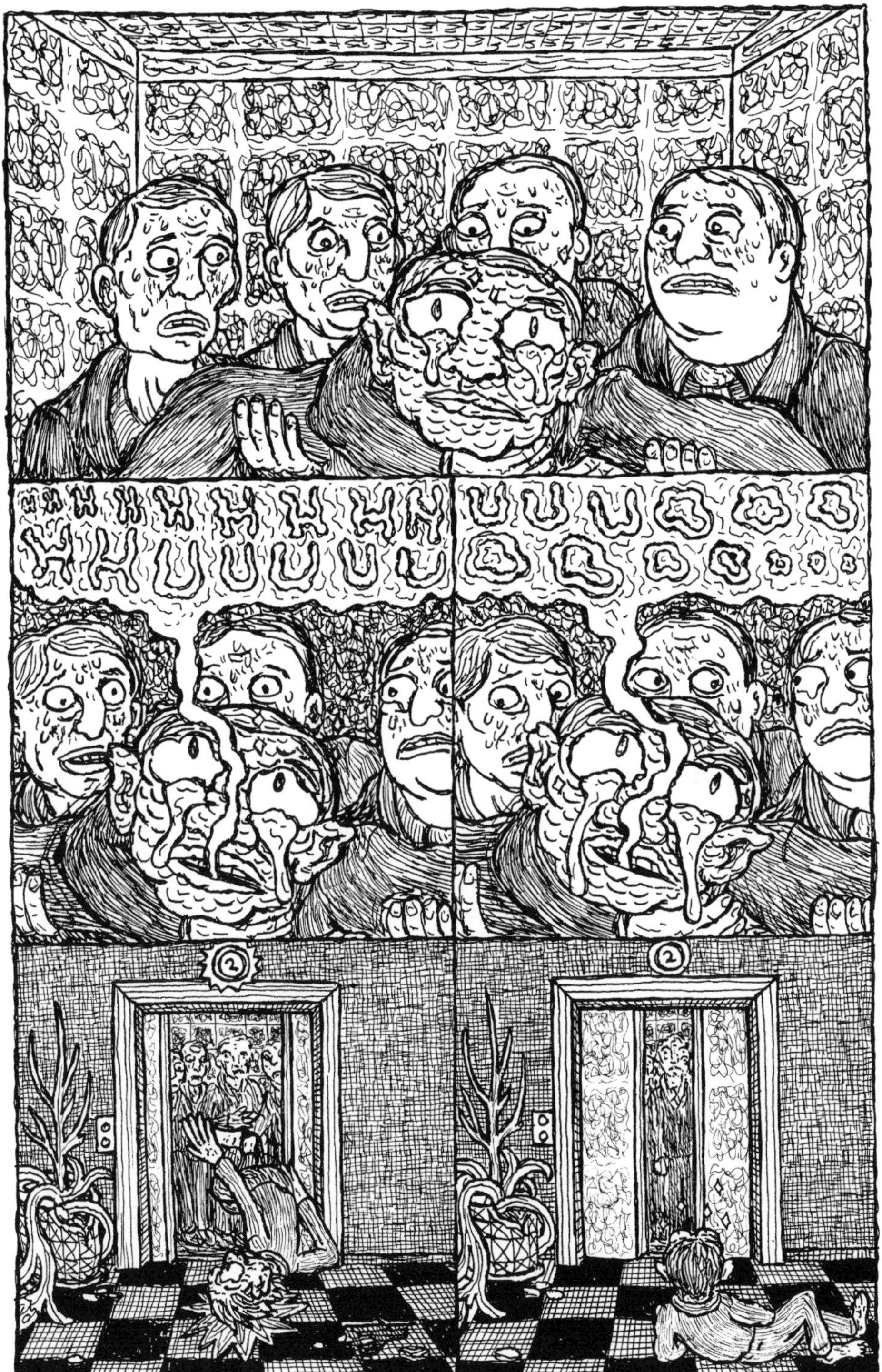
HHHHHHHH
HHUUUUUU
UUUOOO
OOOOOOO

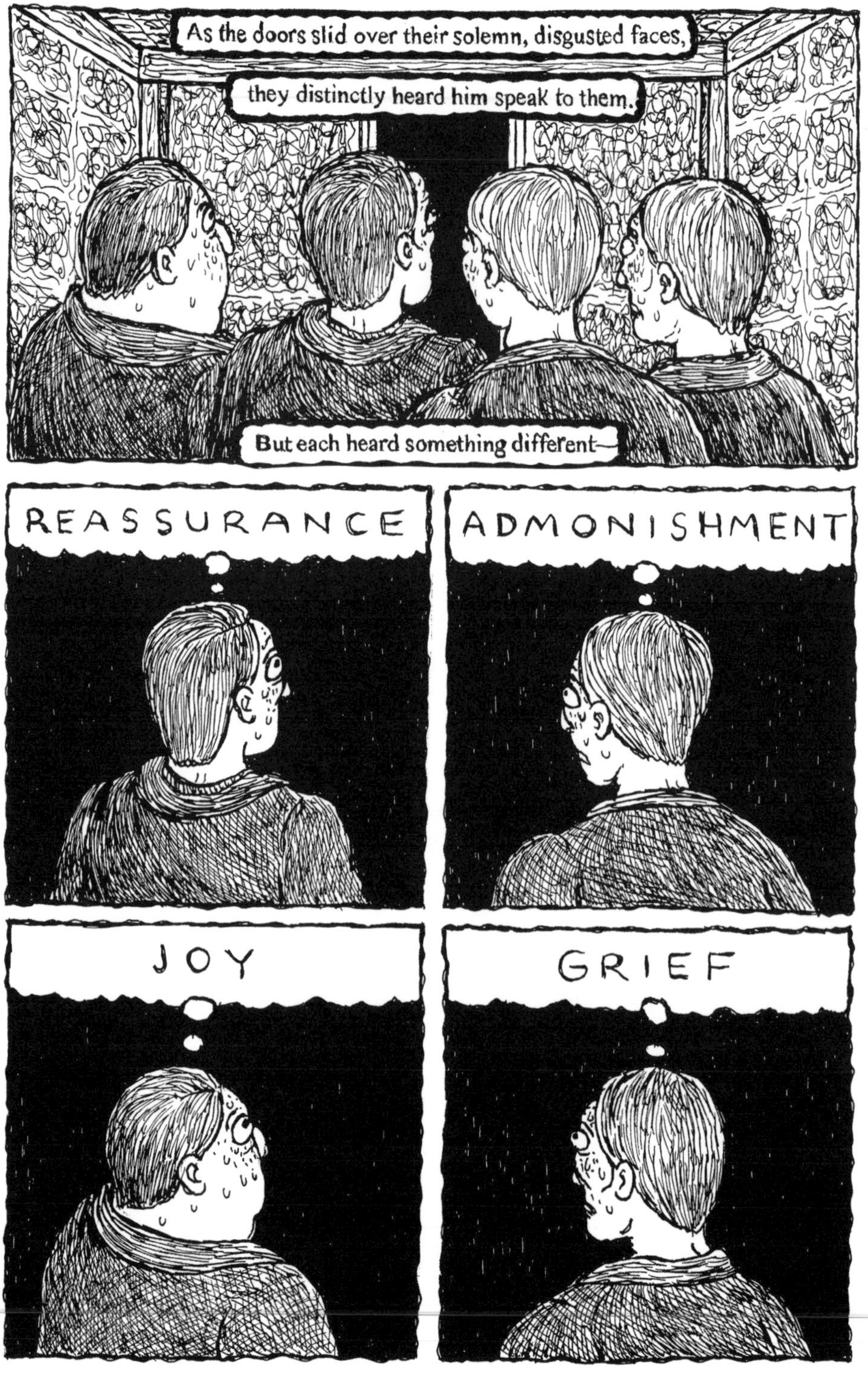
As the doors slid over their solemn, disgusted faces,
they distinctly heard him speak to them.
But each heard something different—
REASSURANCE
ADMONISHMENT
JOY
GRIEF

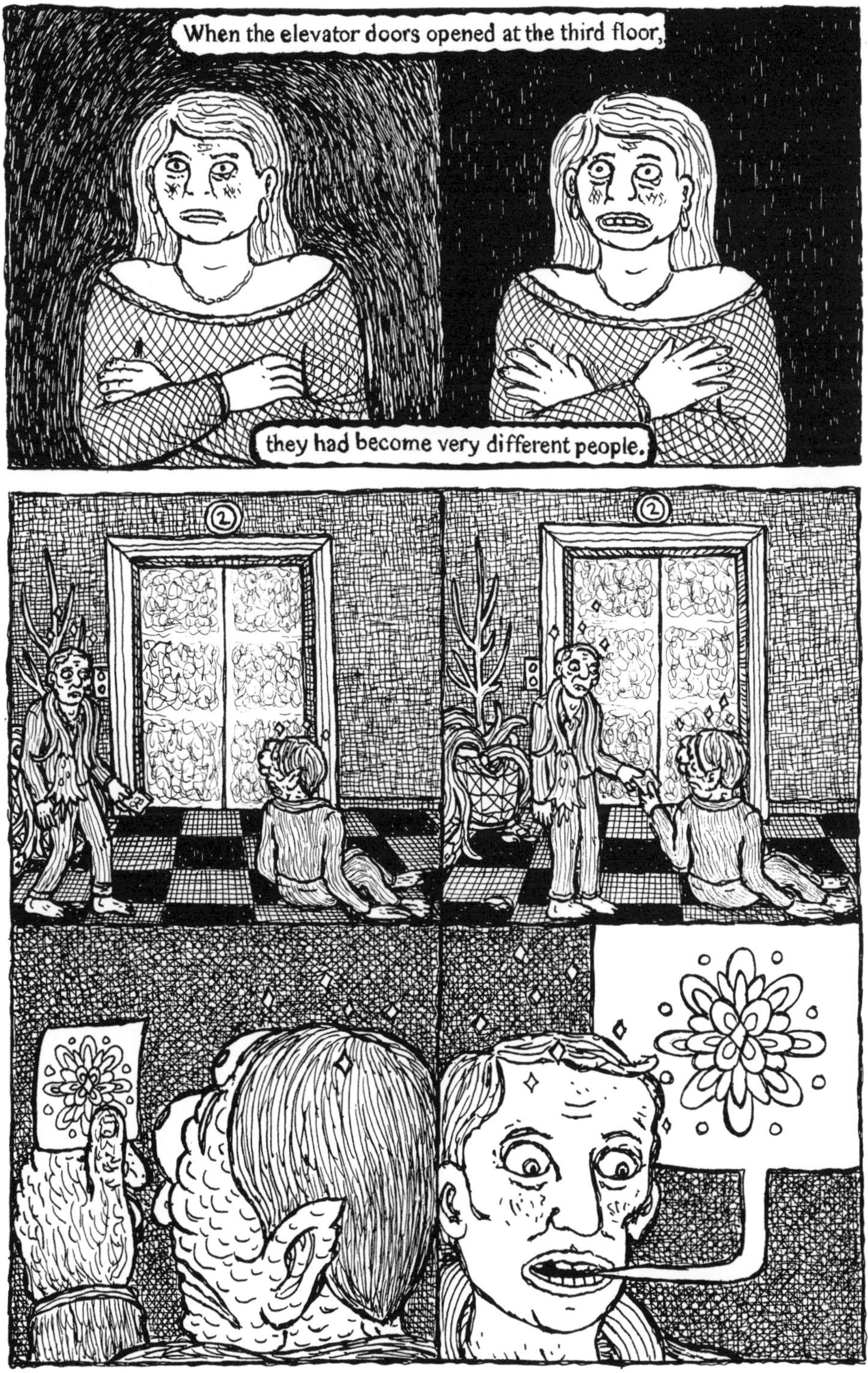
When the elevator doors opened at the third floor,
they had become very different people.

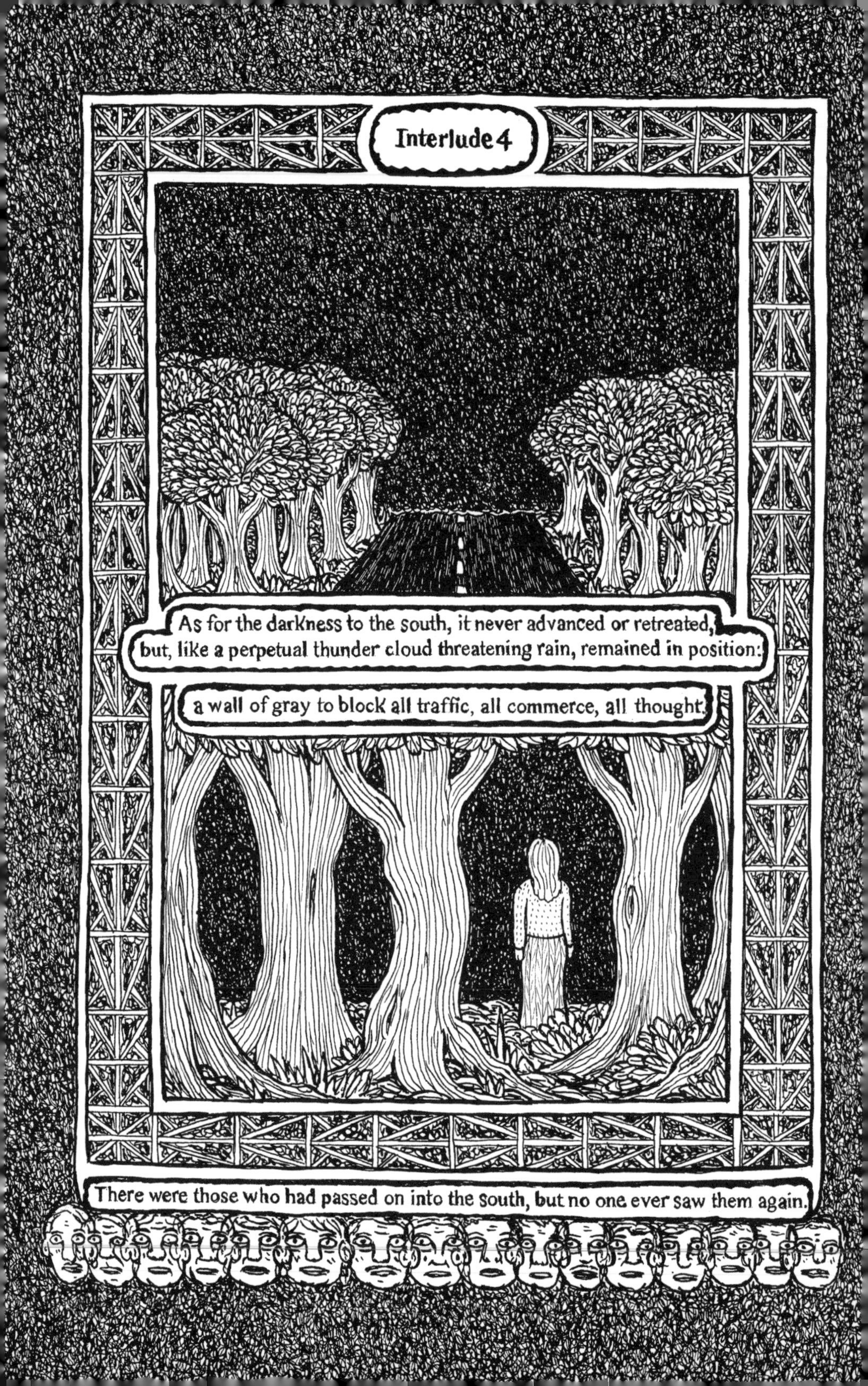
Interlude 4
As for the darkness to the south, it never advanced or retreated, but, like a perpetual thunder cloud threatening rain, remained in position:
a wall of gray to block all traffic, all commerce, all thought.
There were those who had passed on into the south, but no one ever saw them again.

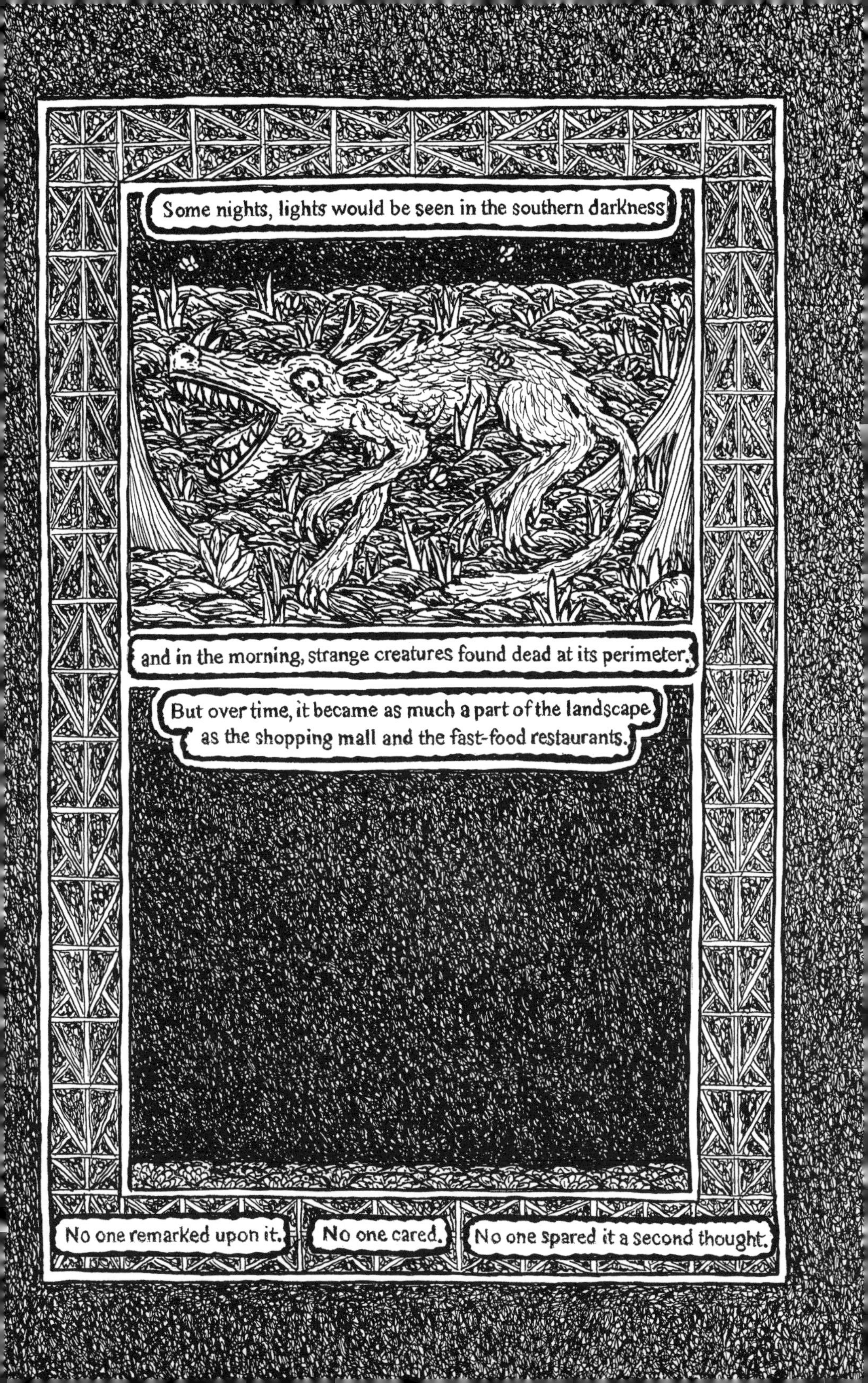
Some nights, lights would be seen in the southern darkness
and in the morning, strange creatures found dead at its perimeter.
But over time, it became as much a part of the landscape as the shopping mall and the fast-food restaurants.
No one remarked upon it.
No one cared.
No one spared it a second thought.

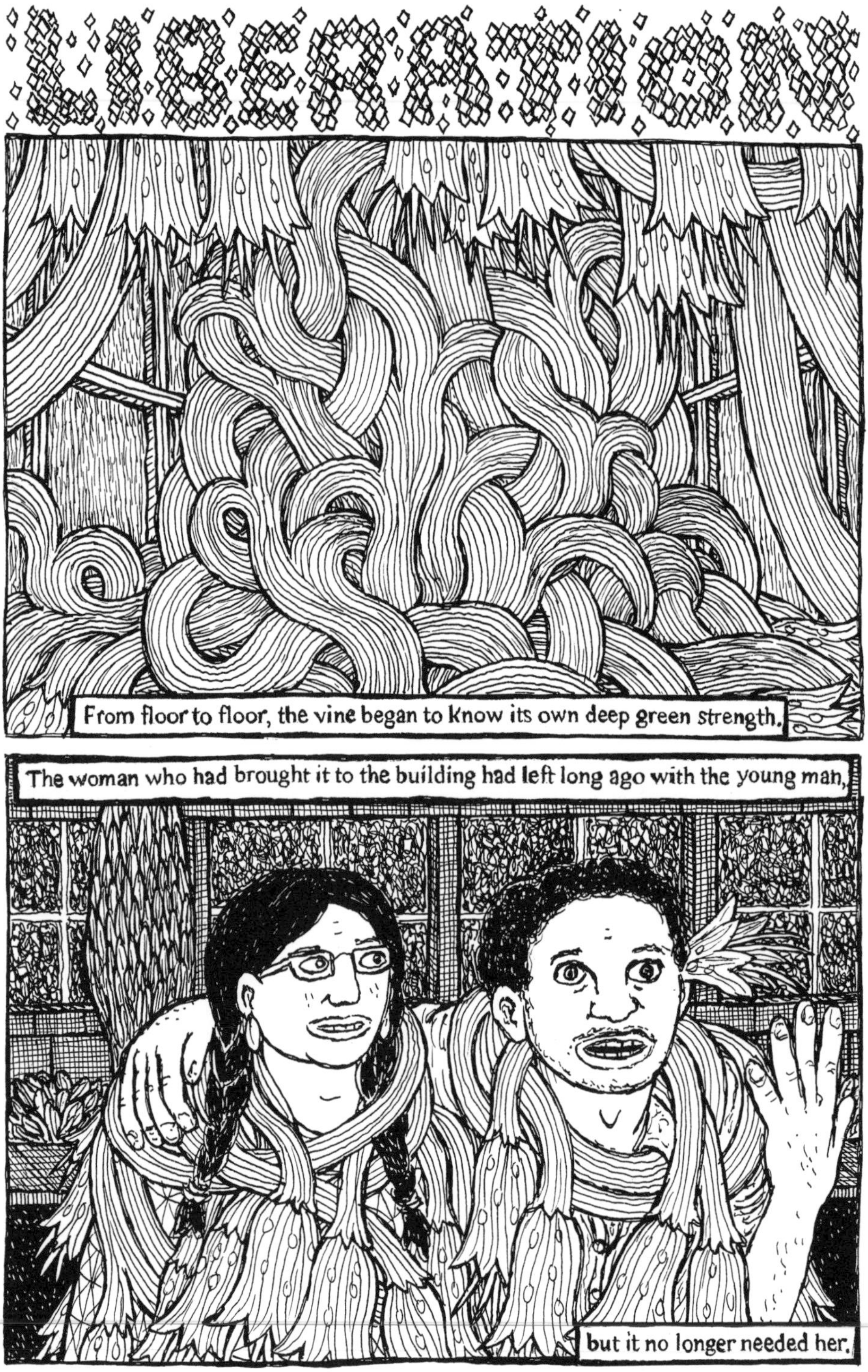
LIBERATION
From floor to floor, the vine began to know its own deep green strength.
The woman who had brought it to the building had left long ago with the young man,
but it no longer needed her.

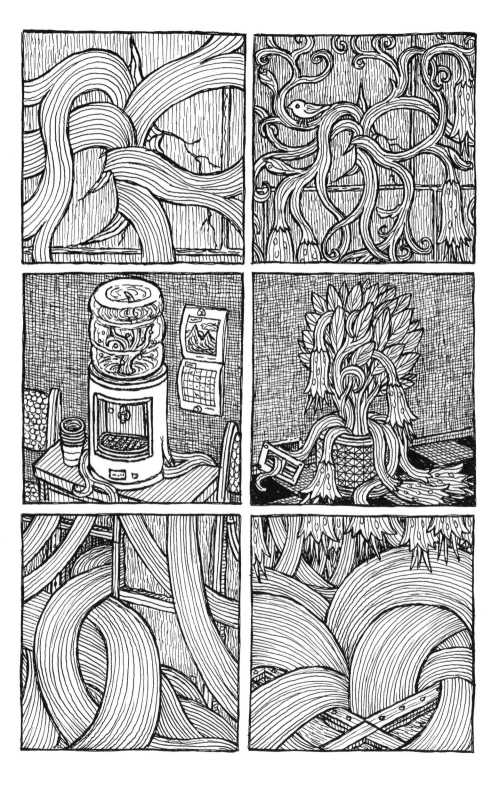

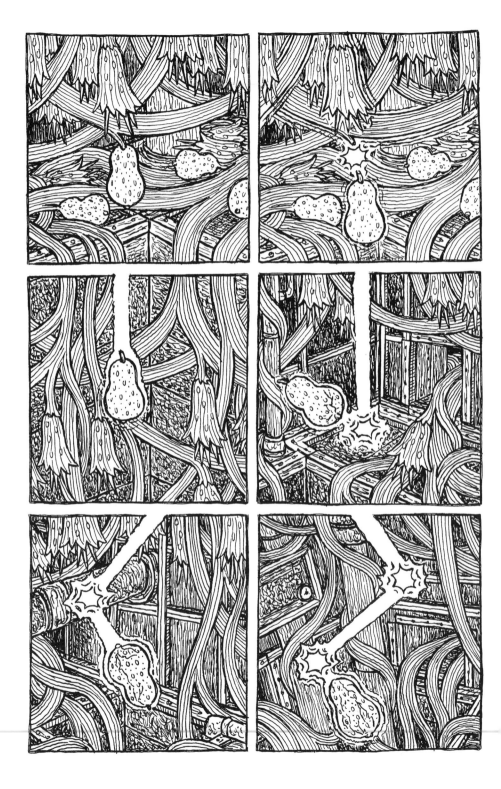

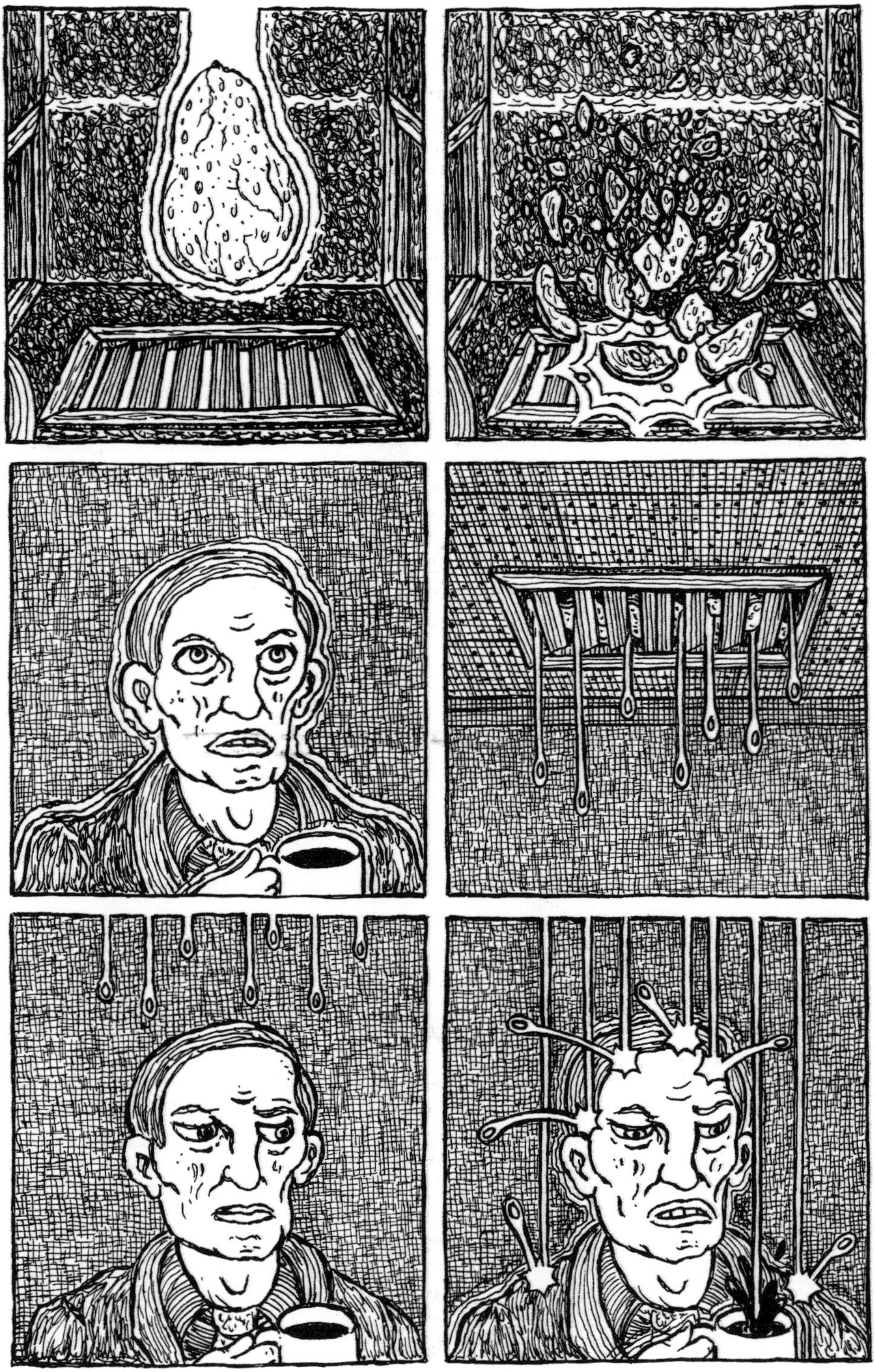

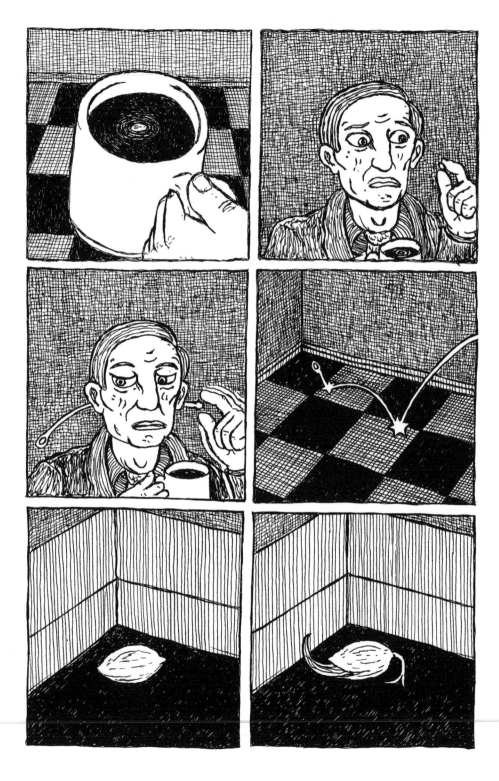

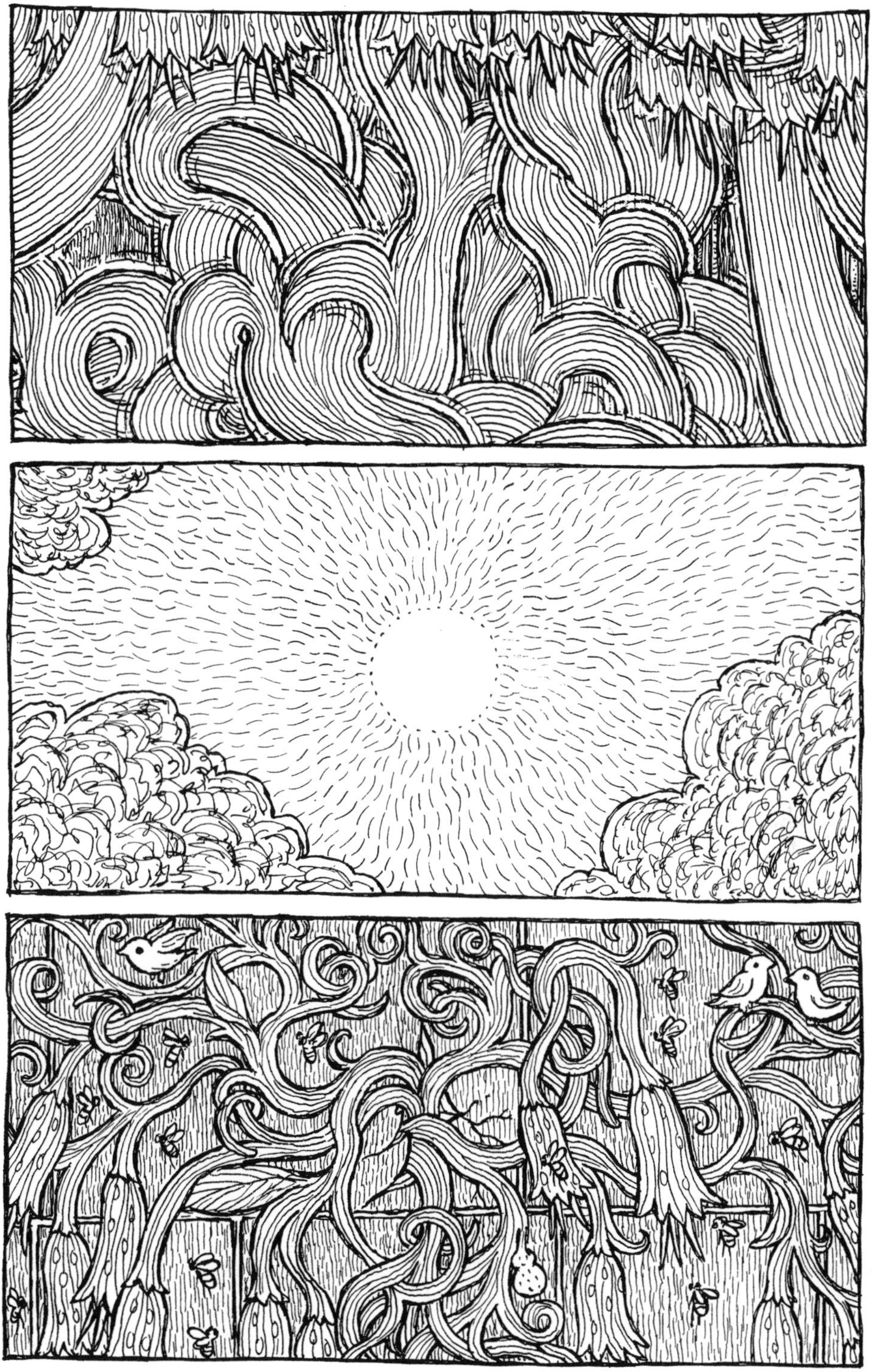

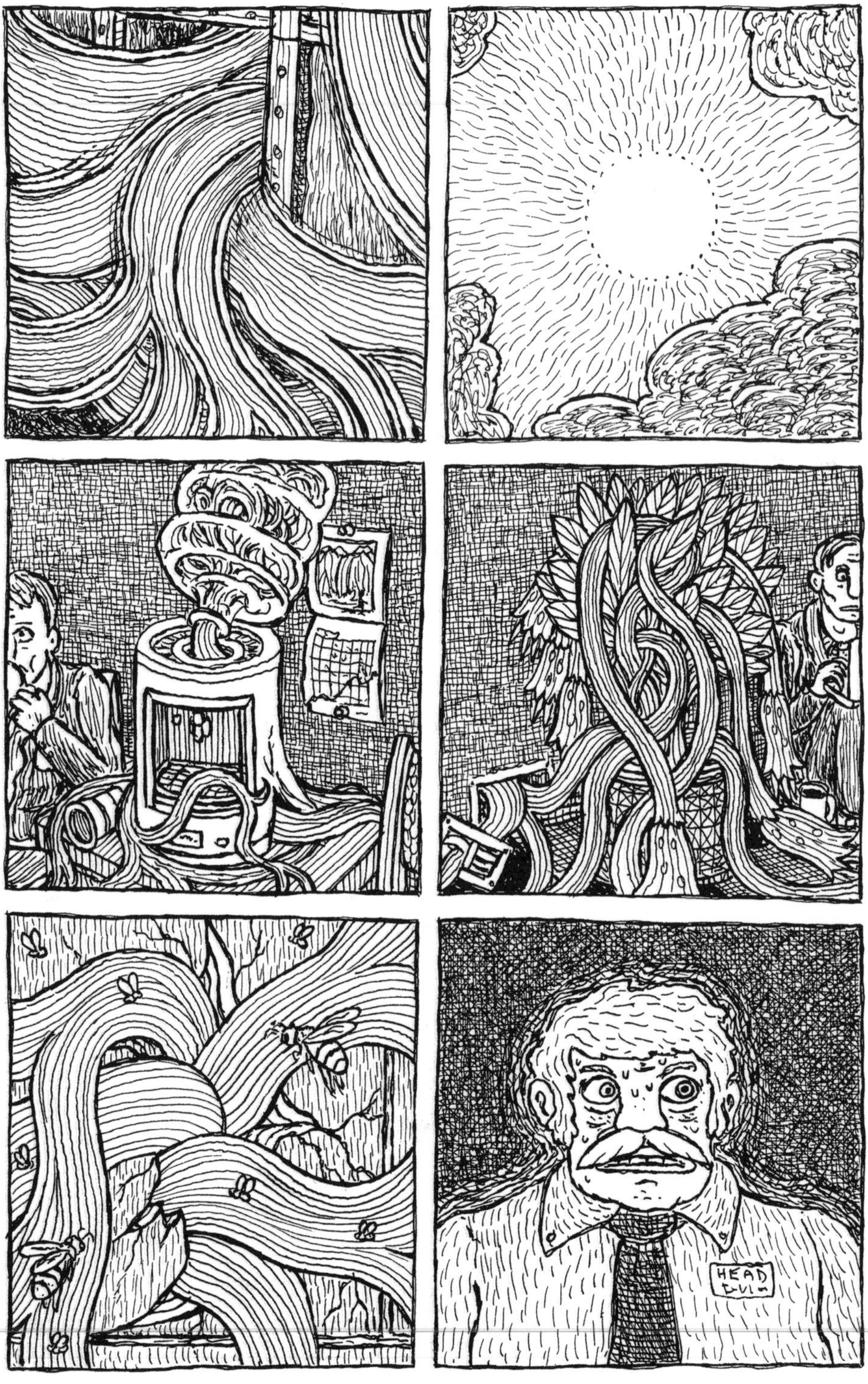
HEAD

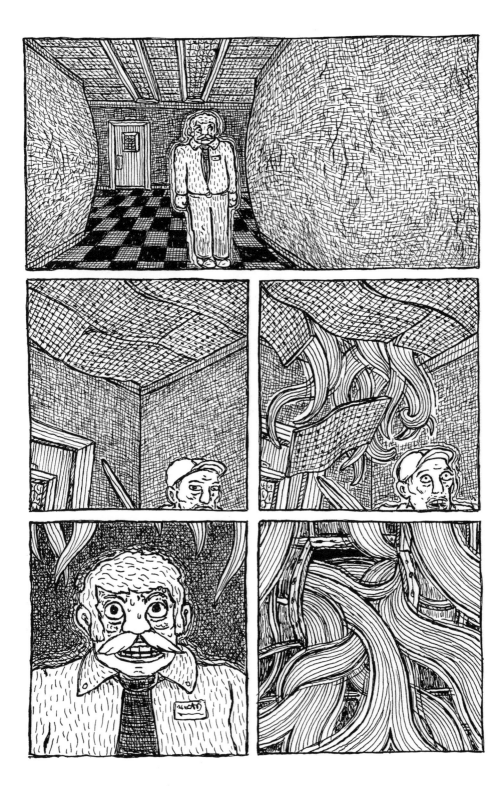

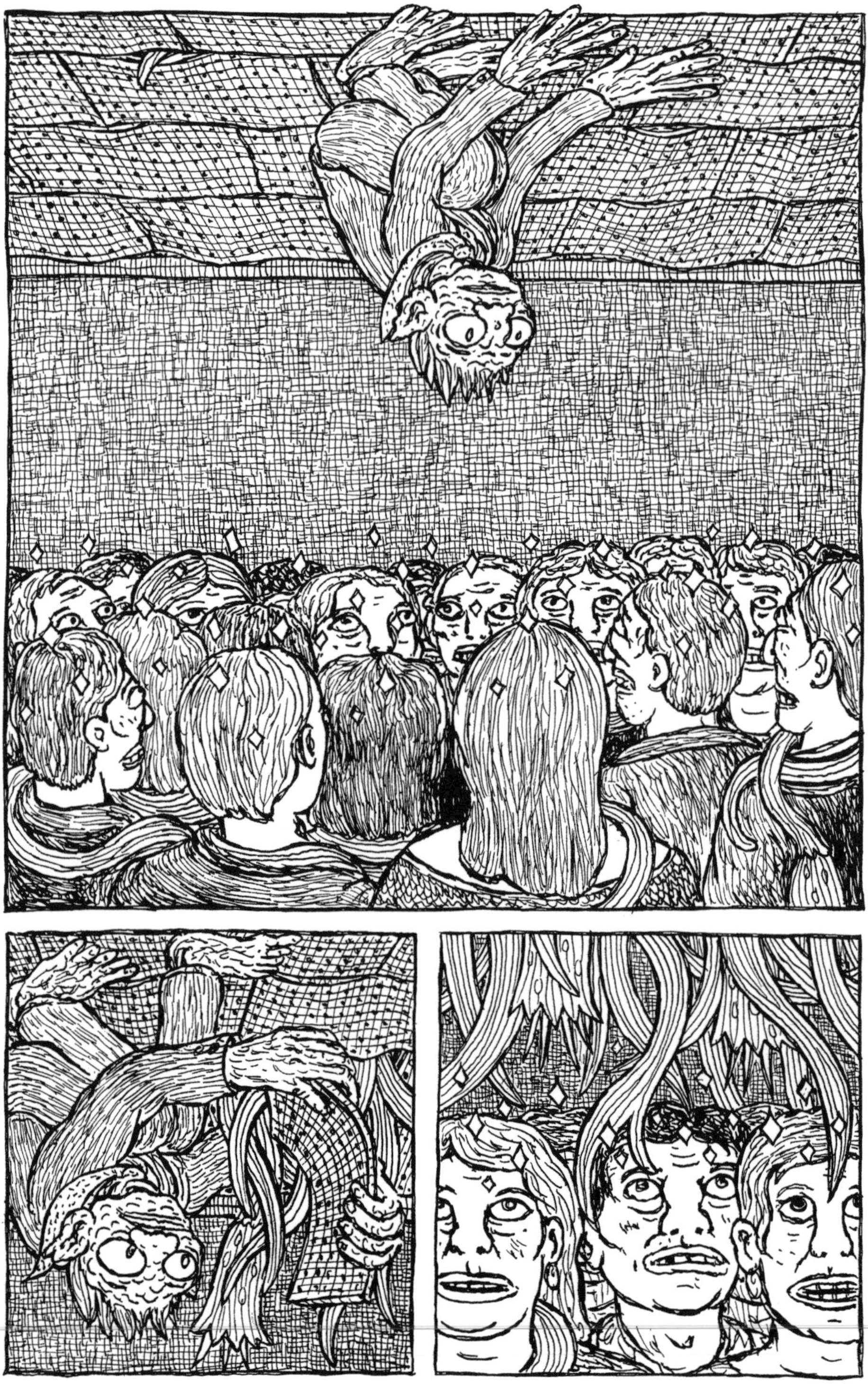

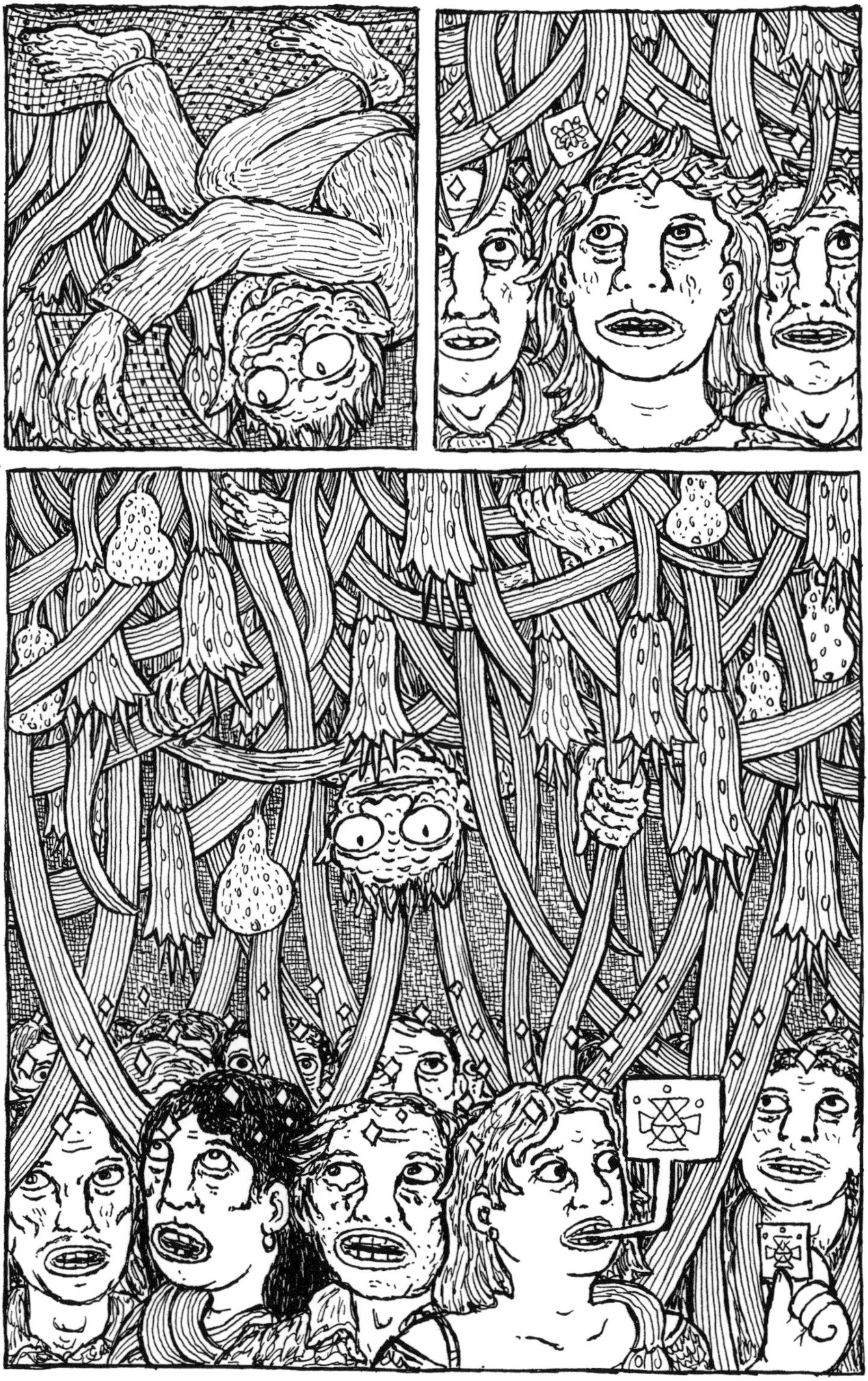

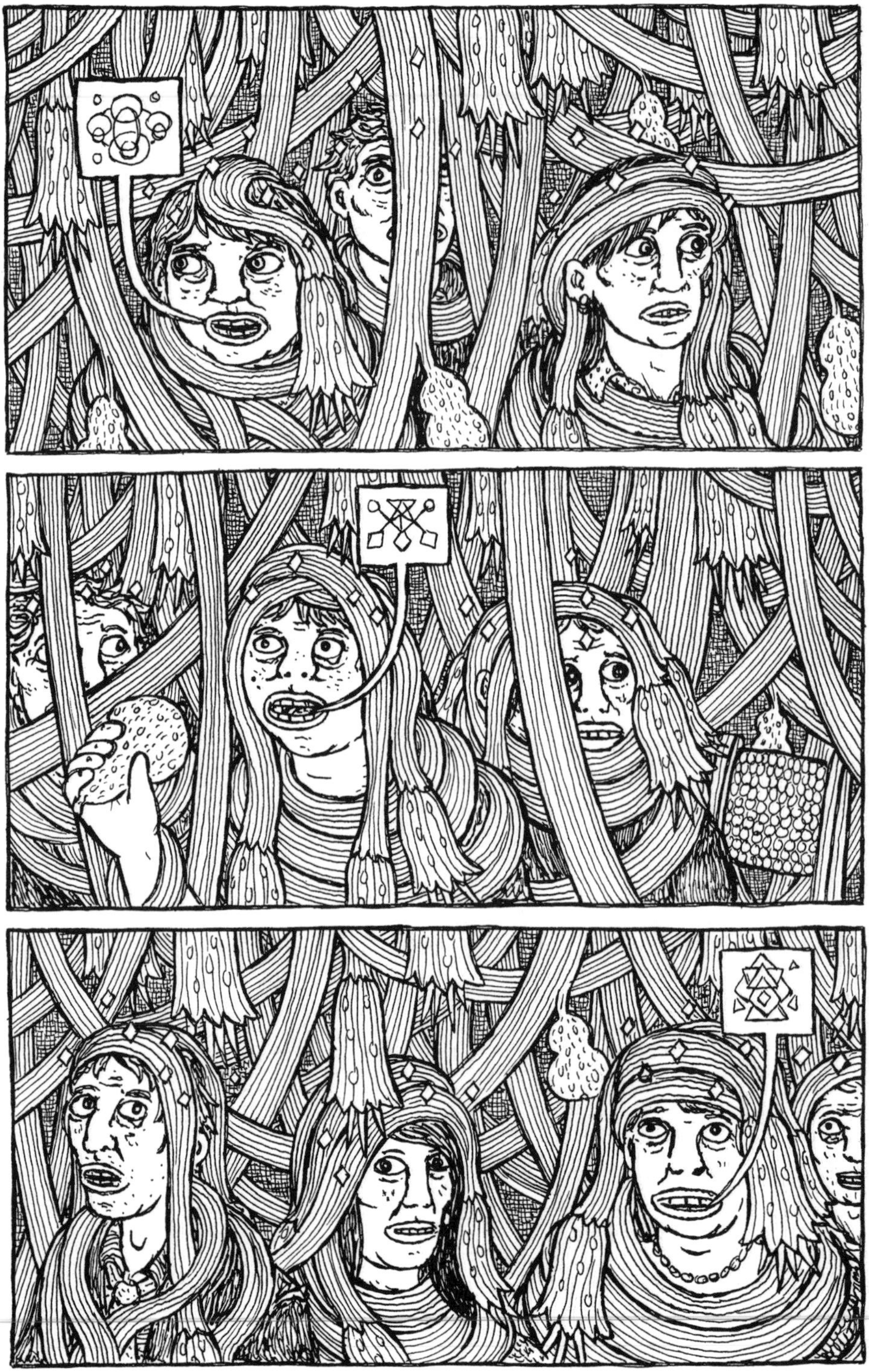

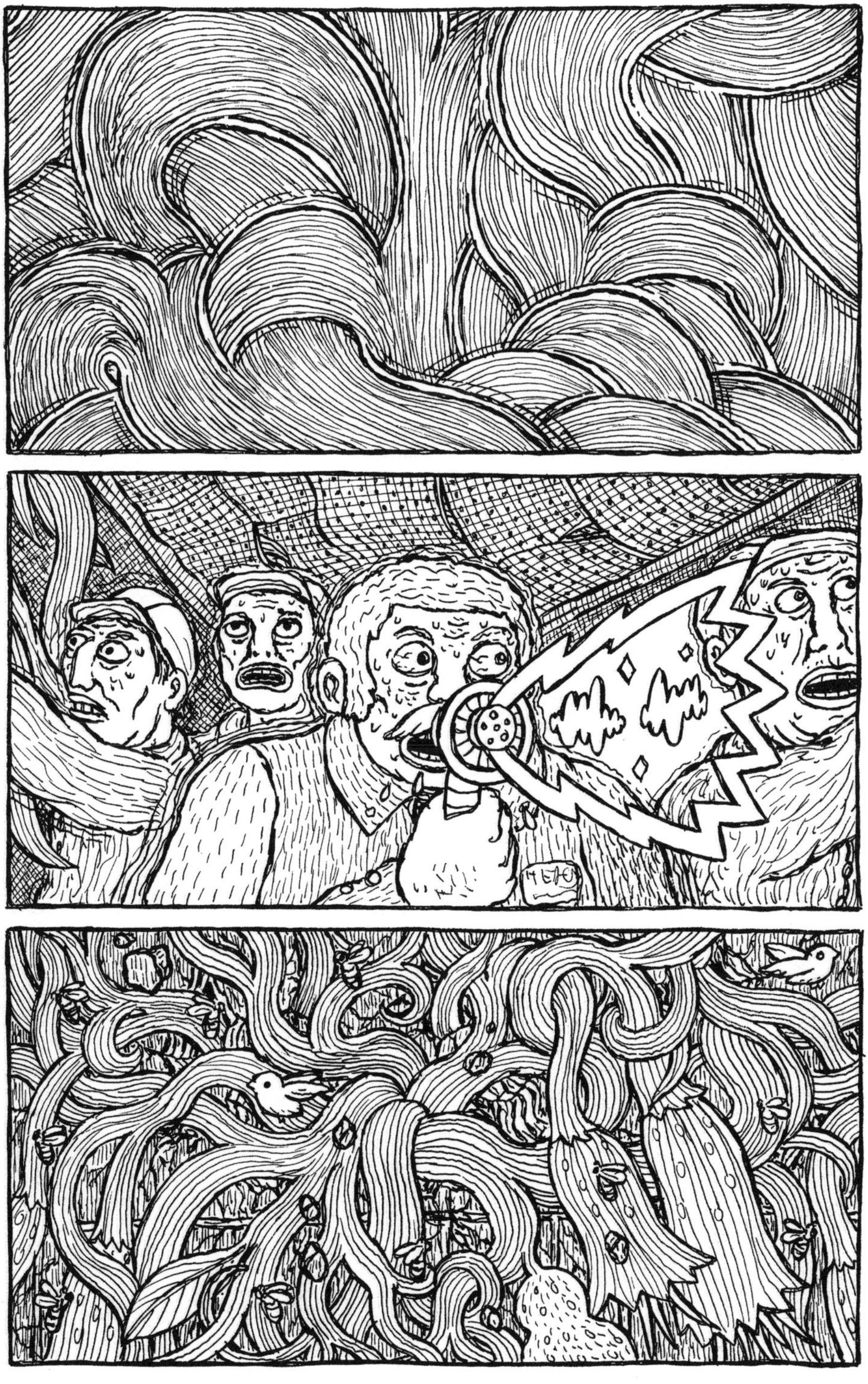

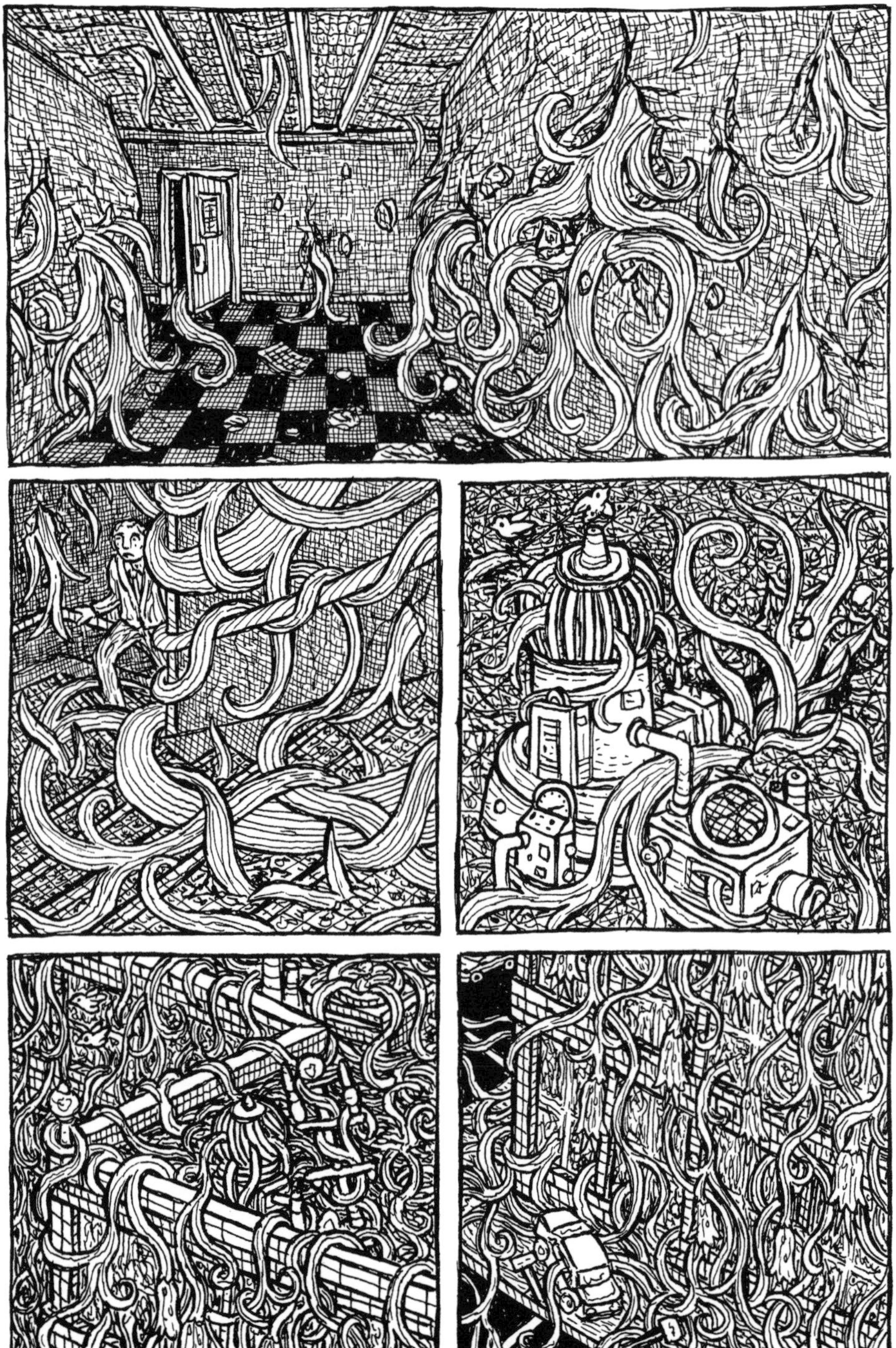

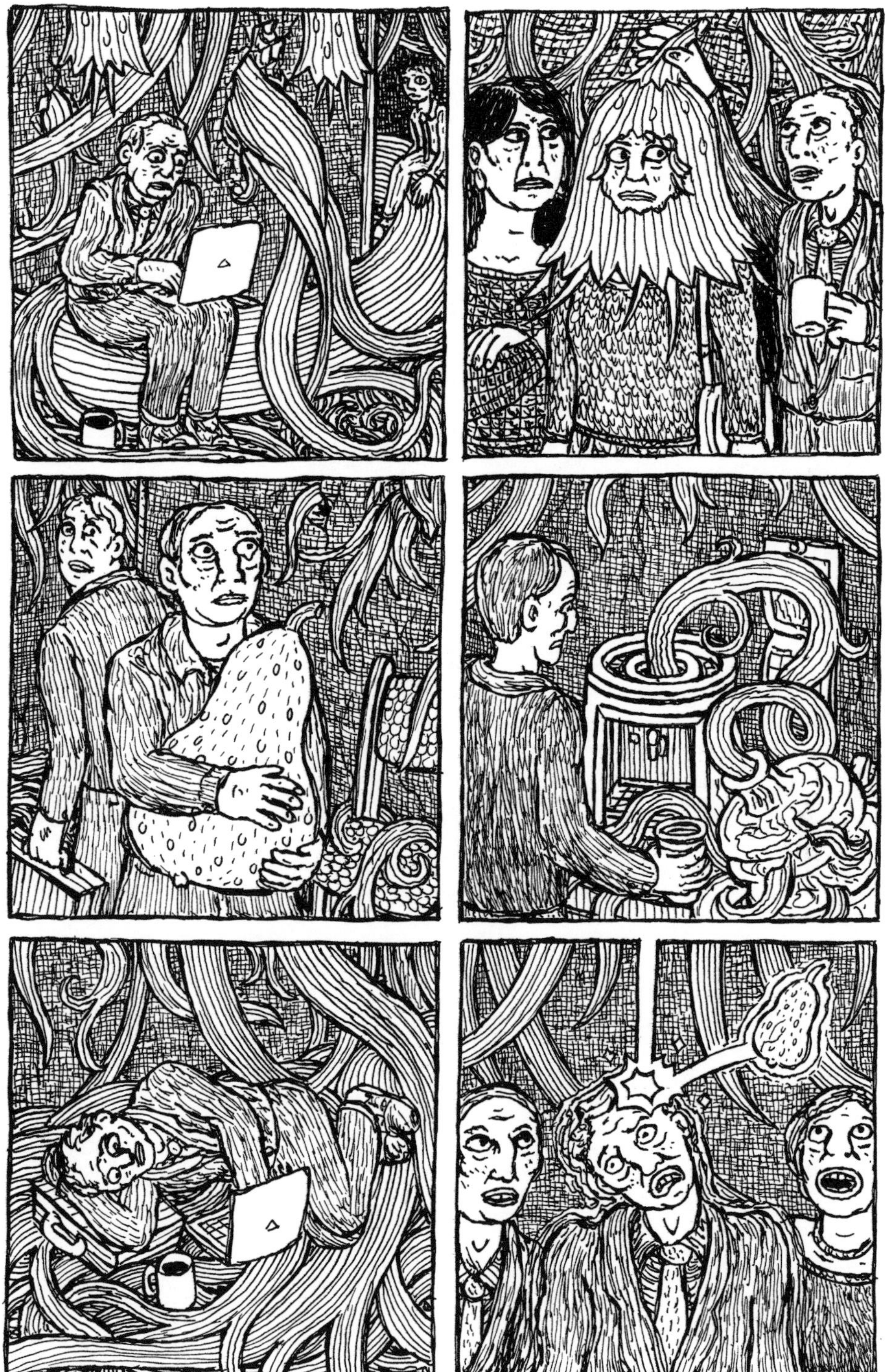

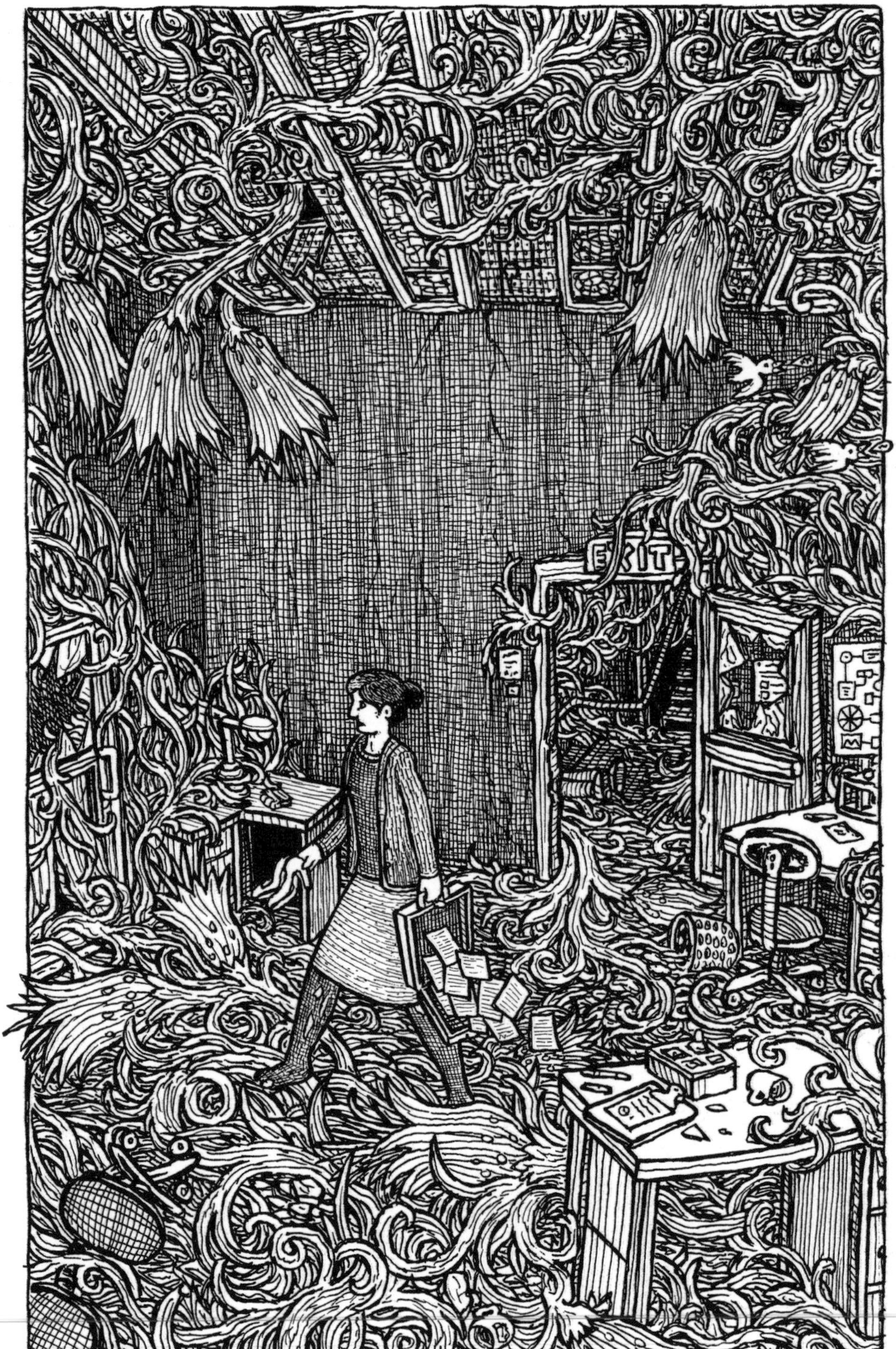
EXIT

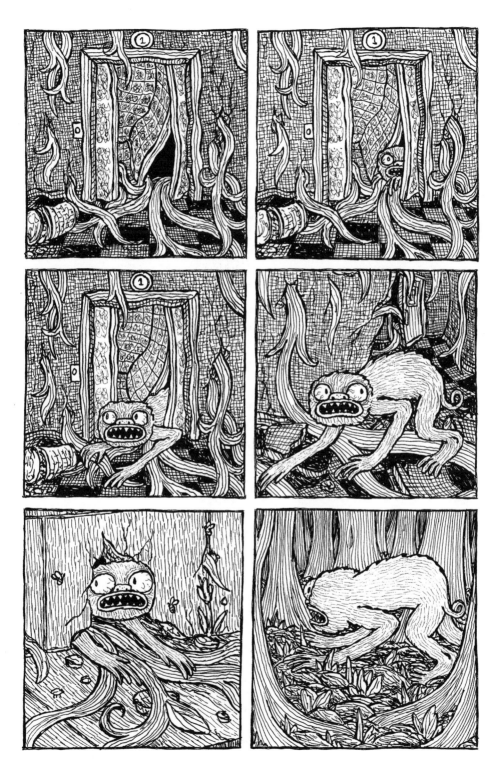

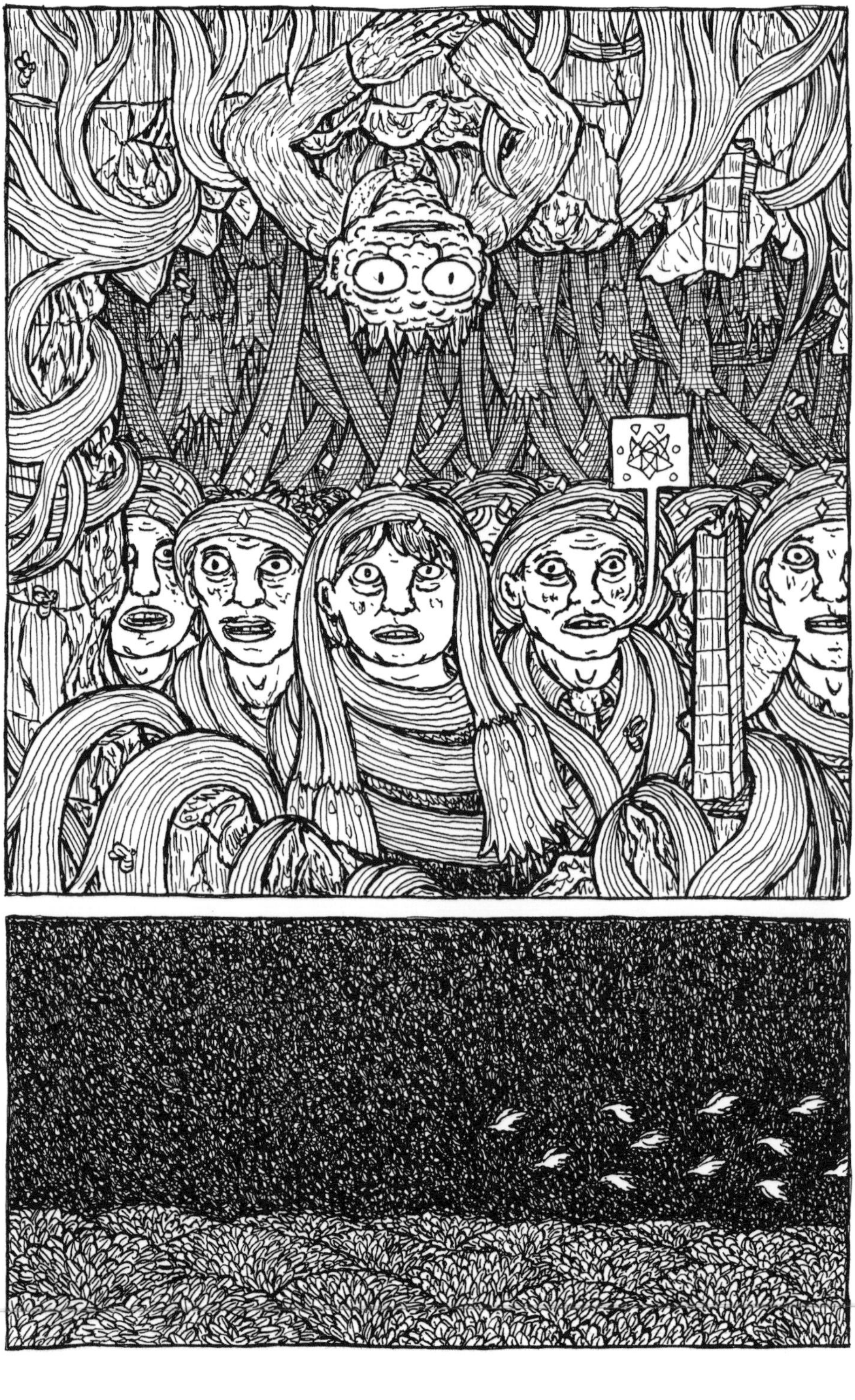

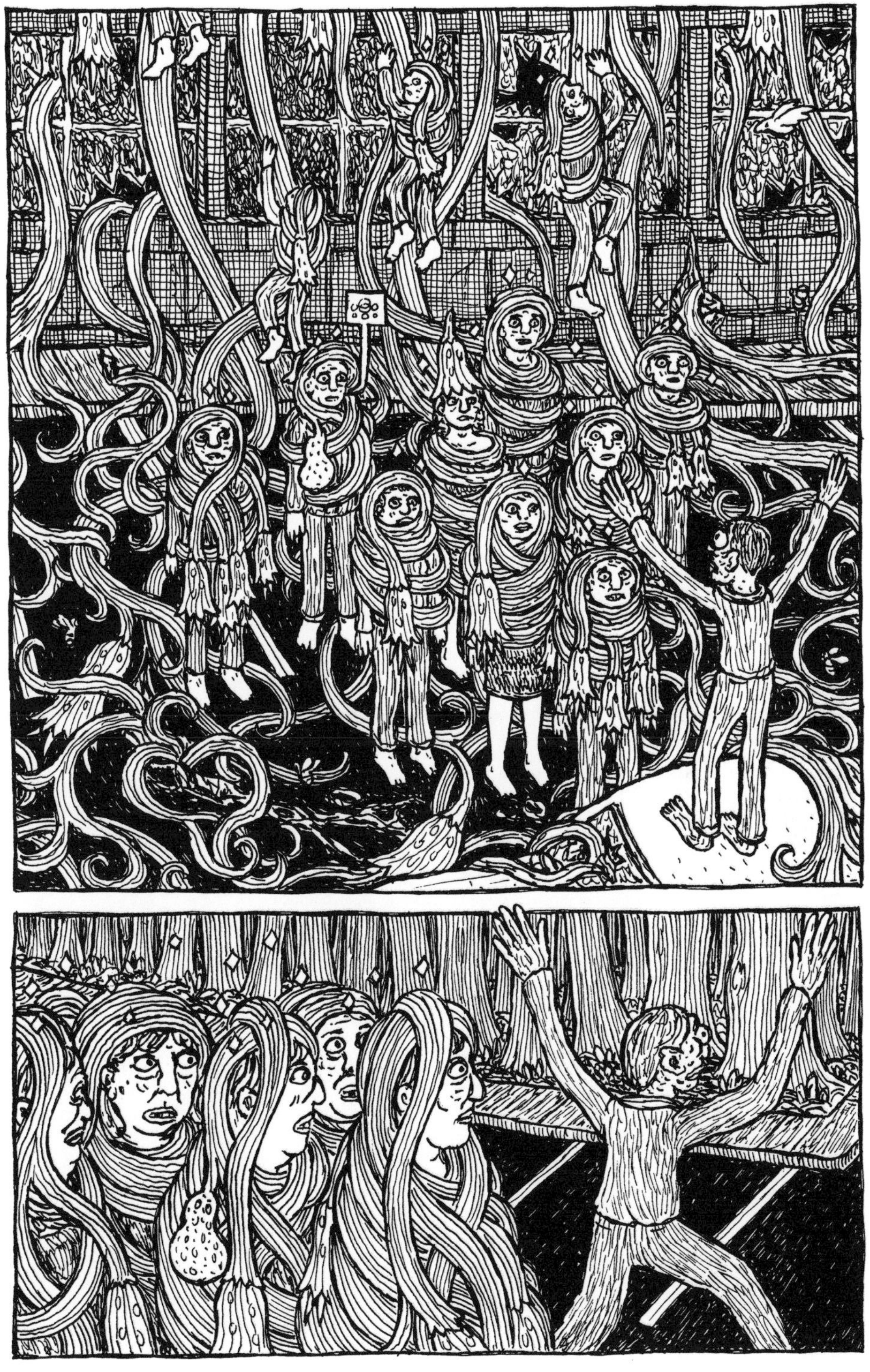

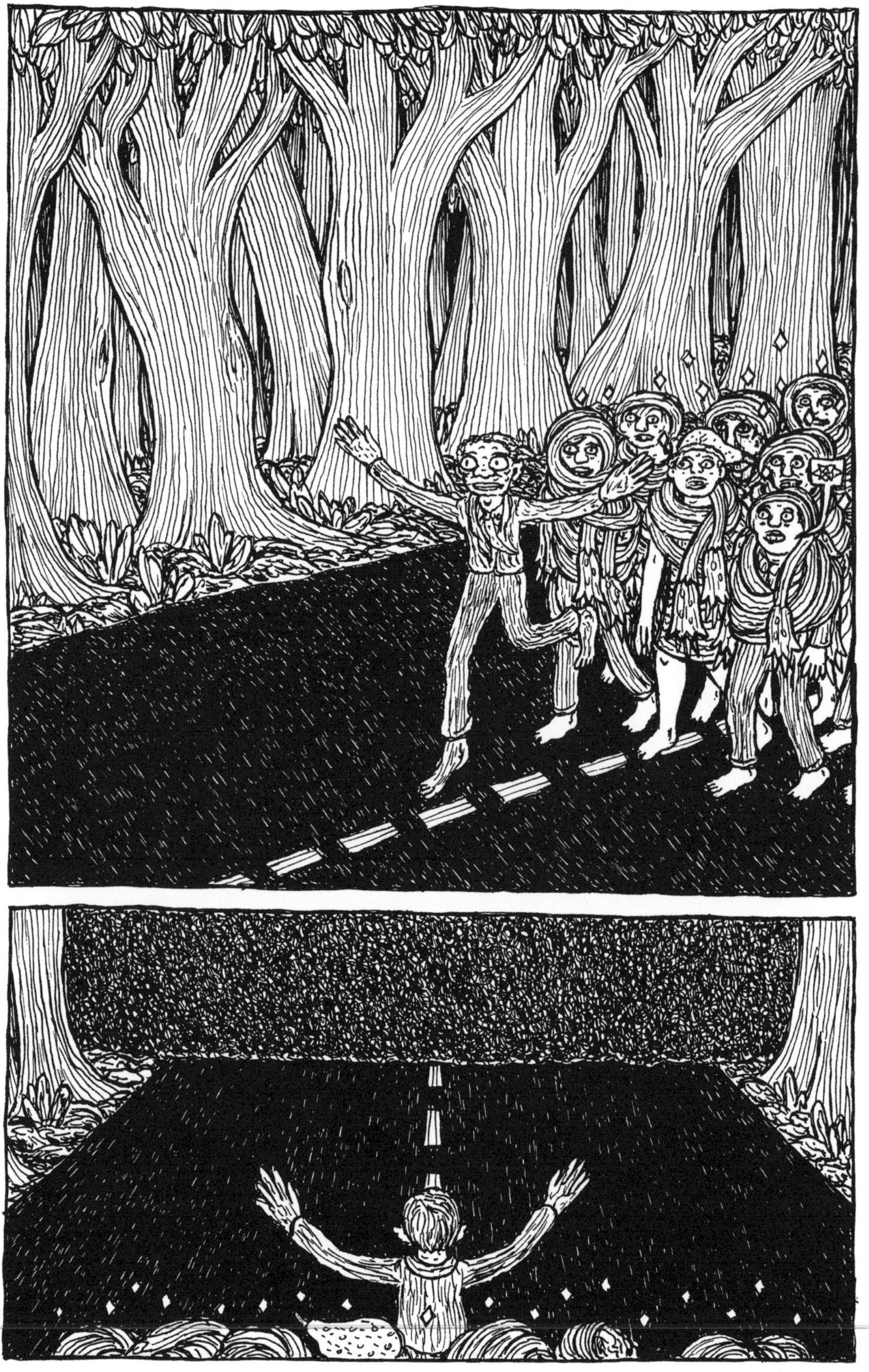

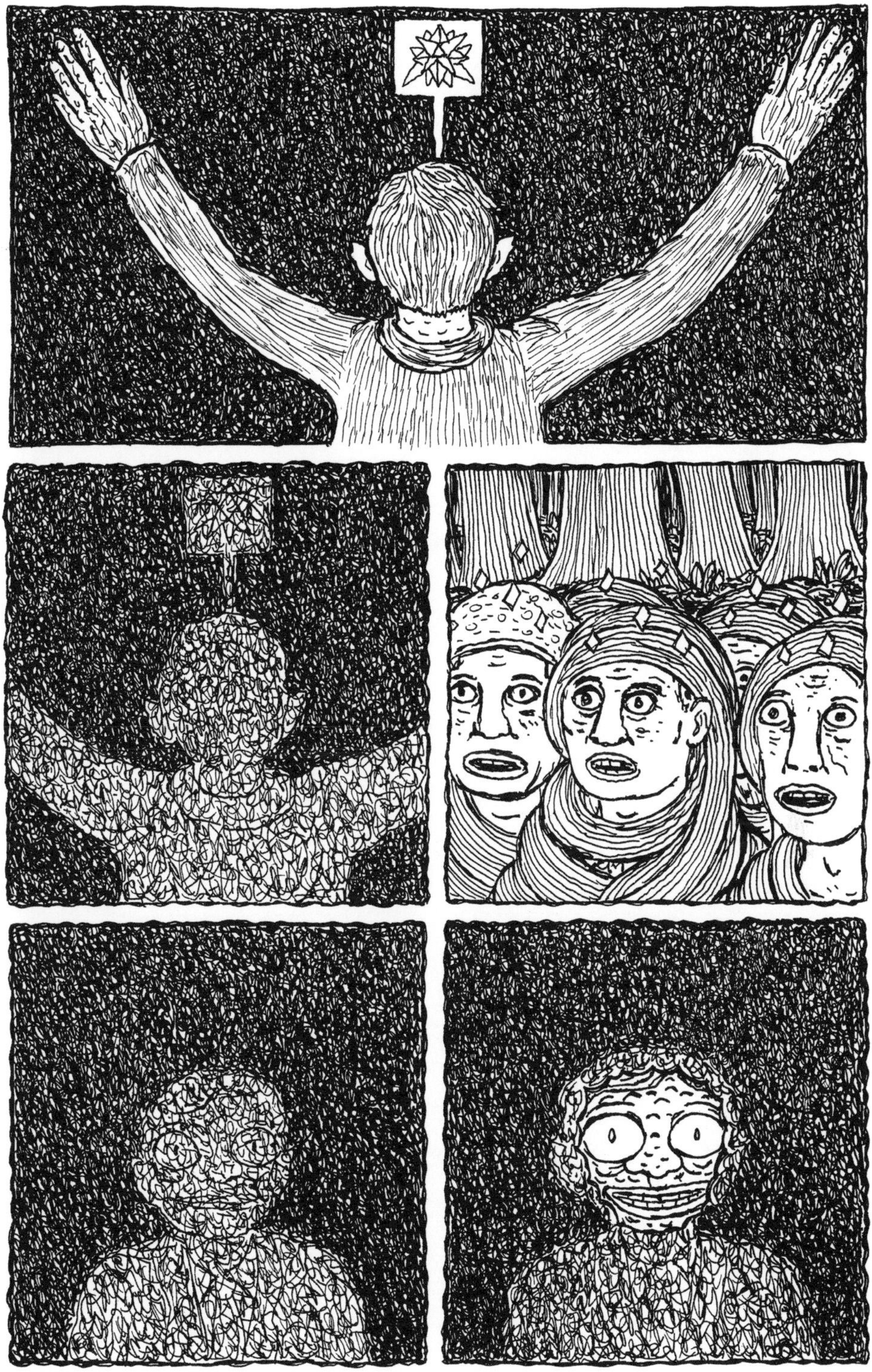

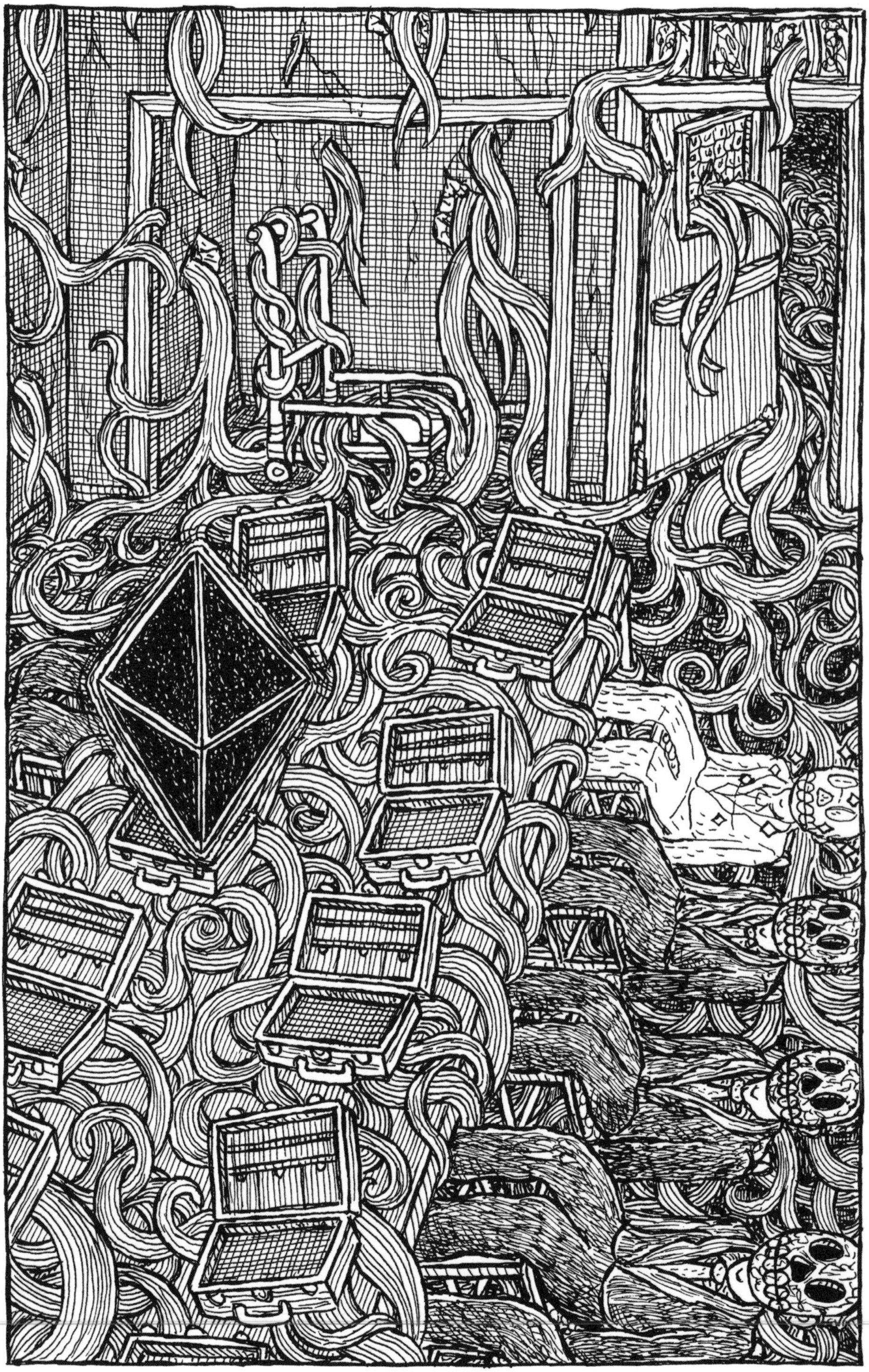

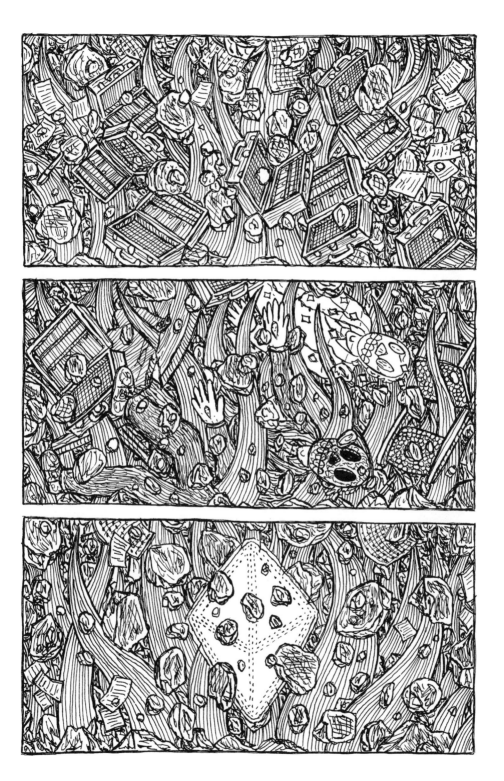

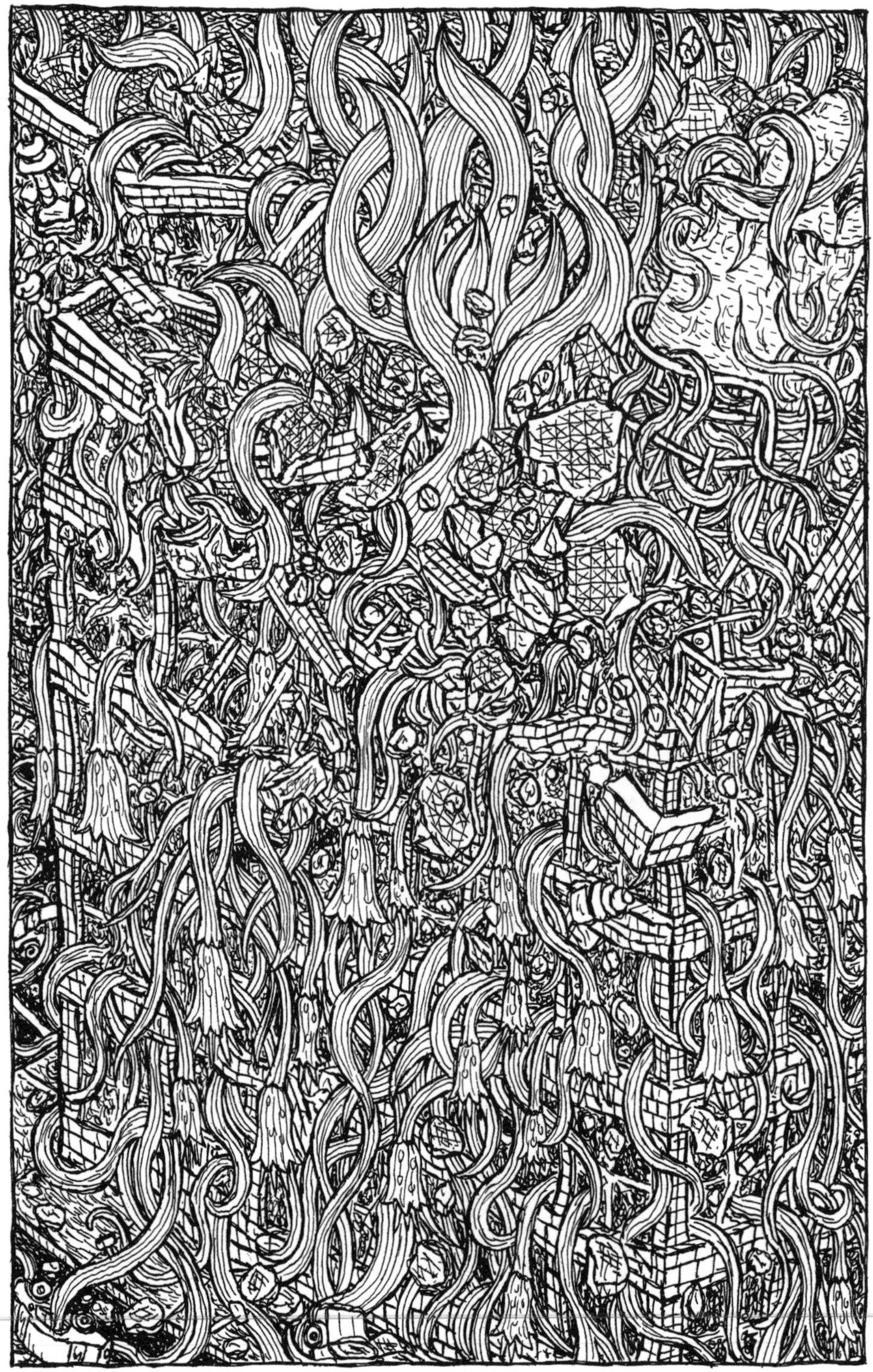

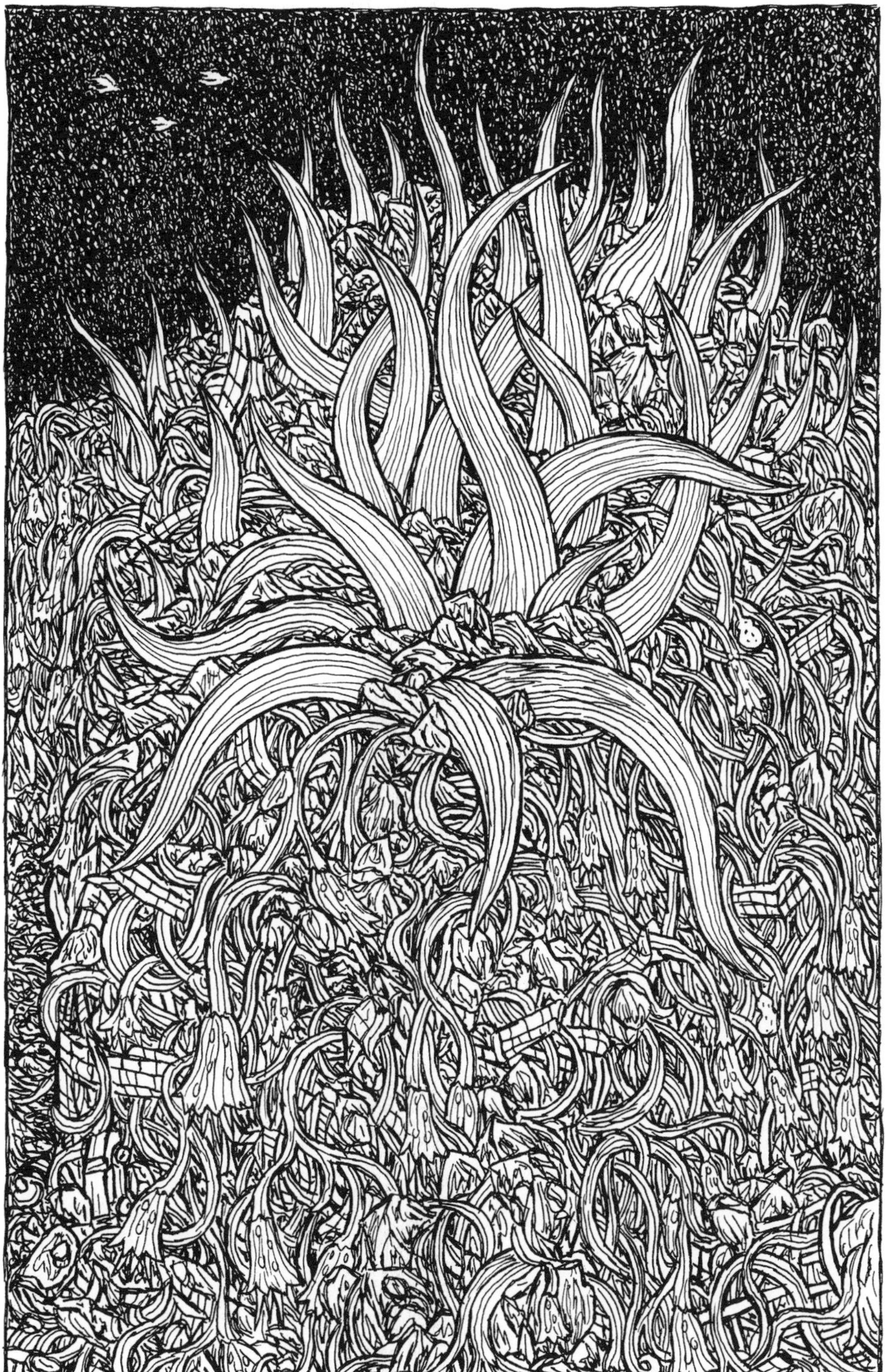

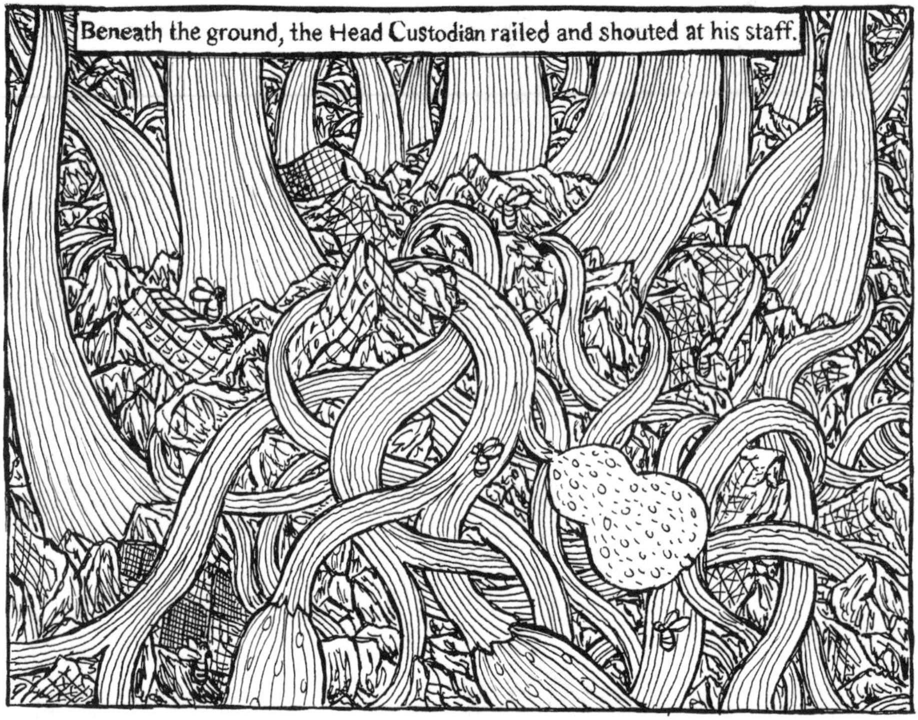
Beneath the ground, the Head Custodian railed and shouted at his staff.

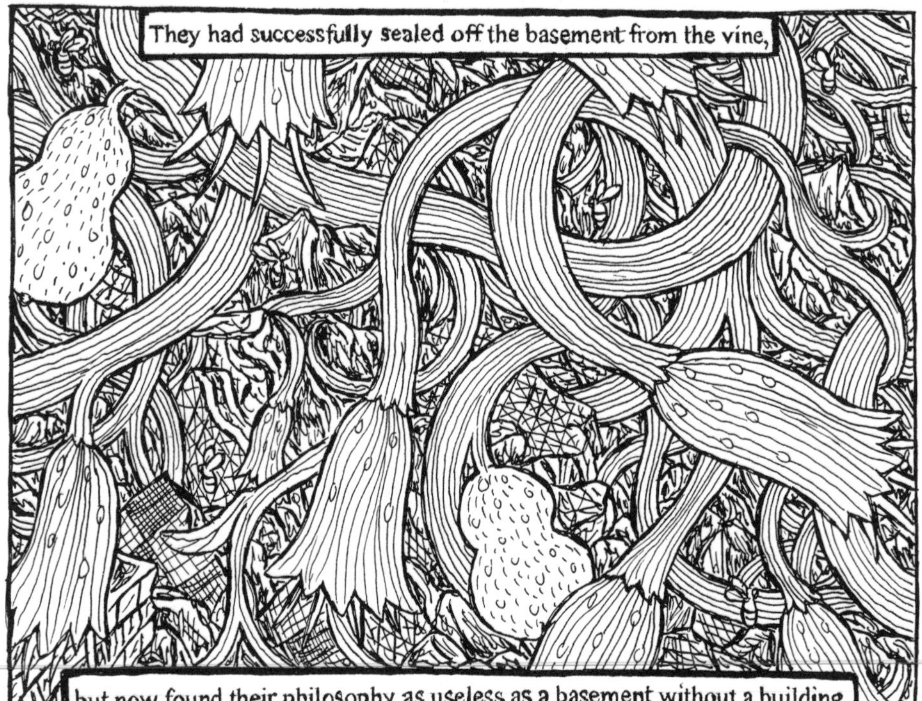
They had successfully sealed off the basement from the vine,
but now found their philosophy as useless as a basement without a building.

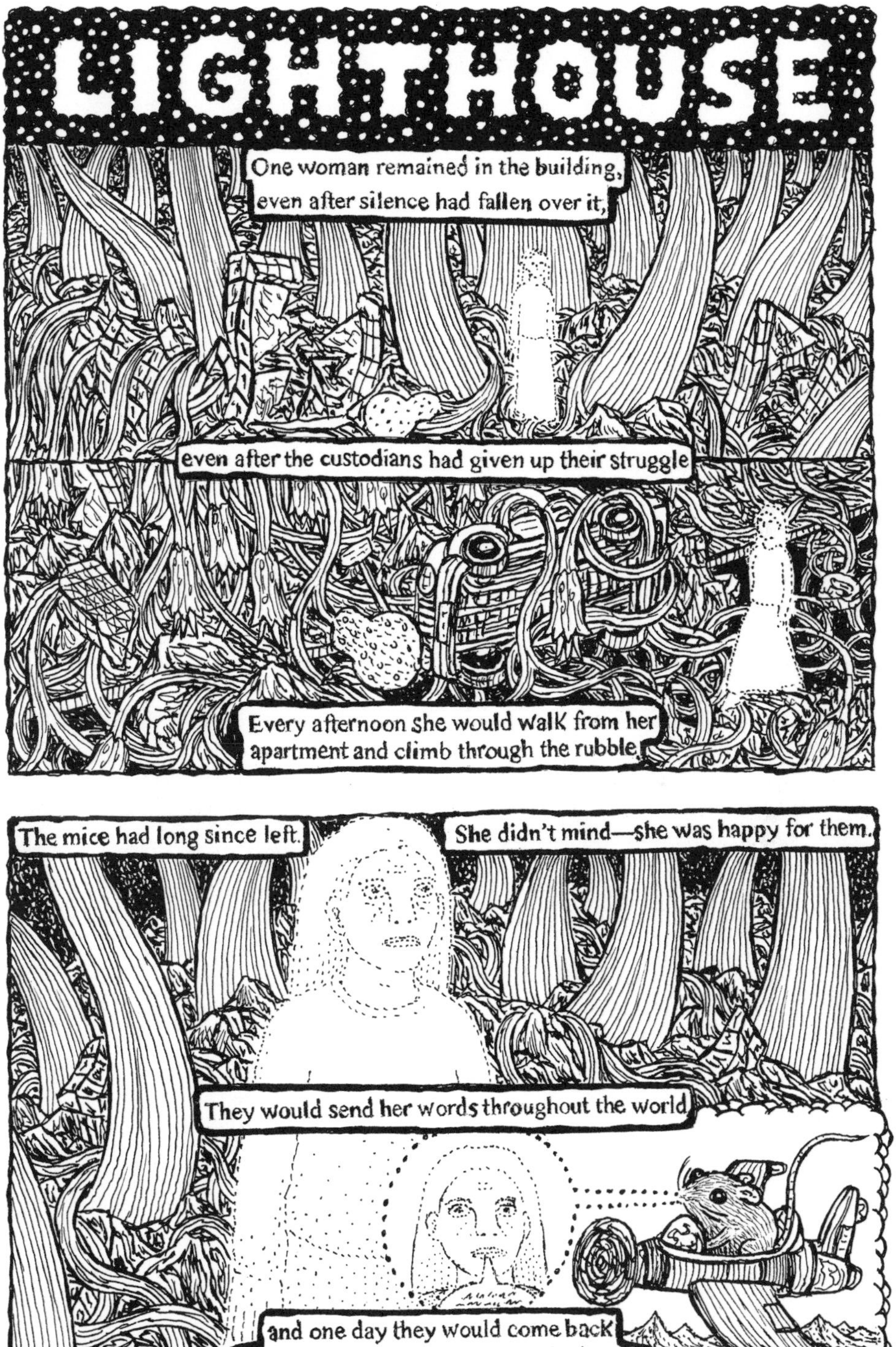
LIGHTHOUSE
One woman remained in the building, even after silence had fallen over it,
even after the custodians had given up their struggle
Every afternoon she would walk from her apartment and climb through the rubble.
The mice had long since left.
She didn't mind—she was happy for them.
They would send her words throughout the world
and one day they would come back and tell her tales of where they had been.

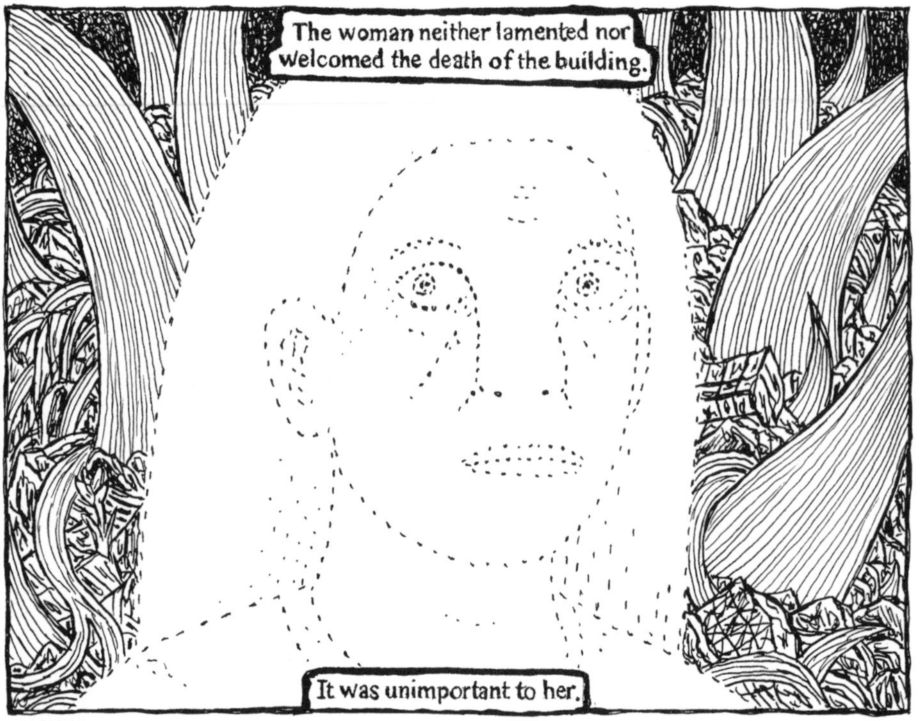
The woman neither lamented nor welcomed the death of the building.
It was unimportant to her.

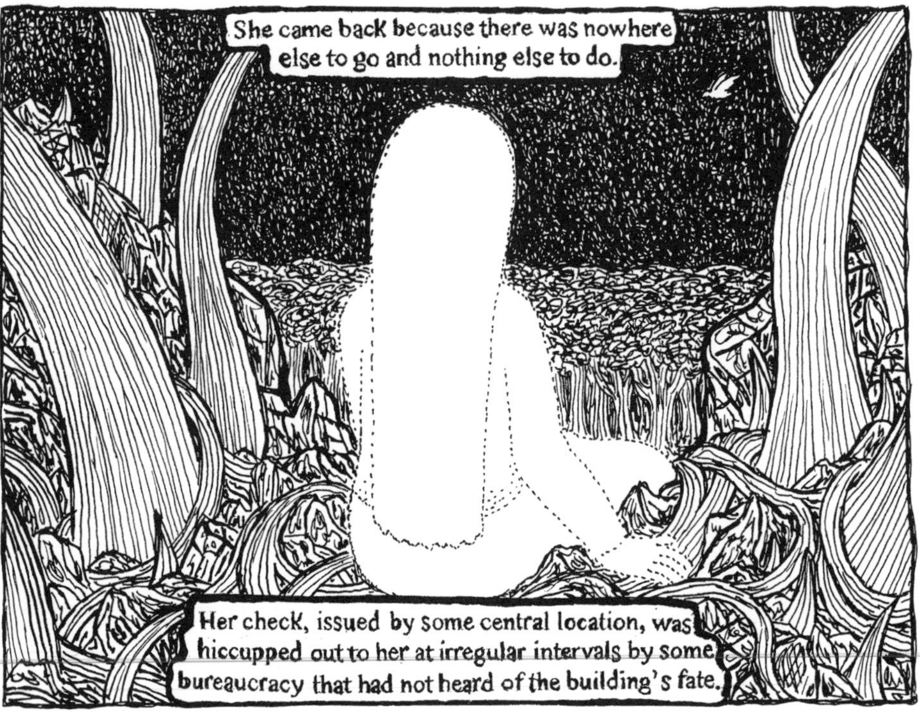
She came back because there was nowhere else to go and nothing else to do.
Her check, issued by some central location, was hiccupped out to her at irregular intervals by some bureaucracy that had not heard of the building's fate.

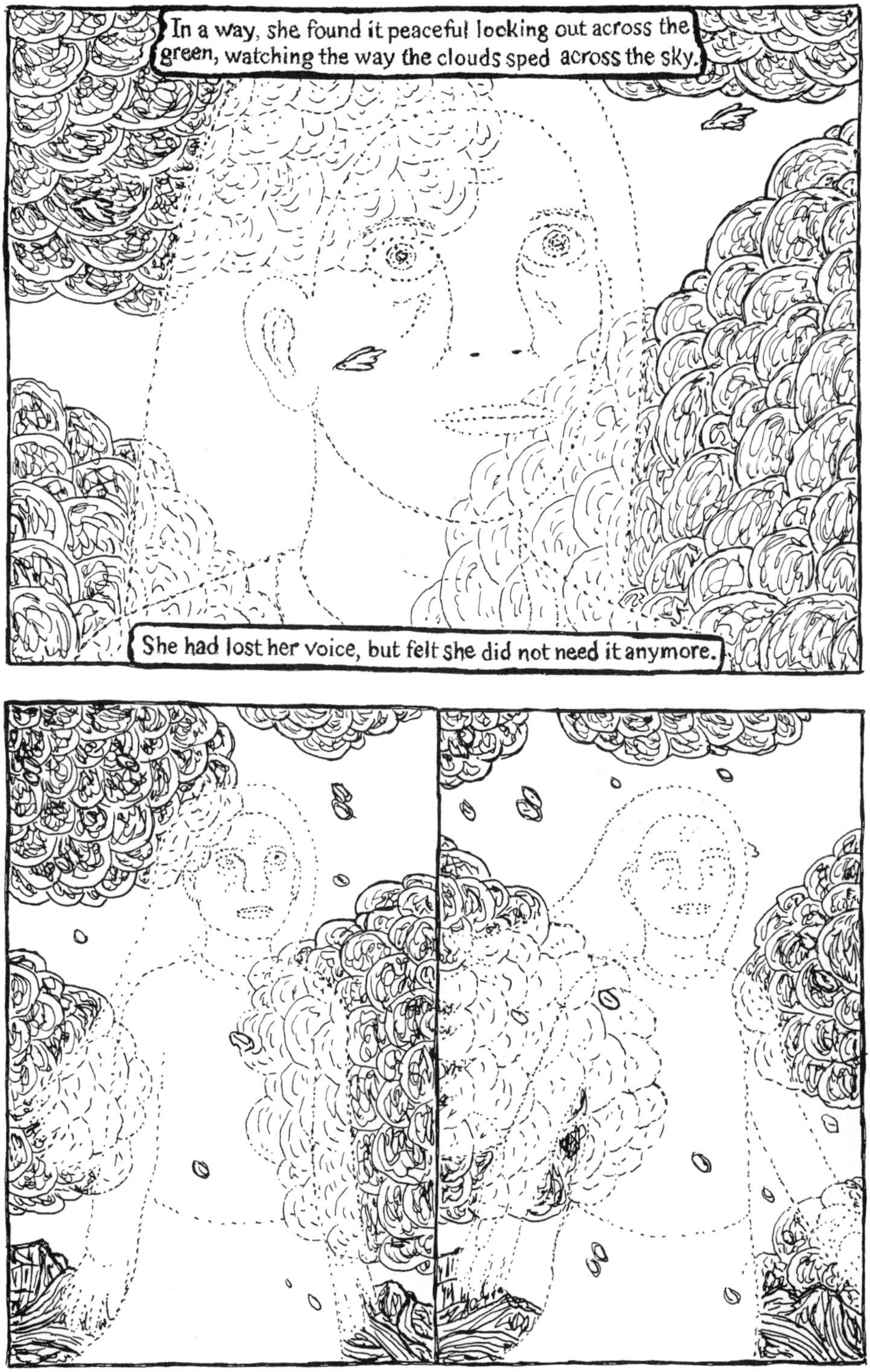
In a way, she found it peaceful looking out across the green, watching the way the clouds sped across the sky.
She had lost her voice, but felt she did not need it anymore.

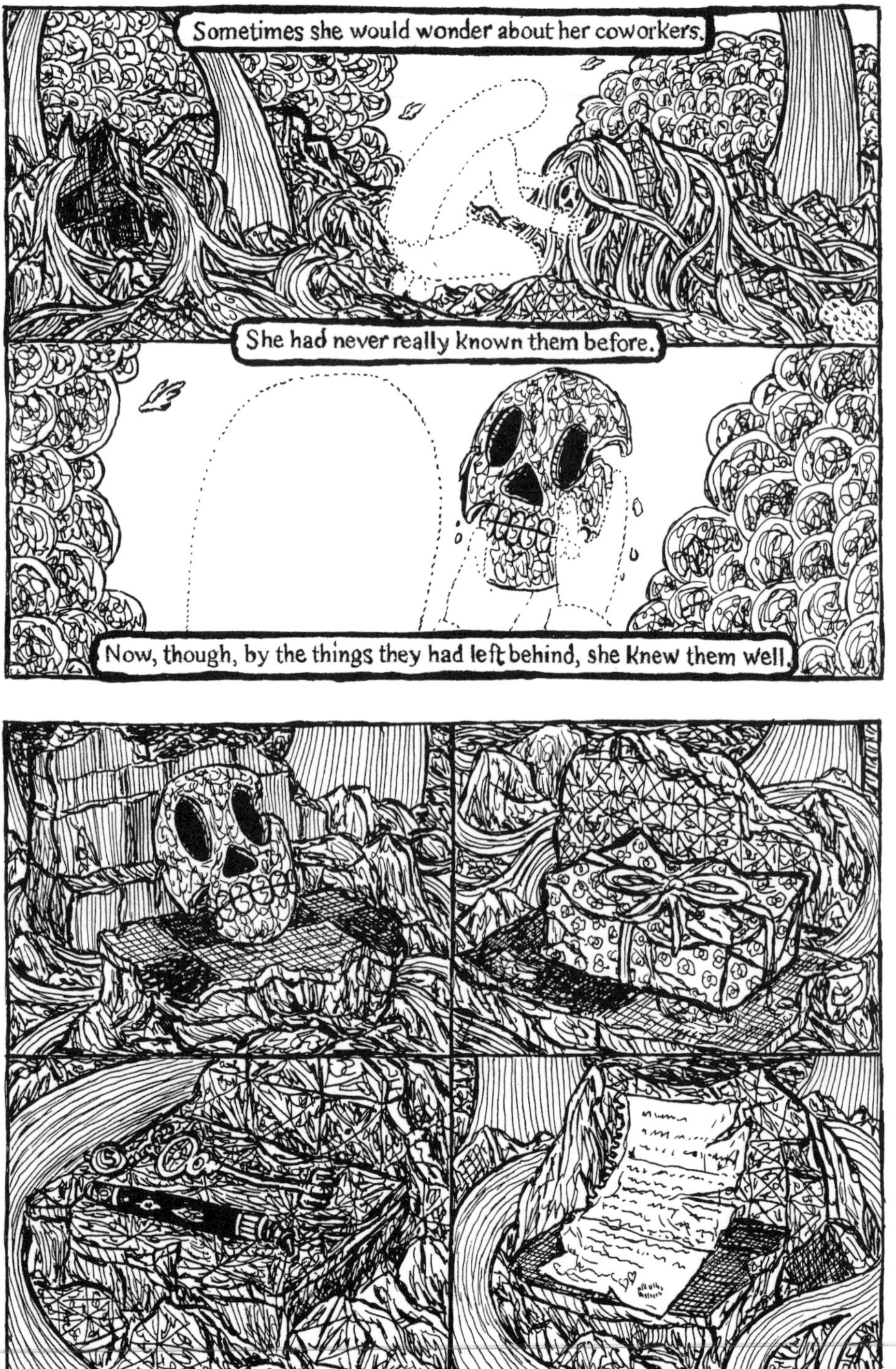
Sometimes she would wonder about her coworkers.
She had never really known them before.
Now, though, by the things they had left behind, she knew them well.

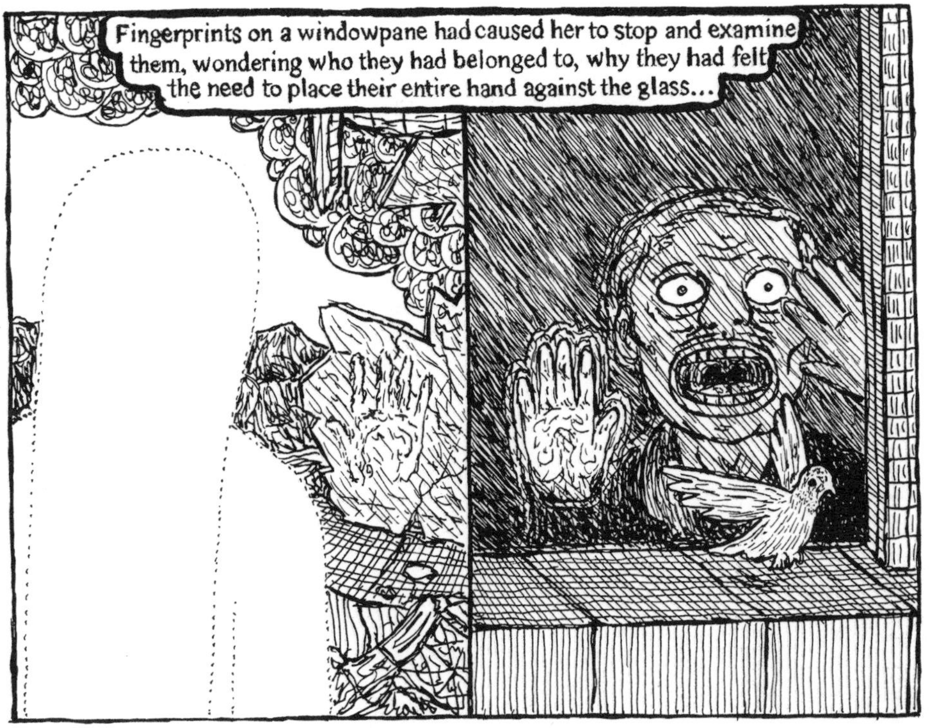
Fingerprints on a windowpane had caused her to stop and examine them, wondering who they had belonged to, why they had felt the need to place their entire hand against the glass...

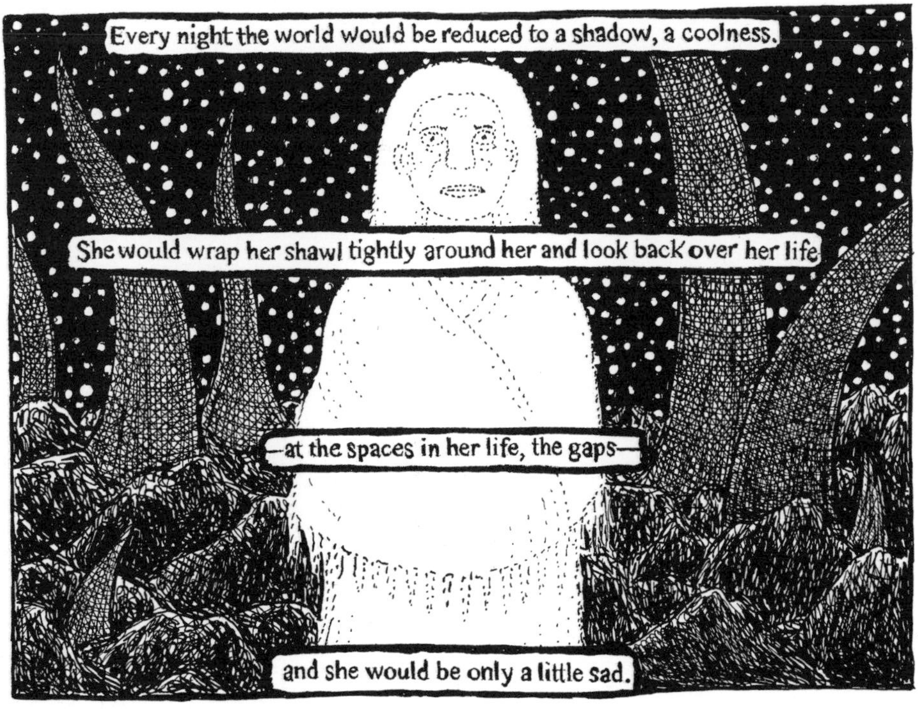
Every night the world would be reduced to a shadow, a coolness.
She would wrap her shawl tightly around her and look back over her life
—at the spaces in her life, the gaps—
and she would be only a little sad.

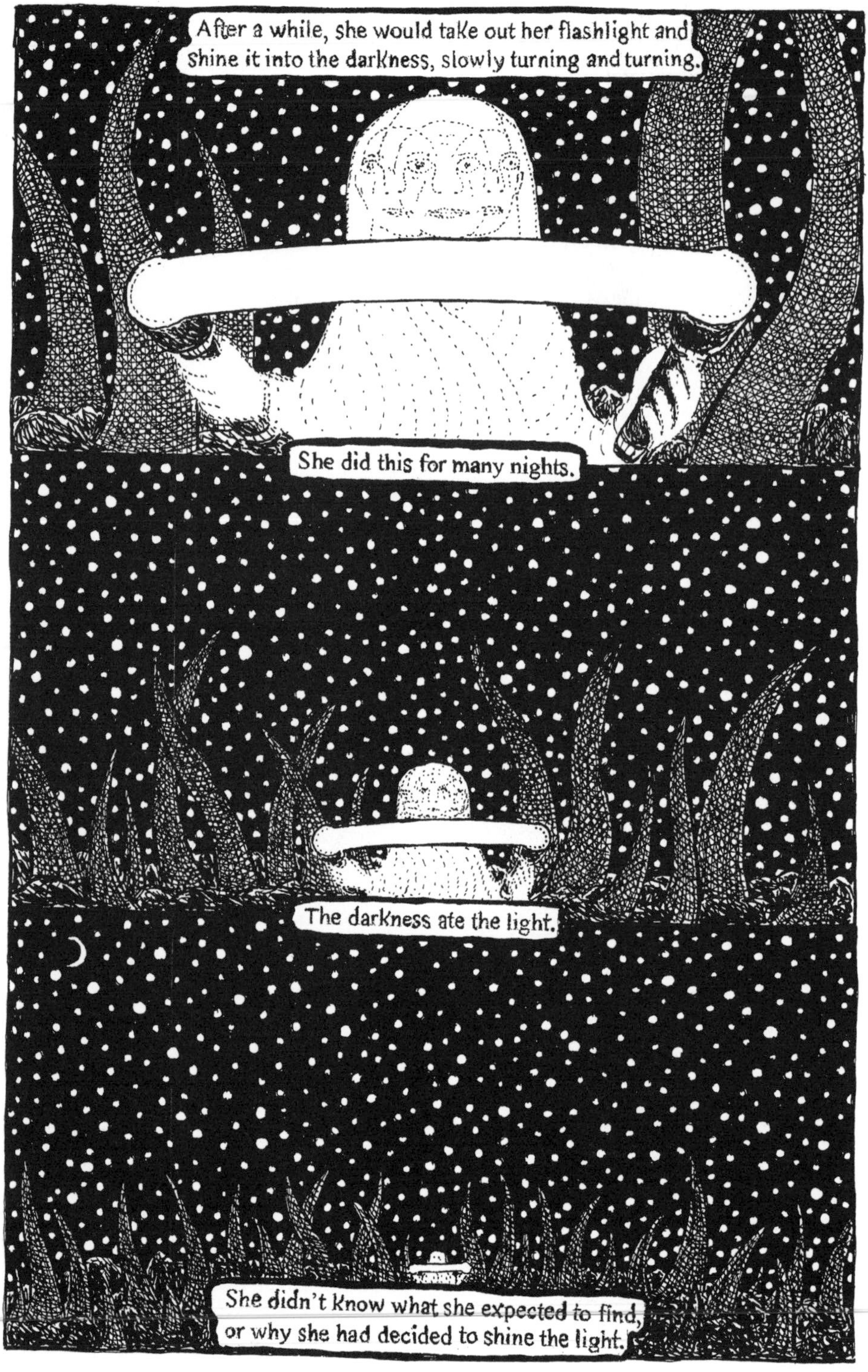
After a while, she would take out her flashlight and shine it into the darkness, slowly turning and turning.
She did this for many nights.
The darkness ate the light.
She didn't know what she expected to find, or why she had decided to shine the light.

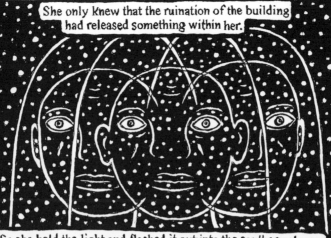

She only knew that the ruination of the building had released something within her.

So she held the light and flashed it out into the southern gloom.

Then one night a light shone back at her:

a violet light, small but intense.

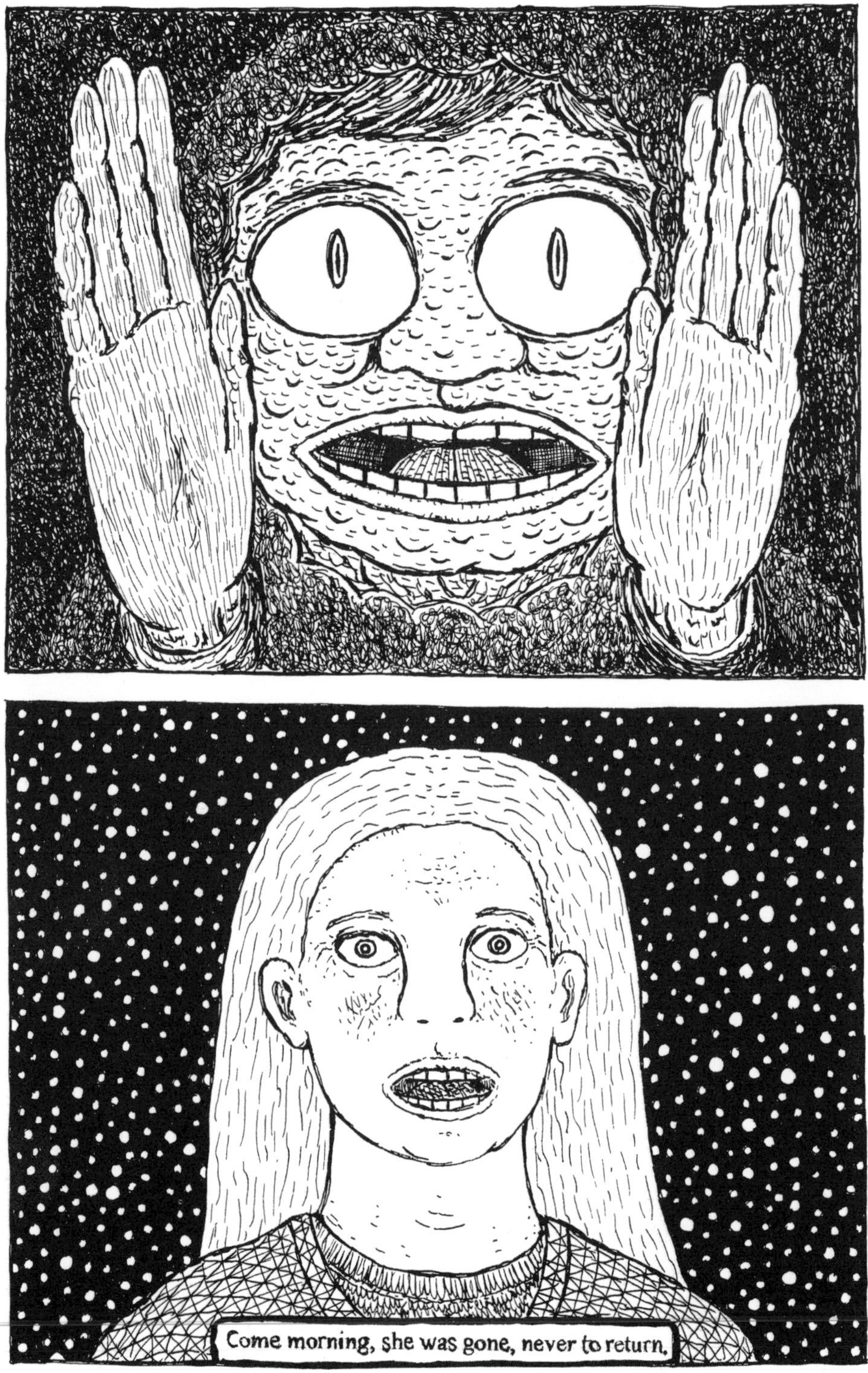
Come morning, she was gone, never to return.

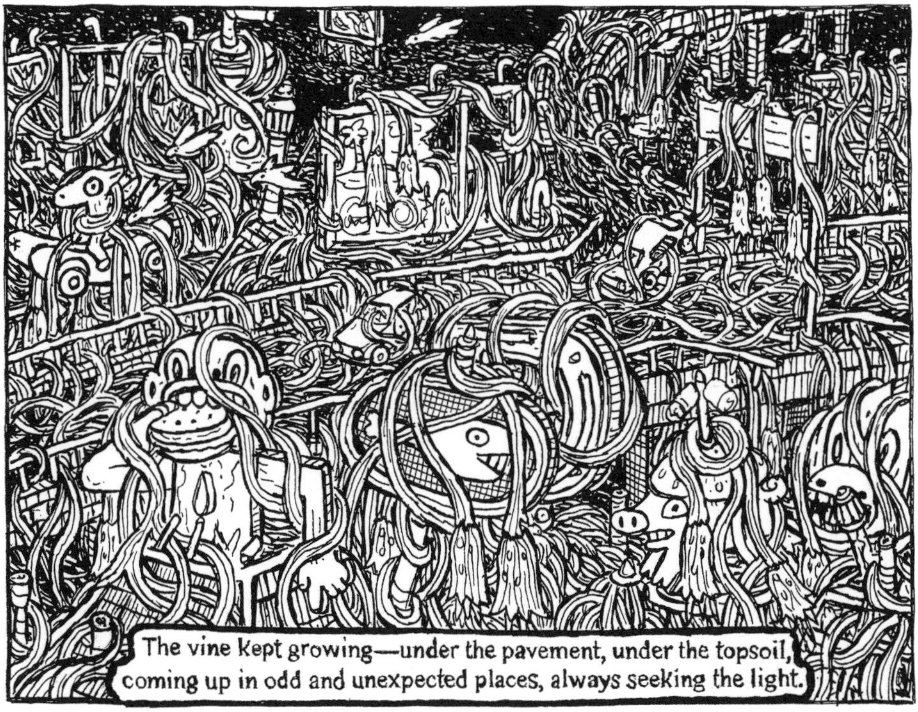
The vine kept growing—under the pavement, under the topsoil, coming up in odd and unexpected places, always seeking the light.

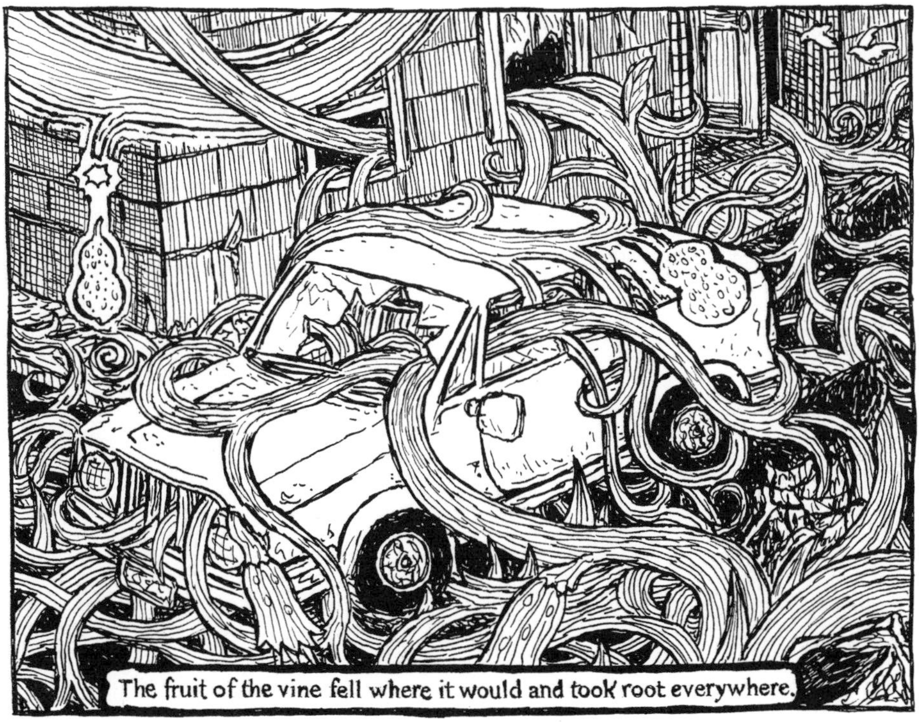
The fruit of the vine fell where it would and took root everywhere.

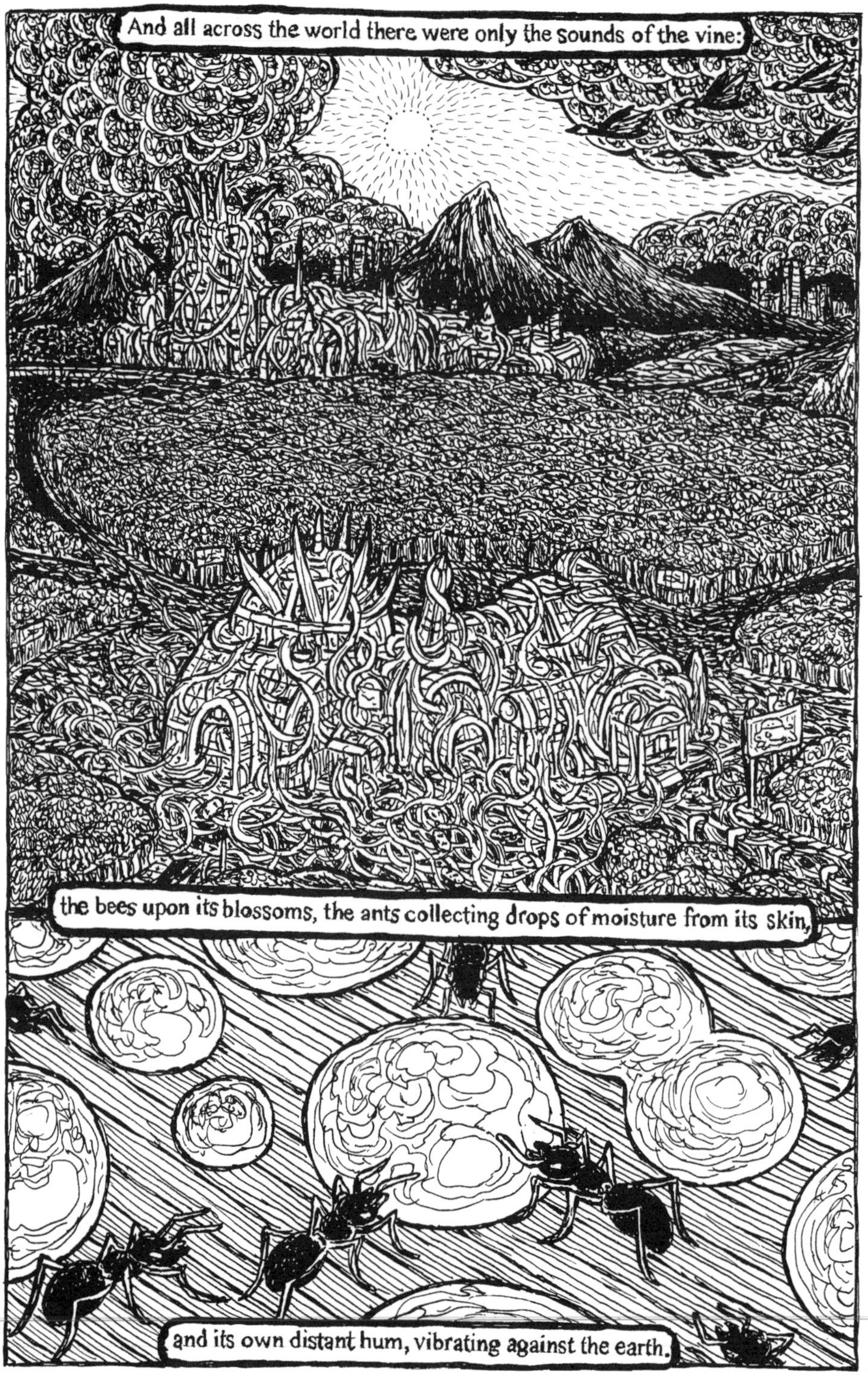
And all across the world there were only the sounds of the vine:
the bees upon its blossoms, the ants collecting drops of moisture from its skin,
and its own distant hum, vibrating against the earth.

drawnandquarterly.com

ISBN 978-1-77046-403-2
First edition: September 2021
Printed in China
10 9 8 7 6 5 4 3 2 1

Cataloguing data available from Library and Archives Canada.

Published in the USA by Drawn & Quarterly, a client publisher of Farrar, Straus and Giroux. Published in Canada by Drawn & Quarterly, a client publisher of Raincoast Books. Published in the United Kingdom by Drawn & Quarterly, a client publisher of Publishers Group UK.

Thank you

To Jeff VanderMeer, for trusting me with this, for the kind encouragement, and for showing my art to a capybara that one time. To Sally Harding for connecting me with D+Q and to Tom Devlin for working with me. Thanks to the D+Q staff: Peggy Burns, Tracy Hurren, Julia Pohl-Miranda, Ann Cunningham, Rebecca Lloyd, Alison Naturale, Kaiya Smith Blackburn, Megan Tan, Lucia Gargiulo, Tomoko Kanai, Jiyeon Cha, Trynne Delaney, and Shirley Wong. To Michael Greytak for scanning assistance, and Mike Emmons for connecting dots.

To all the indie bookstores and comic shops and to everyone who's published, commissioned, exhibited, or supported my work in the past.

To family and friends for so many priceless things! To Heather, Griffin, and Rowan, forever.

Drawn with a Rapidograph pen on Bristol board at the Brunswick Building and at home, mostly during a global pandemic.

Theo, 2021

Theo Ellsworth is a self-taught artist living in Montana. His previously published comics include *Capacity*, *The Understanding Monster*, *Sleeper Car*, and *An Exorcism*. *The New York Times* once called his work, "Imagination at firehose intensity." He has been the recipient of the Lynd Ward Honor Book Prize and an Artist Innovation Award. He loves creative collaboration, cooking, and making family folk art with his kids. He is constantly making invisible performance art in his head that no one will ever see.

Jeff VanderMeer is *The New York Times*-bestselling author of the *Southern Reach Trilogy*, the first volume of which, *Annihilation*, won the Nebula Award and the Shirley Jackson Award for best novel, and was adapted into a movie by Alex Garland. His novels set in the Borne universe are being adapted for TV by AMC, and Netflix has optioned his next novel, *Hummingbird Salamander*, for film. Called "the weird Thoreau" by *The New Yorker*, VanderMeer speaks and writes frequently about issues relating to climate change as well as urban rewilding. He lives in Tallahassee, Florida, on the edge of a ravine with his wife, Ann VanderMeer, and their cat Neo.